MINOANS
AND
MYCENAEANS

FLAVOURS OF THEIR TIME

GENERAL EDITORS
Yannis Tzedakis - Holley Martlew

ISBN: 960-7254-80-5

© Copyright 1999
GREEK MINISTRY OF CULTURE, GENERAL DIRECTORATE OF ANTIQUITIES

PRODUCTION K KAPON EDITIONS

25-27 Makriyanni str., Athens, Greece 117 42, Tel.: 01-9235098 Fax: 01-9214089

GREEK MINISTRY OF CULTURE • NATIONAL ARCHAEOLOGICAL MUSEUM

MINOANS AND MYCENAEANS

FLAVOURS OF THEIR TIME

NATIONAL ARCHAEOLOGICAL MUSEUM

12 July - 27 November 1999

ATHENS 1999

The Exhibition "Minoans and Mycenaeans Flavours of Their Time" is the result of international cooperation between Greek, British, American and Italian scholars, and was funded by the Greek Ministry of Culture and the European Union. It is designed to give prominence not only to the important role played by the natural sciences in modern archaeology, but also to their contribution to a more detailed, profounder understanding of the prehistoric past. Some important aspects of Minoan and Mycenaean society - aspects very familiar to us today, despite chronological distance separating us - such as diet, are illuminated in an original, scientifically sound manner, through analyses of bones and organic remains found in vases from selected excavations.

"You are what you eat" is the apt title of one of the sections in the Exhibition, reminding us that food and drink are not simply a biological necessity, but elements in our cultural identity. Through the gastronomic preferences and habits of the two most important Bronze Age cultures in the Aegean, we come to know the environment, technology, rituals, and daily life of the 3rd and 2nd millennia B.C. The section of the Exhibition devoted to the sacred medicine practised by the Minoans is also of great interest, and a reminder that prehistoric archaeology in Greece has further revelations in store.

ELISAVET PAPAZOI
Minister of Culture

ORGANISING COMMITTEE

YANNIS TZEDAKIS
Doctor of Archaeology
General Director of Antiquities, Em.

HOLLEY MARTLEW
Doctor of Archaeology
British Collaborator

DR. ROBERT ARNOTT
Dept. of Ancient History and Archaeology
University of Birmingham, U.K.

ALEXANDRA KARETSOU
Director 23th Ephorate

MARIA ANDREADAKI-VLAZAKI
Director 25th Ephorate

ELSIE SPATHARI
Director 4th Ephorate

BESSIE DROUNGA
Architect

SAPPHO ATHANASSOPOULOU
Archaeologist

EPHTIHEIA PROTOPAPADAKI
Archaeologist

We are grateful to the authors for the articles they have contributed to this Catalogue. Each of them is an expert in his or her field, and consequently these articles are presented without editorial comment. The views expressed and the conclusions drawn, are those of the individual authors.

This Catalogue does not include the detailed presentation of the scientific data that led to the conclusions presented in this Exhibition. They will be included in a companion volume of scholarly papers that will be published in the year 2000.

ABBREVIATIONS NOTE

ARCHAEOLOGICAL MUSEUMS

A.N.M.	Aghios Nikolaos Museum
CH.M.	Chania Museum
F.	Phaistos Stratigraphical Museum
H.M.	Herakleion Museum
N.M.	National Museum
M.N.	Nauplia Museum
M.M.	Mycenae Museum
R.M.	Rethymnon Museum
T.M.	Thebes Museum

CATALOGUE ENTRIES

E.A.	Dr. Eleni Andrikou
R.G.A.	Dr. Robert Arnott
F.B.	Frederique Baltzinger
C.D.	Prof. Costis Davaras
D.E.	Dr. Doniert Evely
E.B.F.	Dr. Elizabeth French
G.H.	Gordon Hillman
Ath.K.	Prof. Athanasia Kanta
A.K.	Alexandra Karetsou
E.K.	Elisavet Kavoulaki
D.M.	Dimitra Mylona
El.P.	Dr. Eleni Palaeologou
E.P.	Ephtiheia Protopapadaki
S.P.	Sophia Preve
A.S.	Dr. Anaya Sarpaki
G.W.	Prof. Gisela Walberg
P.W.	Prof. Peter Warren

ORGANIC RESIDUE ANALYSIS

EUM	Every sherd that was submitted for organic residue analysis was assigned a project number with the prefix EUM. The number is unique to a vase.

MUSEUM NUMBERS

All vessels have museum numbers. Any quantity of sherds has a museum number. When only one or two sherds survived, they do not have a museum number.

CHRONOLOGY

EM	Early Minoan
MM	Middle Minoan
LM	Late Minoan
MH	Middle Helladic
LH	Late Helladic

The chronology in the Catalogue is based on *Aegean Bronze Age Chronology*, Warren, P. and Hankey, V. (1989) Bristol.

GENERAL

H:	Height
D:	Diameter
W:	Width
L:	Length
Exc. No.	Excavation number
Cat. No.	Catalogue number
FM	Furumark motif: Furumark, A. (1941a) Mycenaean Pottery: analysis and classification, Stockholm.
FS	Furumark shape: Furumark, A. (1941a) Mycenaean Pottery: analysis and classification, Stockholm.

ACKNOWLEDGEMENTS

We wish first of all to acknowledge those who made the Project, and this Exhibition possible, by their support and funding in general or of individual contributors: The Raphael Programme of the European Union (Directorate-General X), the Ministry of Culture of the Hellenic Republic, the Holley Martlew Archaeological Foundation, the U.S. National Science Foundation (Grant SBR 96-00254), the Wellcome Trust, the Universities of Birmingham and East London (U.K.) and Vassar College (U.S.A.).

The Directors of the Project wish to thank the following contributors to the success of the Exhibition and for their work on the Catalogue: Maria Andreadaki-Vlazaki, Dr. Eleni Andrikou, Dr. Vassilis Aravantinos, Dr. Robert Arnott, Sappho Athanassopoulou, Michaela Augustin-Jeutter, Frederique Baltzinger, Professor Dr. Curt W. Beck, Eileen Chappell, Adrien A. Chase, Professor Costis Davaras, Nicole DeRosa, Dr. John Evans, Dr. Doniert Evely, Dr. Elizabeth B. French, Professor Louis Godart, Professor Robert E. M. Hedges, Gordon Hillman, Professor Spyros E. Iakovidis, Professor Athanasia Kanta, Alexandra Karetsou, Elisavet Kavoulaki, Dr. Olga Krzyszkowska, Karen C. Lee, Dr. Patrick E. McGovern, Prof. Eleni Manjurani, Dimitra Mylona, Richard Neave, Dr. Eleni Palaeologou, Nikos Papadakis, Dr. John Prag, Sophia Preve, Dr. Michael Richards, Dr. Martin Richards, Dr. Anaya Sarpaki, Elsie Spathari, Edith C. Stout, Anastasia Tsigounaki, Professor Gisela Walberg, Diana Wardle, Professor Peter Warren, Darlene Weston and David K. Whittaker.

This Exhibition would not have been possible without the support and co-operation of the Director, Dr. Ioannis Touratsoglou, the Curator of the Prehistoric Collection, Dr. Eleni Papazoglou, and the staff of the National Archaeological Museum, to whom we owe a great deal as the Exhibition approached its opening. We would also like to acknowledge the extensive co-operation of the Ephors and the Museum staffs of Western, Central and Eastern Crete, Boeotia, and the Argolid and also to offer our thanks for the loan of objects from museums in their care. We would specifically like to express our deep gratitude to the Exhibition designer, Bessie Drounga of TAP, and to Moses and Rachel Kapon of Kapon Editions and their staff for the production of this Catalogue. Our personal thanks to Vassilis Charalambakos who supervised the copy presentation in English and in Greek. No list of acknowledgements would be complete without expressing our special appreciation to Ephtiheia Protopapadaki (Project Assistant) and to Dr. Robert

Arnott (Project Consultant) for their tireless efforts during the many months it took to prepare the Exhibition and its Catalogue.

There are those who have contributed to this project in their professional capacities and here we acknowledge the valued assistance of: Stefanos Alexandrou (photographer), Dr. Dorothea Arnold, Artful Studio (UK):Phillip Daniels and Edward Hamilton (graphic designers), Andrew Bayliss of Lloyds Bank, Cheltenham (UK), Butser Ancient Farm (UK), Irini Chochlakidi, Dr. Stella Chryssoulaki of the Ministry of Culture, Dr. Peter Day (consultant), Yannis Dilaris, Photis Dimakis (restorer), Dot Imaging: Director Grigoris Kokoris and Dina Panou, Antonis Dragonas (consultant), Manolis Floures (photographer), Dr. David Hardy (translator), the Herakleion Museum (reproduction of slides), Dionissios Konstantopoulos (illustrator of "The Little Tripod Cooking Pot"), Dr. Kelly Kouzelli, Antonis and Manos Lignos (construction of museum cases), John Martlew and Co. and Thorpe and Thorpe, Solicitors (UK), Metropolitan Museum of Art, New York, U.S.A. (reproduction of slides), Dr. Mark Nesbitt (environmental consultant), Graham Norrie (photographer), Dr. Frederick I. Ordway, Pallis S.A. (publishers), Antonis Pandazis (restorer), Angeliki Panoutsou (translator), the Museum Restoration Departments of Chania, Aghios Nikolaos, Argos, the National Museum and Thebes, Dr. Delwyn Samuel (environmental consultant), Roy Savage of 5th Scents (UK), Stefanos Stournaras (photographer), Dr. Metaxia Tsipopoulou, the University of Birmingham (U.K.), the University of Manchester (U.K.) (reproduction of slides), and Costis Velonis (electrician).

The project has had many friends who have performed vital tasks behind the scenes, to whom we wish to express our gratitude: Maria Andreadaki-Vlazaki (special thanks for helping to set up the Exhibition), Rayna Andrew, Dr. Christos Boulotis, Manolis Danbounellis, Jeff Fendall, Mr. and Mrs. Daniel Gardner, Stelios Katharos, George Landers, Lambrini Limantzaki, Dimitra Marangaki, Dr. Jonathan Musgrave, Anna Mylona, Dr. Kim Shelton, Roy Treherne, Mrs. Era Vardaki, and the ladies at The Ballroom (UK).

Some names may have been excluded, not by design, but by accident. Our apologies and our thanks to everyone who helped us.

DR. YANNIS TZEDAKIS   DR. HOLLEY MARTLEW

CONTENTS

EPIRUS

THESSALY

AEGEAN SEA

AETOLIA

BOEOTIA

EUBOEA

Thebes ●

ATTICA

Menidi ●
● Athens

Mycenae ●
Midea ●

PELOPONNESE

CYCLADES

IONIAN SEA

Akrotiri
TH

Pylos ●

Chania ●

CRETE

Gerani ● ● Chamalevri
● Armenoi

Kno

Monastiraki ●
● Apodoulou

● Phaistos   M

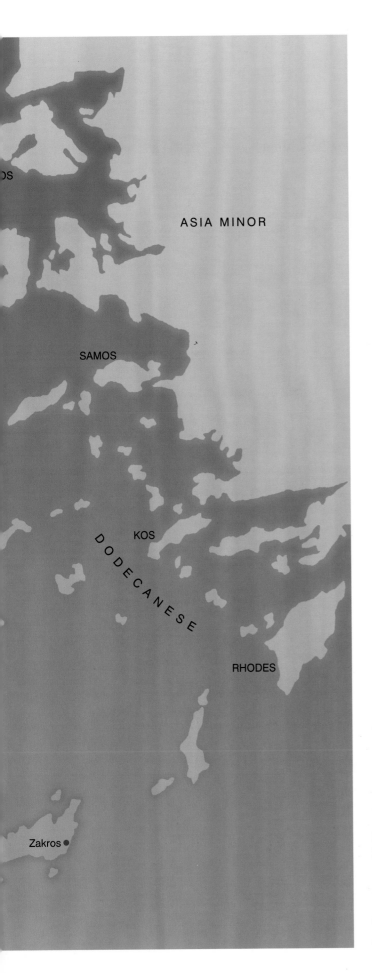

ASIA MINOR

SAMOS

KOS

DODECANESE

RHODES

Zakros ●

**MAP OF GREECE AND THE AEGEAN IN THE
BRONZE AGE**

*The sites which are marked are those which are the subject
of the research project and the source of objects and other
material displayed in the Exhibition.*

INTRODUCTION

ARCHAEOLOGY MEETS SCIENCE

When this project was begun two and a half years ago, it was decided to initiate an in-depth application of state of the art scientific analyses to a group of Minoan and Mycenaean ceramic artefacts. If successful, the tests would tell us what had been cooked, eaten, stored, or drunk. The intention was to establish concrete evidence of a kind never before produced. This information would give us a deeper understanding of diet, demography, health status, and social conditions in the Bronze Age Aegean, which would in turn be of great significance to the study of European social history as a whole.

We should make clear why we wanted to do this. The tests we were about to undertake had only been available for a few years, and their possible application to archaeological subjects had been clear even more recently. It was new ground, which is always exciting. The most important thing, however, was that it gave us the chance to place aspects of archaeological research on a firm scientific base. Our work, if successful, would turn theory into fact. It would disprove theories. It would provide information that had not even been the stuff of dreams.

It was an exciting prospect, but it was not without problems. It required financial backing. For this we are grateful to the European Union, to the Ministry of Culture of the Hellenic Republic, to national and private foundations, and to institutions of higher learning. It required courage. We might do all the work, spend all the money, and find out nothing.

When we started, it was not at all clear that the project would meet with any success. It was a way forward, the time was ripe, and positive results would be extremely significant, not just for Greek archaeology, but for archaeology as a whole.

When the first samples were taken, it did indeed concentrate minds. To process each sample was an expensive undertaking.

There was a fundamental question: would any organic signals have been retained in pots that had been buried in soil for between 3000 and 4000 years. There were other problems. At the beginning of the project, we perforce were working with samples that had been cleaned in an acid solution. We knew that with such cleaning procedures, we ran the risk that organic signals that had survived through time could have been destroyed through traditional methods of cleaning. We were daring fate, and we dared fate in another way: we had submitted samples from decorated vessels as well as coarse ware. Before the first results came through, we were faced with another problem: plastic bags. The samples were showing up a lot of contaminants, and it was suspected they came from storage in plastic bags. We then had to submit a tiny piece of each plastic bag from which we had taken a potsherd, so that the organic chemists could check the chemical properties of the bags against the results from the pots.

When the first results came through on the first group of sherds from the Room with the Fresco in the Cult Centre at the palace of Mycenae, they were astonishing. Every vessel told us something. The large tripod cooking pot found near the altar in the Room with the Fresco had held meat, lentils, and olive oil. A stirrup jar nearby had contained wine. When additional sherds were submitted, the organic residue tests on a large cooking pot jar from this cult room revealed the pot had contained not just wine, but resinated wine, not just resinated wine, but true retsina.

Never before had anyone known the exact contents of a Mycenaean cooking pot. Never before had anyone known with scientific precision, that a particular vessel had contained wine, resinated wine, and most important, wine treated with pine resin. We had discovered that retsina was known in the Greek Bronze Age.

As it became clear that the analysis of pottery was proving to be a successful undertaking, more sites were added to the list from which ceramic samples were submitted for analysis. In this Exhibition, you will see results from one Neolithic Cretan site dating 6000-3800 B.C., and ten Minoan and Mycenaean sites, dating from 2200 B.C. to 1100 B.C.

As it became clear what success we were having in the field of organic residue analysis on potsherds, we discussed an innovative test on skeletal material that, if successful, would reveal the protein content of diet. We had access to the Late Minoan Cemetery of Armenoi, with 227 tombs. The special process that established the types of protein consumed by an individual was called stable isotope analysis. We were told that depending on the survival of collagen in the bone, the protein sources for diet for the 10 years preceding death could be established.

Samples from a representative group were taken from the Cemetery of Armenoi: this meant for example, taking samples that were male and female in equal numbers. When the results from the first 80 skeletons had provided interesting and worthwhile information, the study was expanded to include a Neolithic cave in Crete, a group of Late Helladic chamber tombs at Mycenae, Grave Circle B at Mycenae, and then it was decided to seek for results on material from one of the most well known of all Bronze Age sites in Greece, Grave Circle A at Mycenae. In all cases, the tests proved to be successful, and they have provided us with a great deal of new information.

For example, a generally held theory about Bronze Age diet that meat was reserved for high days and holidays, has been disproved. All Bronze Age results indicate that Minoans and Mycenaeans had diets rich in animal protein. In the one case where we could differentiate between rich and poor burials, the Late Minoan Cemetery of Armenoi, both rich and poor had a lot of meat in their diets. Another great surprise for archaeologists and laymen alike: the inhabitants of Armenoi between 1390 and 1190 B.C. were not eating fish.

Bone analysis made us think about how the sequencing of DNA could assist with our research. Work has been initiated with such interesting preliminary results, that it was recommended that the DNA project be continued and expanded into further population studies and the search for diseases from which Minoans and Mycenaeans suffered.

It is impossible to think about food, drink, health, plants, pots and bones, without including something about Minoan and Mycenaean healing and medicine. Like all early societies, they practiced medicine, had an effective *materia medica* and undertook basic surgery. Whether they differentiated between the religious and the practical, we do not know, but the section of the Exhibition dedicated to our understanding of the use of medicine in everyday life, shows examples of both.

Ultimately we decided that an in-depth environmental study of a Bronze Age site would also be a worthwhile endeavour, and would provide a fitting introduction to the Exhibition and to our main subject. Our reward for this undertaking was a landmark discovery: proof of the production of olive oil in Minoan Crete at a time prior to the building of the first palaces.

THE EXHIBITION IS IN FIVE PARTS.
Section I: What Did They Produce?
Section II: What Did They Cook?
Section III: What Did They Drink?
Section IV: Food and Drink.
Section V: You Are What You Eat.

Organic residue analysis: the methods used by Prof. Dr. Curt W. Beck, Vassar College, U.S.A.; Dr. John Evans, the University of East London, U.K.; and Dr. Patrick

E. McGovern, MASCA, University of Pennsylvania Museum, U.S.A., are explained in their own words, at the beginning of the Exhibition; these pertain to Sections I, II, III and IV. Stable isotope analysis: the method is explained at the beginning of Section V, by Prof. Robert E. M. Hedges, Acting Director, and Dr. Michael Richards, Research Laboratory for Archaeology and History of Art, University of Oxford, U.K.

The wall panels that introduce Sections II, III and V explain the systems that were followed in visual terms.

A GUIDE TO THE ORGANIC RESIDUE ANALYSIS IN THE EXHIBITION

A sherd from each vessel, which is identified in the Exhibition as having an "organic residue result", was submitted to a series of scientific tests, the results of which were then analysed by an organic chemist. What the visitor sees on display is the original vessel, or in cases where just a diagnostic sherd survived and was analysed, the type and shape of vessel from which the sherd would have come, is exhibited. This is made clear in each case.

Three chemists worked in three different geographical locations, two in the United States, and one in England. These men were scientists known and respected in their field, but they were not knowledgeable about Bronze Age Greece *per se*. This means that their results were not clouded by any preconceived ideas of what they might find, because they had none. In most cases they had only a sketchy knowledge of the types of vessels with which they were dealing, so again their conclusions could be trusted as unbiased and objective in a way that could not have been achieved if they had started with specialised knowledge in the field. Samples were chosen by us with great care and intent, but we did not share this knowledge with our chemists, except in a few instances when a result was particularly perplexing, and we or they wanted to double check a result, the men collaborated, but otherwise they worked completely independently.

Upon occasion it was reminiscent of the discovery of the planet Neptune by two astronomers within months of each other, in the mid 1840's. The astronomers did not know each other, and they lived in different places, Adams in Cambridge, England, and Versier in Paris. McGovern and Evans, the former in the United States and the latter in England, and who have never met and whose day by day work was not known to each other, confirmed the existence of mead, beer and wine in individual vessels, and both suggested the possibility of a mixed fermented beverage. The vessels dated to the Late Bronze Age, from Minoan sites (McGovern) and from Mycenaean Thebes (Evans) between the dates of 1500 and 1250/1100 B.C. Occurrences like this point to a homogeneity of taste in the Minoan/Mycenaean world, which is not surprising, but it is significant to have it confirmed on such a level. As for us, we were being bombarded with information about the contents of pots, day by day, so much so that sometimes it was unsettling, not least when we were told about the possibility of what was to us a strange and very potent, mixed fermented beverage that consisted of honey mead, wine, and beer. But the fact that two men, their work unknown to each other, reached the same type of result, one on Minoan material and the other on Mycenaean, was impressive and it was re-assuring.

The visual focal point of Section IV is the reconstruction of the area near the altar of the Room with the Fresco in the Cult Centre at Mycenae. The original contents are on display, and they include the vessels that were submitted for analysis, as well as the other interesting and beautiful artefacts found *in situ*.

A GUIDE TO THE RESEARCH ON SKELETAL MATERIAL AND MEDICINE

Tiny pieces of a bone from each of a representative group of skeletons from each cemetery, or group of tombs, underwent stable isotope analysis. Actual collagen taken from the bone of a Minoan is displayed in the introductory panel.

Individual wall panels present a summary of results for each group.
These are:

Crete:
Neolithic Cave of Gerani (c. 6000-3800 B.C.)
Late Minoan III Cemetery of Armenoi (c. 1390-1190 B.C.)

Of the 227 tombs that have been excavated to date at Armenoi, only one larnax contained a multiple burial. The skeletons from the larnax from this chamber tomb 132, were examined by an osteoarchaeologist, and found to be a man and a woman. A special display has been mounted to present the results, and as part of it, reconstructions of the heads of the couple were made, and they are exhibited along with the original skulls.

The reconstruction of a chamber tomb from the Late Minoan Cemetery at Armenoi provides the visual focal point of Section V. One of the painted terracotta larnakes which were primarily a phenomenon of the Late Minoan world, is included, with a representative range of grave goods, from exquisitely painted pottery, to the cooking pots and kylikes which were used for ritual ceremonies.

Mainland:
Grave Circle B at Mycenae. Also on exhibit are reconstructions of the heads of a male, Sigma 131, and a female, Gamma 58, from Grave Circle B (17th-16th century B.C.).

A Group of Late Helladic Chamber Tombs (c. 1600-1200 B.C.).
Grave Circle A. We were successful in obtaining results from the surviving skeletal material from Grave Circle A, first excavated by Schliemann in 1876 (16th century B.C.).

Evidence for Minoan and Mycenaean healing and medicine is exhibited. Such information is naturally linked to a study of health and diet, and is found in a number of forms. The presentation includes skeletal material that offers evidence of disease, trauma and surgery and plant remains that will have been used for medicines. Also included are tools and objects used by the healers; the Linear B tablets, probably giving us the word **i-ja-te** or "doctor"; and from peak sanctuaries, some votive offerings which were the forerunners of the modern talismans, and were placed in the sanctuaries to invoke a cure.

HIGHLIGHTS OF THE EXHIBITION

A few have already been mentioned. Other highlights include the discovery of a vegetable stew in a Neolithic bowl; a Minoan aromatic workshop dating to the time before the first palaces, c. 2000 B.C., and a Minoan stew prepared in the 15th century B.C.

Honey is difficult to trace, so the incidence of finds of honey/beeswax is important. They culminate in the presence of what is presumed to have been honey mead in drinks in the Late Bronze Age in Crete and on the Mainland.

Almost everything that is revealed in Section III on drink can be classified as a highlight: wine that appears to have been resinated, at around 2200 B.C., in Crete; a definite find of resinated wine at the time of the first palaces in Crete at about 1900 B.C.; the possibility of mixed fermented beverages (wine, beer, and mead) in the Late Bronze Age both in Crete and on the Mainland; wine with rue found in a tripod pot in an area of the Cult Centre at Mycenae. It is astonishing for us to remember that in the very early stages of the project, when the first scientific results were coming in, we had a serious discussion about the worrying possibility of not having much to say or show in the section we had planned on drink.

For the lay person and the scholar who are interested in the finer points, noting the organic residue results obtained from decorated vases and from the "enigmatic" vessels of the Minoan/Mycenaean world, is worthwhile. Examples of the former are decorated stirrup jars from several sites, a juglet from Armenoi, and a stemmed bowl from Mycenae. Examples of enigmatic or unusual vessels are an industrial vessel from Chamalevri; Minoan baking basins; a "mug" and a pierced neck jar from Mycenae; a feeding bottle and a rhyton from Midea.

Our work has added to the list of enigmatic vessels. One is a tiny phial found in what we now know was a Minoan aromatic workshop at the site of Chamalevri on the north coast of Crete. The organic residue result was "oil of iris and a beeswax mixture with a strong cereal presence". What was the role this tiny vessel played in the production of aromatics?

We have discovered a commodity, oil of iris, which was heretofore not a known substance in the Greek Bronze Age. There is no known Linear B sign for it. Oil of iris is historically, however, a very important ingredient in the production of aromatics, and it is the most expensive ingredient used in today's perfume industry, selling for about 3000 pounds sterling a kilo. The Minoans therefore had identified and were using one of the rarest and now most valuable commodities known to the perfume trade, 4000 years ago at a time before the first palaces were built.

Finally... We believe that the scientific work that was carried out, has allowed the Minoan/Mycenaean civilisation to come alive in a way that was not possible before. It is the detail that is important and which gives the results presented in the Exhibition a meaning beyond the purely scientific. The results give a real sense of life's carrying on in ways with which we can identify. The years that separate us vanish.

To find out what kinds of food and drink were in use, and had possibly formed part of a cult meal, at Mycenae, at roughly the time of the Trojan War. That was luck.

To find out what was contained in storage vessels in a Minoan settlement that dates to c. 2200 B.C., was luck.

To find out the probable contents of a Minoan cocktail. That was luck.

Tremendous luck, but then archaeology does depend on luck. Archaeology depends on perseverance, insight, and luck. Perseverance we had. Luck we had. Insight? After visiting this Exhibition, and being among the very first people to find out what our Bronze Age ancestors ate and drank, we hope our project team will be credited with having insight as well.

We have accomplished a great deal, and you will see the results in the Exhibition, but we view our work as unfinished. We view our work as beginning. Nothing has stopped, we are continuing every aspect of this work, and advancing into new areas. In the next stage of our project, currently in progress, we are 1) bringing areas of our research into sharper focus by expanding the base of ceramic and skeletal material submitted for tests to new sites; 2) pioneering new and innovative scientific techniques which we did not embark on earlier either for reasons of money, time, or the simple fact that they were not then available. The intention of the project team is to be, and to remain, at the cutting edge where... archaeology meets science.

DR. YANNIS TZEDAKIS   DR. HOLLEY MARTLEW

INTRODUCTION TO ORGANIC RESIDUE ANALYSIS

The main objective of MINOANS AND MYCENAEANS - FLAVOURS OF THEIR TIME, was to try to find out what food remains survived inside the fabric of vessels that had been used in the Greek Bronze Age. When a pot is used for cooking, eating, or drinking, particles of food and drink soak into the fabric. The aim was to try to find out 1) what particles had survived the intervening years; and 2) to identify them. The formal title for such work is:

Organic Residue Analysis.

Each successfully tested potsherd provides a list of organic components. This list of components provides the clues. The organic chemists then have the task of analysing each group of components to ascertain what foodstuffs are indicated. This is the most difficult and time-consuming part of the procedure, and the chemists must have specialised knowledge and experience.

The vessels that were tested, by name and number(s):

Name: Each vessel is called by its traditional name.

Museum number: All vessels have museum numbers. Any quantity of sherds has a museum number. When only one or two sherds survived, they do not have a museum number.

EUM number: Every sherd that was submitted for organic residue analysis has an EUM project number. The EUM number is unique to a vase.

Vessels on display: A sherd from each vessel which is identified in the Exhibition as having an organic residue result, was submitted to a series of scientific tests, the results of which were then analysed, as indicated above, by an organic chemist. What the visitor sees on display is: 1) the original vessel, or 2) a substitute vessel: in cases where just a diagnostic sherd survived and was analysed, the type and shape of vessel from which the sherd would have come is exhibited. This is made clear in each case.

Please refer to the texts that appear below, on the various methods used to carry out organic residue analysis. These texts have been written by the men who carried out the work. It is their results that are presented in the Exhibition: Prof. Dr Curt W. Beck, Dr John Evans, and Dr Patrick E. McGovern.

Please also refer to the diagrams on Organic Residue Analysis that introduce Section II and Section III.

DR. HOLLEY MARTLEW

METHOD OF ANALYSIS

Sherds weighing from 2.5 to 5.0 grams were ground to a fine powder in a stainless steel mill and extracted with 10 millilitres of a solvent mixture of equal volume of dichloromethane and diethyl ether at room temperature by ultrasonic agitation. The extract was filtered through a Kontes No. 74812-0000 disposable polyethylene Hirsch funnel with a sintered disc of 20 micron pore size and evaporated to dryness at 30 degrees C in a stream of nitrogen. The organic residue was weighed and redissolved in 1 millilitre of the solvent mixture. It was then treated with diazomethane to convert any acid components to their more volatile methyl esters.

Most of the methylated extracts were analysed by injecting 1 microlitre into a Hewlett-Packard Model 5995C/96A gas chromatograph-mass spectrometer system equipped with a Model 5997A computer workstation; more recently (after September 1, 1998) a new Hewlett-Packard Model HP 6890 gas chromatograph coupled with a HP 5973 Mass Selection Detector (MSD) and equipped with a HP MSD ChemStation computer was used. Both chromatographs were fitted with Alltech AT-1 capillary columns 15 meters long and having a diameter of 0.25 millimetres. The stationary phase was poly (dimethylsiloxane); the carrier gas helium. The oven containing the capillary column had an initial temperature of 50 degrees C, which was raised at the rate of 5 degrees C/minute immediately after sample injection until it reached 250 degrees C after 40 minutes.

Some samples were run a second time after preliminary evaluation of the total ion chromatograms produced by the mass spectrometer. If one component (usually a contaminant) was present in so large an amount that it reduced the other components to very small peaks, the second analysis was programmed with the mass detector turned off in the region of the dominant peak in order to enhance the minor components.

Structures of the components were assigned using hard-copy and computer-searchable collections of mass spectra components compiled by The Mass Spectrometry DATA Centre of the Royal Society of Chemistry (U.K.); by the Wiley/ NBS Registry of Mass Spectrometry Data (F. W. McLafferty and D. B. Stauffer), 5th and 6th editions; and by the Amber Research Laboratory at Vassar College, U.S.A.

This work was supported by the United States National Science Foundation with Grant SBR 96-00254 (Anthropology) and by Vassar College

PROF. DR. CURT W. BECK
EDITH C. STOUT, KAREN C. LEE,
NICOLE DEROSA, ADRIEN A. CHASE
Vassar College, Poughkeepsie, N.Y., U.S.A.

METHOD OF ANALYSIS

X-RAY FLUORESCENCE (XRF)

This technique enables us to investigate the major elemental make-up of the sherd. By comparing both sides of the sherd it may be possible to detect the original presence of aqueous systems from an excess of calcium and magnesium on the inner face. Equally the presence of such elements as phosphorous, sulphur, zinc, etc. can also be indicative.

PREPARATION OF SHERD FOR ANALYSIS

The outer surfaces of the potsherd were removed and the remaining sherd ground to powder. Approximately 3 gr. of powder was then placed into a paper thimble and sequentially extracted with a series of solvents:

- hexane
- chloroform
- 2-propanol

Each extraction took 24 hours. The extracts were then concentrated and investigated by infrared spectroscopy and chromatography.

INFRARED SPECTROSCOPY (IR)

IR analysis enables us to see if we have extracted any organic substances from the sherd. In theory each organic chemical substance has a unique "fingerprint". Hence it can give us some insight into the nature of substances present, which in turn makes the subsequent chromatographic investigations more straightforward.

CHROMATOGRAPHY

Chromatography is a group of techniques that enable us to break complex mixtures down into their constituent parts (a little like breaking a word into its letters). There are two major systems:

- gas chromatography (GC).
- high performance liquid chromatography (HPLC).

Both were used in this investigation. The former for looking especially at fats and oils and the latter at proteins.

DR. JOHN EVANS
University of East London, U.K.

METHOD OF ANALYSIS

Organic contents analysis is shedding new light on diet, materials processing, trade and economics, plant domestication, and a host of other cultural, scientific and medical concerns of the ancient and modern worlds. Three complementary analytical techniques – infrared spectrometry, liquid chromatography, and wet chemical analyses– are used to detect organics.

INFRARED SPECTROMETRY

Infrared spectrometry takes advantage of the nature of chemical bonds that stretch and bend when exposed to infrared light. This light is not visible to the human eye, and is of a slightly lower frequency (or longer wavelength) than ordinary light. Any given chemical compound absorbs infrared light at specific frequencies that can be precisely measured and shown on a spectrum. The technique is extremely versatile and precise, requiring as little as a milligram of material.

A very small sample, which has been obtained by

extracting the ancient pottery sherd with an organic solvent (such as methanol or chloroform), is ground up together with the transparent solid, potassium bromide. The mixed sample is then placed in a micro cup that is inserted into the optical bench of the spectrometer, which no longer measures the infrared absorptions at individual frequencies, but uses a statistical technique called Fourier transformation. By this method, multiple passes of infrared light are rapidly reflected off the sample and recombined with the reference beam by a moving mirror, to yield an "interferogram." After Fourier-transform processing, the "interferogram" provides a very precise absorption spectrum for the ancient sample, with minimal background noise.

LIQUID CHROMATOGRAPHY

Liquid chromatography is rapidly becoming the main tool of biochemical research generally, even more so than gas chromatography, because many more compounds can be dissolved in a solvent than can be volatilised. The compounds are most efficiently separated by a technique called chromatography. Chromatography, in principal, is very simple: the "unknown" ancient sample is dissolved in a suitable organic solvent, which is then passed through a column that is lined with a material that preferentially absorbs the compounds of interest. Depending on how strong the affinity is between the compound, moving solvent, and stationary substrate, the compound will take more or less time to pass through the column. The goal is to separate the "unknown" into its component constituents, which can then be identified by analytical techniques, whether infrared spectrometry, mass spectrometry, or nuclear magnetic resonance.

After extraction of the ancient pottery, the sample is dissolved in a suitable solvent and a 10-microlitre volume is typically injected into the column. As materials come off the column, ultraviolet light (of higher frequency/shorter wavelength than visible light) is passed through them and their absorption spectra compared with an ever-growing database of modern and ancient standards. Ultraviolet light is selectively absorbed by electrons in molecules, depending on the nature of the chemical bond. The absorption spectrum is not as precise as infrared analysis or mass spectrometry, but, combined with an adequate separation of compounds, it can be an extremely powerful technique.

WET CHEMICAL SPOT TESTS

Two standard wet chemical tests, provide corroborative evidence for wine and barley beer. The presence of tartaric acid/tartrate, which occurs in large amounts in nature only in grapes (and therefore in wine), was confirmed by dissolving and heating the ancient sample in concentrated sulphuric acid. Dinaphthol is then added, to convert tartaric acid to a compound that exhibits green fluorescence under ultraviolet light. The specific test for barley beer focuses on calcium oxalate, which is a principal component of "beer stone" which settles out at the bottom and along the sides of barley beer processing and storage vessels. The oxalate is reduced by zinc granules in an acidic medium to glyoxalic acid, followed by reaction with phenyl hydrazine and hydrogen peroxide, to give a distinctive pinkish red colour.

DR. PATRICK E. McGOVERN
MASCA, University of Pennsylvania Museum, U.S.A.

EVERY VESSEL HAS A STORY TO TELL

A jug with dark–on–light floral decoration... an animal figurine... an elegant jug with reed decoration... a large stirrup jar with a tightly packed leaf design... a stirrup jar decorated with a delicate olive leaf pattern... These five vases illustrate the preoccupation in the Greek Bronze Age with motifs from the natural world, and the uncanny ability of the Minoan vase painter and potter to translate the beauty of the natural world onto the surface of a clay pot.

These five are present for the pleasure they afford the eye.

The sixth vessel, a tiny stirrup jar from the Late Minoan Cemetery (c. 1390-1190 B.C.) at Armenoi, yielded the important and unique organic residue result of "pure olive oil".

This stirrup jar and its important scientific result therefore serve to introduce the guiding principle behind "Minoans and Mycenaeans-Flavours of Their Time", a combination of pleasure for both eye and mind.

Beautiful vases and sturdy cooking vessels abound in Bronze Age Greece, but the quest behind this Exhibition was for something more: to try to find out what secrets lay beneath the elegant exteriors of decorated vases and the plain rough surfaces of ordinary domestic wares. This was done through the application of scientific tests to the fabric of Minoan and Mycenaean potsherds. The aim was to discover the purposes for which individual pots were used.

This was the inspiration. From this original idea sprang the environmental study and the study of skeletal material –all using different tests, but all the tests had the same objective: to reveal the secrets beneath the surface of pots, of plants, of shells, of bones – the secrets held beneath the surface of the material remains of Bronze Age Greece.

DR. YANNIS TZEDAKIS   DR. HOLLEY MARTLEW

1 JUG

R.M. 21837

MM I B (c. 2000-1900 B.C.)
Chamalevri, 1994. Pateras House. Room B.
On floor Z. Exc. No 11
H: 22.5 cm.; D: body 18 cm., base 9.8 cm.

Almost complete; restored. Light brown clay. Beaked jug with cutaway neck. Biconical body; narrow neck; roll handle, arched from rim to shoulder, flat base. Black and red paint covers the whole surface of the vase. Alternating orange and white (faded) three-leafed sprays decorate the upper part of the body.

M.A.-V.

2 JUG WITH REED PATTERN

H.M. 3962

LM I B (c. 1480-1425 B.C.)
Phaistos, Second Palace
H: 30 cm.; D: base 6 cm.

Piriform vase with tall neck, beak spout and strap handle. Relief ring at junction between neck and shoulders. Surface of vase covered with ochre-grey slip and decorated with dense black-painted reed pattern. Around the base, a band of the same colour defines a floral motif which is probably a stylised rendering of plant roots. Handle and interior of spout painted solid. Fine, pure, yellowish fabric. Excellent example of neopalatial, floral style. Firing and paint excellently executed. Mended from a large number of fragments and restored. Body and rim chipped.

A.K.-E.K.

3 STIRRUP JAR

CH.M. 4464

LM I B (c. 1480-1425 B.C.)
Chania, 1977. Kastelli hill - Greek Swedish Excavations. LM I House I - Room M.
Above floor. Exc. No 36
H: 46 cm.; D: body 35 cm., base 14 cm.

Almost complete, restored. Light brown, gritty clay; buff slip, red paint. Ovoid body; narrow flat base. Circular disk pierced by two holes. Cylindrical neck; two bosses attached to the rounded rim. Two small vertical handles, elliptical in section. Solid paint on both necks and on handles. On the body, tightly packed reed plants, naturalistically rendered, are growing from a groundline indicated by four horizontal bands. Traces of burning outside.

M.A.-V.

3

4 ANIMAL FIGURINE

. . . .

R.M. 7591

MM II (c. 1900-1700 B.C.)
Peak Sanctuary, Vrysinas
H: 10 cm.; Length: 13.5 cm.

The right front leg and the corresponding horn are restored. Brown buff gritty clay. Two discoid protuberances depict the eyes, cylindrical holes depict the nostrils, and an elongated deep incision depicts the mouth. Incisions also indicate female sex. A small incision marks each hoof. The tail is long and coils back against the body.

E.P.

5 STIRRUP JAR

. . . .

R.M. 1575

LM III B (c. 1340-1190 B.C.)
LM Cemetery of Armenoi. Tomb 6
H: 14.2 cm.; D: 19.2 cm.

Complete. Light brown clay. Squat, biconical body. The false neck and spout are tubular. Handles elliptical in section. Ring base. The main decorative theme is located on the shoulder of the vessel. On one side, two wide leaves filled with lines (FM 16); on the other side, the same motif, but it faces in the opposite direction. Additional motifs are sea anemones on the left and right of the rim. Bands encircle the body down to the base and two semi-circles decorate the disk on the top. The brown/reddish paint on yellowish slip is characteristic of the fine production of the Kydonia workshop.

E.P.

6 SMALL STIRRUP JAR

. . . .

R.M. 21121   EUM-332: Wall sherd

PURE OLIVE OIL

This is an important result. There was no indication of any other detectable ingredient. To have a "pure" substance of any kind is extremely unusual. This result is unique for this project.

Beck: See method of analysis.

LM III A2 (c. 1370-1340 B.C.)
LM Cemetery of Armenoi. Tomb 201
Sherds submitted for analysis averaged between 4 and 6 centimetres in diameter. The type is similar to that of R.M. 6593.

R.M. 6593 is a substitute for R.M. 21121/EUM-332, which only survived in sherd condition and could not be restored.

4

5

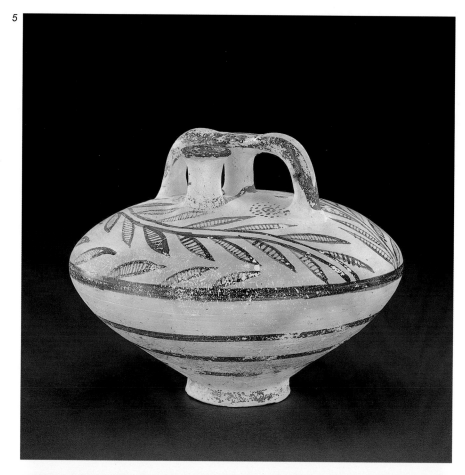

5 a

6   SMALL STIRRUP JAR
. . . .
R.M. 6593

LM III A2 (c. 1370-1340 B.C.)
LM Cemetery of Armenoi. Tomb 198
H: 6.4 cm.; D: body 6.9 cm.

Complete. Light brown clay, yellowish
slip. Brown to orange paint. Globular
body with sloping shoulders. Narrow false
neck. Cylindrical spout with rounded rim.
Handles elliptical in section. Flat base.
An unvoluted Minoan flower decorates
one side of the shoulder. Two systems of
concentric semi-circles decorate the other.
Bands run around the vase from belly to
base.

E.P.

What did they produce?

THEY PRODUCED OLIVE OIL

The choice for the environmental study was the Tzambakas House, Chamalevri, because it was rich in material. The date of MM I A (c. 2160-2000 B.C.) was strictly fortuitous. As it has turned out, the results of the study are more valuable than they otherwise might have been, because they date to a time before the Minoans built the first palaces.

The results of the environmental work carried out on Tzambakas House show how advanced methods of agricultural production were at the turn of the second millennium B.C.

DR. HOLLEY MARTLEW

The Importance of the Olive Tree

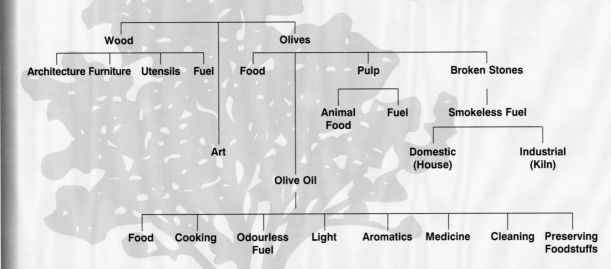

- Wood
  - Architecture
  - Furniture
  - Utensils
  - Fuel
  - Art
- Olives
  - Food
    - Olive Oil
      - Food
      - Cooking
      - Odourless Fuel
      - Light
      - Aromatics
      - Medicine
      - Cleaning
      - Preserving Foodstuffs
  - Pulp
    - Animal Food
    - Fuel
  - Broken Stones
    - Smokeless Fuel
      - Domestic (House)
      - Industrial (Kiln)

Production of Olive Oil

Olives

Stage 1: Preparation
① Pounding   or   ② Soaking in hot water

Stage 2: Pressing
① Pouches   or   ② Egyptian Method   or   ③ Wooden Clogs

Archaeological Evidence of Production

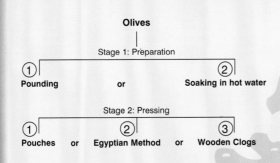

MM I A c. 2160-2000 B.C.

A landmark discovery at the prepalatial Minoan site of Chamalevri, West Crete: The earliest clear evidence for the systematic retrieval of broken olive pieces in great quantity.

LM I A c.1600-1480 B.C.

Lever press at the site of Alafouzos, Therasia (nr. Thera)

CHAMALEVRI-TZAMBAKAS HOUSE

Chamalevri is a village on the coast 10 km. east of Rethymnon. The results of two surface surveys in the past and a large number of recent excavations suggest that it was the site of a large, highly important Minoan settlement, the life of which covered the entire Minoan era. Linear A scholars identify it as the site of the city *da-*22-to*.

A MM I (c. 2160-1900 B.C.) building with a large number of rooms and an upper storey, covering an area of 355 square m. Built at a high point of the Tsikouriana hill, it controlled the surrounding farmland and looked over the ocean to the north, in the direction of the coastal settlement of Stavromenos. Other similar houses or building complexes are gradually coming to light not far away. The rock in this area is a soft limestone that was always conducive to the growing of olives and vines. It was, in fact, precisely the need to reorganise the cultivation of olives that was the occasion of this particular excavation (1994-1996), and indeed most of the excavations at Chamalevri.

Two main building phases have been identified in the building, associated with the MM I A and B periods (c. 2160-1900 B.C.). In the first phase, some of the floors on the ground floor were covered with red plaster, while others were simple earth floors. A number had circular depressions/hearths as sources of heat and light. In the second phase, the floors were of beaten earth. At this time there was radical reorganisation of the rooms, involving the destruction of old walls and the erection of new ones. It was possibly during this phase that the upper storey was added over part of the ground floor, and its walls covered with a layer of mainly white plaster. The kitchen complex occu-

pied the west part of the building, and had the characteristic furnishings and equipment, and large hearths/ pyres with ash and charcoal.

In the east part of the south corridor was installed a loom, judging by the large number of clay loomweights collected from the surrounding area. In order to admit abundant light, a triple opening/window was created in the outer wall next to it, and the bedrock that formed the bottom part of this wall was dressed for the purpose. This need for lighting perhaps presages the Minoan polythyron, the earliest example of which is the MM II A (c. 1900 B.C.) polythyron at Malia.

To the south of the triple opening an open area was created, in which were concentrated rubbish pits containing large quantities of pottery, animal bones, barnacles, whole vases –most of them cups– obsidian blades and flakes, fragments of stone vessels and stone tools. At this point, a wall with a different orientation was erected during the final years of the life of the building. On the floor of the now confined space were a large number of cups, a layer of ash and many barnacles, which are connected with the final destruction of the building.

Rubbish pits have also been located at various other points outside the building. In particular, the spaces left between the area dug for the foundations of the building and the walls that were erected and, also, the area along the entire outer east side, were filled with waste building material and pottery.

During the excavation of the Tzambakas house soil was systematically collected for archaeobiological investigation, the results of which are analysed below by An. Sarpaki. The most significant finding of this study was the identification of a large number of crushed olives. This points to the production of olive oil at Chamalevri about c. 2000 B.C., and also indicates that the pits were used as heating fuel for houses, a practice still to be found in Cretan villages today. The two-nozzled, low-footed lamp R.M. 21935, the tripod brazier R.M. 21839, and the hearths in the floors of the rooms in the Tzambakas house are further evidence of the association of the site with olives, olive oil, and the use of pits as heating fuel.

The MM I A (c. 2160-2000 B.C.) pottery consists of handleless deep carinated and one-handled globular cups, bowls with straight or slightly incurved sides, teapots, bridge-spouted jugs with a high carinated shoulder and beak-spouted jugs with a high, cutaway neck. In MM I B (c. 2000-1900 B.C.), the handleless cups are plainer, deep conical cups, while the one-handled version is wheel-made with a body that tends toward the conical. The shoulders on the bridgespouted jugs are lower, and in the case of beak-spouted jugs, the base is wider, the body is now carinated and the neck lower. Cooking vessels are invariably found in abundance.

The decoration is light-on-dark (dotted bands and straight lines in a variety of compositions) and dark-on-light (solid circles and semi-circles, hatched patterns). The MM I A (c. 2160-2000 B.C.) pottery is characterised by incised and barbotine decoration and an early use of colour, and in the following phase there is an increase in the coloured and barbotine examples.

MARIA ANDREADAKI-VLAZAKI
Director 25th Ephorate, Chania
Ministry of Culture

Chamalevri. Plan of the Tzambakas House.
(Architectural drawing by G. Christodoulakos).

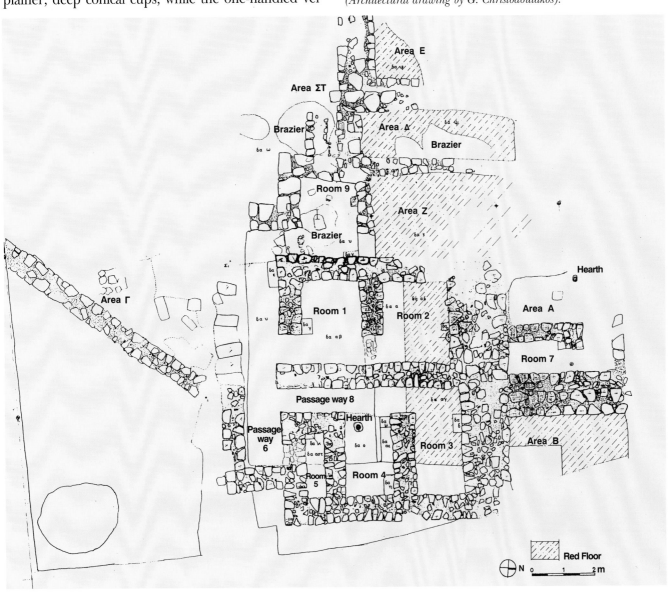

METHOD OF DATA RETRIEVAL

The procedure used for data retrieval is as follows: a water flotation machine is used to wash soil from archaeological excavations and to help separate the heavy fraction, the residue, which is composed of inorganic and organic matter, whose specific gravity is heavier than water. The light fraction, the so-called flot, floats up and away into two small sieves, whose mesh size is 1.00 and 2.50 microns. These capture all floating matter, most of which is organic, such as seeds, charcoal, shells, snails, insects, foraminifera and so forth. After the sorting and retrieval of environmental data from both residue and flot, these are submitted for further study by archaeological specialists. Sorting of the residue is done by eye, whereas the flot is separated into its components with the aid of stereoscopic microscopes.

The categories of organic remains are many and depend on the survival of organic and inorganic material. How much survives depends on specific environmental and taphonomic conditions at the site,

Flotation Machine

as well as, and most important, on the behaviour of its inhabitants.

Tzambakas House, Chamalevri, has provided a representative sample of plant material and many bones. Most of the former would have been totally missed, had the water flotation method not been implemented. This is of extreme importance and shows that the study of the archaeology of a site is not complete without detailed study of its surviving environmental data.

The collecting, washing and sorting procedure is followed by study. The archaeological material is identified using the relevant modern comparative collections. This method of comparing archaeological with modern material is suitable for all environmental data extracted from archaeological sites.

DR. ANAYA SARPAKI
Institute of Mediterranean Studies, Rethymnon, Crete

THE ARCHAEOBOTANICAL STUDY OF TZAMBAKAS HOUSE, RETHYMNON, CRETE

Tzambakas House is unique in Minoan archaeology for having had 129 soil samples submitted to rigorous environmental study. These represent in great detail Middle Minoan I A (c. 2160-2000 B.C.) which precedes the first palaces, and Middle Minoan I B (c. 2000-1900 B.C.) which coincides with the appearance of the palaces. All environmental and economic information, which contributes to the explosive change in social and economic structures, during this time, needs to be studied closely. The preliminary results of the archaeobotanical study are presented here.

The most important archaeobotanical finding was, to our great surprise, the large number of minutely broken fragments of **olive** stones. These would surely have been missed, had we not persevered with the work, as the typical method of checking for the archaeobotanical remains lies in the assessment of the charred remains from the coarse flot. At that point a decision is made whether to continue to water-float or not. It was decided not to stop, as we had free student labour. The olive fragments, though, were minute and at first were mistaken for specks of charcoal. When examined under a microscope, they were identified as broken fragments of olive stones.

The **olive** exists since the Early Minoan period in Crete, but there is no means of knowing whether it is the cultivated olive or the wild variety. Secondly, we have no evidence on the extent and the intensity of cultivation. Thirdly, we do not know the early uses of olive, i.e. whether it was cultivated to be eaten or whether the extraction of oil was practised.

The archaeobotanical finds from Tzambakas House have proven, beyond any doubt, that the olive must have been intensively cultivated, as olive oil was already extracted, at this site, prior to the building of the palaces. If not pressed in the building itself, at least pressing must have taken place not far away, as the broken stones seem to be dispersed everywhere in the building. A high concentration was found in Room 1 and in Corridor 6.

We know that olive stones can be given as feed to some animals such as pigs, but the high dispersion of the broken stones and the nature of the building argues against this thesis. Moreover, no whole stones have been found, so the storage of olives as food is, presently, excluded. The information that is imparted is: a) an early proof of the extraction of olive oil (MM I A to MM I B, c. 2160-1900 B.C.); and b) most probably, usage of these broken stones for fuel (cooking and heating), as we can think of no other reason to find the by-product of olive oil extraction in such a building. As we know, the use of olive stones for these purposes is perfect, especially in houses with bad ventilation, since olive stones do not produce smoke as normal wood does.

The other appearance of seeds in great numbers is the **fig**. Although we know that the tree existed locally, the find of fig seeds is ubiquitous at the site. Moreover, it is mostly present in mineralised form - very few seeds are charred. This is a mystery which cannot be explained totally at present.

The **almond** is always found broken and, although it is not found in large numbers, it is present in most samples. This is again an indication that the samples did not come from storage but are by-products of consumption.

The **grape** is not well represented, but is nevertheless present. It is also found fragmented and is, obviously, not a result of storage of dried grapes. The **pear** is also present, but in very small numbers.

Other cultivated plants are **cereals** and **legumes.** They are surely under-represented and by no means reflect the archaeological situation *per se*. Although they are very few, they are indicative, probably, of a real presence.

All of the evidence of cereals – even the fragments marked 'cerealia' – point to the presence of wheat. The only glume base which was found points, with reservation, to **Triticum dicoccum,** emmer wheat. The absence of barley, which is a common crop in the most arid parts of Greece, could imply either that the fields belonging to the economic sphere of Chamalevri were quite fertile, and that, therefore, the cultivation of wheat was economically viable, or that this particular building represents a wealthy household.

On the other hand, the **legumes** are equally represented, a fact which implies that there is a balance between the number of legumes and cereals. Could we be seeing again a case of crop rotation, such as cereal/ wheat - legumes - cereals etc? The presence of faba beans, **Vicia faba,** is perhaps indicative of some kind of garden agriculture, as this plant needs a watering regime. There is also lentil, **Lens sp., Trifolium** and **Medicago sp.** The last two can be used as green fodder and/or green 'manure' for fertilising the fields.

WILD PLANTS

Thymelaea hirsuta: the use of this plant as some kind of broom cannot be excluded, whether it refers to sweeping the threshing floor or the living room floor. Its high presence in Room 4 is intriguing. However, it is also interesting that the tough fibres in its stem have been used for rope-making. Another species', **Thymelaea tartonraira's,** shoots were used for sail-making. So is this plant the result of cleaning, i.e. brooms, or does it indicate the collection of plants brought to the site for rope-making etc?

The presence of **Pistacia sp., Celtis sp.** (cf. australis), the nettle tree, found mineralised, and **Sambucus** gives an indication of the wild fruits which might have been collected not far from the site and, probably, indicates a maquis vegetation.

DR. ANAYA SARPAKI

Institute of Mediterranean Studies, Rethymnon, Crete

7 OLIVE TREE FRESCO FRAGMENTS

H.M. 39

LM I (c. 1600-1425 B.C.)
Palace of Knossos, excavation by A. Evans
Surface: 28.5×28.5 cm.

Fragment of a wall-painting, of lime-plaster. Depiction of olive branches in the fresco technique. Grey-green colour on an off-white background. Mended from 23 fragments.

A.K.-E.K.

8 BRAZIER, TRIPOD

R.M. 21839

MM I B (c. 2000-1900 B.C.)
Chamalevri, 1995. Tzambakas House.
Room 5. Exc. No 63
H: 19.7 cm.; D: small rim 26.5/27.5 cm., base 16.7 cm.

Almost completely preserved; restored. Reddish yellow, gritty clay; red paint. Conical body; broad, rolled rim; flat base; elliptical leg section. Painted inside and out.

M.A.-V.

7

10 QUERN

R.M. 2913

MM (c. 2160-1700 B.C.)
Chamalevri, 1997. Pateras House.
Surface 28.7×28.3 cm.; H: 12.1 cm.

Quern, saddle; regular form. Sandstone, mid-grey; fine grained. A corner
is lost. Its base has a large amount
swollen off; sides with rounded corners,
also may show high levels of polished
surface. Top has all over low polish.

D.E.

11 CRUSHING TOOL

R.M. 2912

MM I A (c. 2160-2000 B.C.)
Chamalevri, 1994. Pateras House.
On the floor. Exc. No ME81
L: 15.1 cm.; W: 9.6 cm.; H: 4.6 cm.

Complete. Probably sandstone, grey with
quartz veins; fine grained. Elongated,
ovoid. Natural pebble, one face and
sides unaltered; lower face may have a
central zone, where the stone's surface
has been pitted by being used to hammer
something.

D.E.

8

9

9 LAMP, PEDESTALLED

R.M. 21935

MM I B (c. 2000-1900 B.C.)
Chamalevri, 1996. Tzambakas House.
Corridor 6. Exc. No 142
H: 7.2 cm.; D: small rim 19.9 cm., foot 9 cm.

Almost completely preserved. Reddish
brown clay, turned to dark grey by fire.
Shallow body; broad, flat rim with two
horizontal wick spouts, and low, hollow
pedestal. Burnished. Heavily burnt.

M.A.-V.

10-11

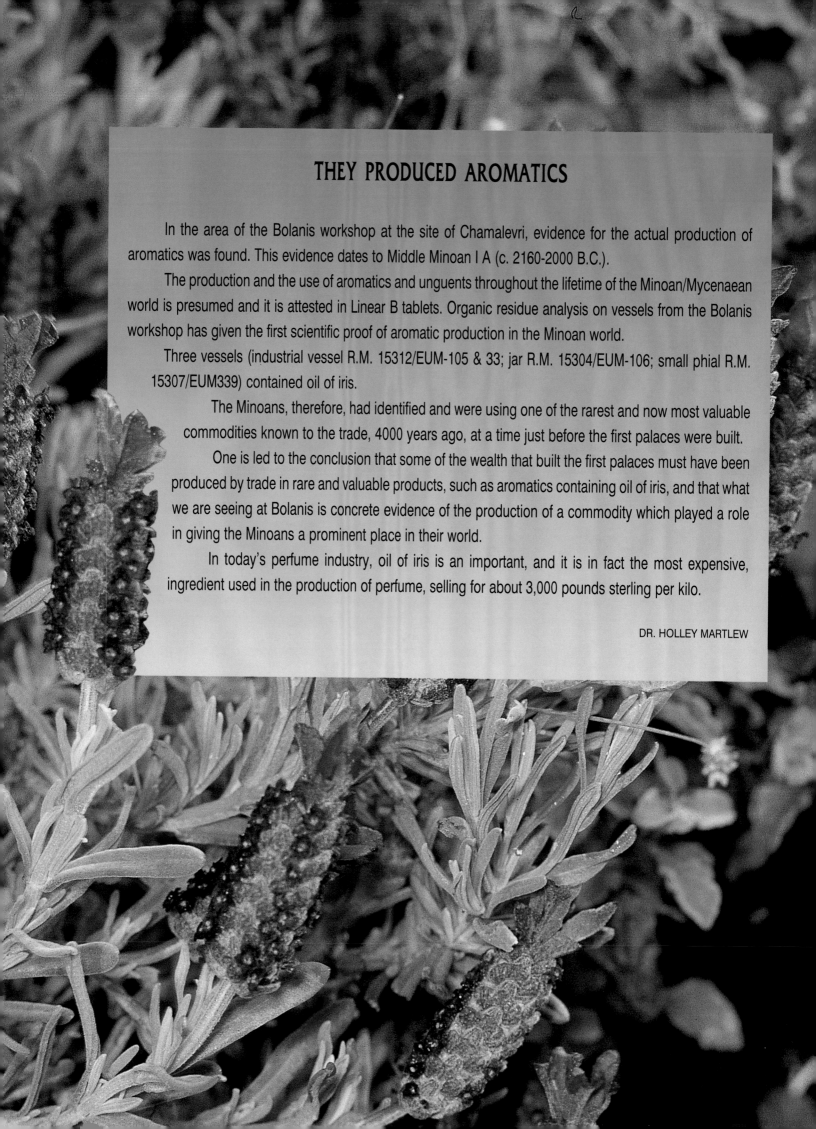

THEY PRODUCED AROMATICS

In the area of the Bolanis workshop at the site of Chamalevri, evidence for the actual production of aromatics was found. This evidence dates to Middle Minoan I A (c. 2160-2000 B.C.).

The production and the use of aromatics and unguents throughout the lifetime of the Minoan/Mycenaean world is presumed and it is attested in Linear B tablets. Organic residue analysis on vessels from the Bolanis workshop has given the first scientific proof of aromatic production in the Minoan world.

Three vessels (industrial vessel R.M. 15312/EUM-105 & 33; jar R.M. 15304/EUM-106; small phial R.M. 15307/EUM339) contained oil of iris.

The Minoans, therefore, had identified and were using one of the rarest and now most valuable commodities known to the trade, 4000 years ago, at a time just before the first palaces were built.

One is led to the conclusion that some of the wealth that built the first palaces must have been produced by trade in rare and valuable products, such as aromatics containing oil of iris, and that what we are seeing at Bolanis is concrete evidence of the production of a commodity which played a role in giving the Minoans a prominent place in their world.

In today's perfume industry, oil of iris is an important, and it is in fact the most expensive, ingredient used in the production of perfume, selling for about 3,000 pounds sterling per kilo.

DR. HOLLEY MARTLEW

CHAMALEVRI, PRE-PALATIAL WORKSHOP AT BOLANIS

In 1992, part of an open-air workshop was discovered at Bolanis, Chamalevri. It dates from the advanced MM I A phase (c. 2160-2000 B.C.) and there are strong indications that it was more than a simple household workshop and suggesting that it was an organised craft-industry of this period: a long paved path affording communication between, and also separating, the individual activities, a large number of hearths and pyres of different types, clay vessels of distinctive shape and specialised function, and large rubbish pits.

DETAILED DESCRIPTION

A paved path traverses the site, dividing it into a north and south part. The north part has been more thoroughly investigated and has accordingly produced more evidence. The path consists of a series of large pebbles with a bedding of sherds, gravel and earth, forming a level walkway. Only the north side of it is carefully finished, with a row of closely set pebbles. The south face cannot be made out.

Two pits (K and Σ) were investigated at the east end of the excavations, the first of which dates from LM III C1 (c. 1190-1130 B.C.), while the second, long, shallow pit is contemporary with the building complex. Two pyres (1 and 2) were found next to the pits. A long, clay vessel resembling a water-spout (R.M. 15521) and the base of a cylindrical vase were found in contact with pyre 2. A small wall to the south formed the boundary of an unexplored area with a great quantity of ash and a large number of sherds from burnt functional vessels. The wall is followed by a curved stone structure, only part of which is preserved. The paved path starts at this point.

Two contiguous hearths were found to the north of the above area. Hearth 1, which is rectangular in shape, has a floor of rectangular bricks with strong signs of burning. The east front is bounded by a row of stones. The bottom of a burnt vase (R.M. 15304), a burnt bowl (R.M. 15311) and a handleless cup were found in a small recess to the southwest. Hearth 2 is oval in shape and has a floor of grey-white clay, the surface of which is burnt and is a red colour, and jet-black at its highest point. Of the northeast part of the

Plan of the excavated area, workshop at Bolanis.

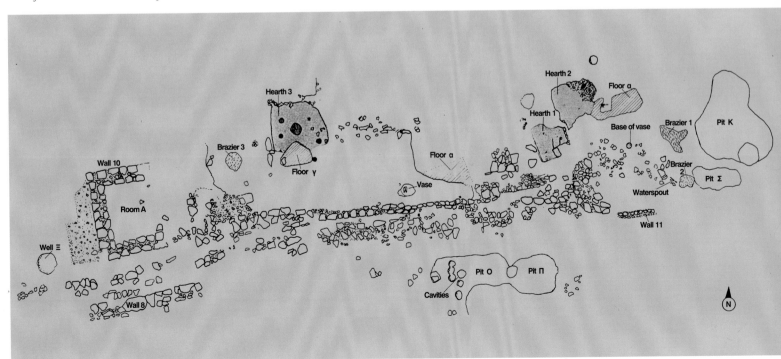

hearth, only the substratum and a few little stones survive. Two trenches were dug to the northeast and northwest of the two hearths. The one to the northeast contained only earth, while the other was dug specially to receive the lid of a pithos (R.M. 15519), which has a large circular hole cut in the centre. The vessel was then inverted and placed in the cutting, forming a completely flat surface; on this rested the base of a cylindrical vase, of which the entire bottom is also missing (R.M. 15313). This structure seems to have been intended for a liquid that, for some reason, had to penetrate down to the bedrock.

To the west was found a clay vessel of specialised function, with holes in the body and bottom (R.M. 15312), and a burnt bowl (R.M. 15311). To the south were found two contiguous pits (O and P), the second of which belongs to the LM III C1 phase (c. 1190-1130 B.C.). Pit O, which has some at present inexplicable cavities at the bottom, contained 22 handleless cups of the MM I A period (c. 2160-2000 B.C.), apparently placed in groups. Together with them was a carbonised clay disc from the bottom of a cylindrical vessel.

A third hearth (hearth 3), found to the northwest, had some very distinctive features. It is a four-sided structure bounded by stones at the west. It has a floor of beaten earth and red clay in places, in which there are five cavities, all of them small ones, apart from the central cavity, which had distinct traces of burning around it. An intact jug (R.M. 15302) had been placed next to the southeast cavity. Pieces of obsidian and quartz were found on the floor of the hearth, along with a clay weight bearing 39 impressions made by a seal with a floral motif (R.M. 13247). The continuation of the pit to the northeast has not been excavated, but there are many sherds from burnt cooking pots on the surface here. To the southwest is another pyre (pyre 3), which had a large number of obsidian blades on the surface. The two miniature vases (R.M. 15307 and 15308) from this general area and the area of hearth 3, which exhibit signs of fierce burning, are certainly to be associated with the particular workshop activities of this installation.

At the west end of the explored area was found

room A, on either side of which were open areas paved with pebbles. Another building begins on the south side of the path, directly opposite room A.

The pottery is characterised by the presence of handleless carinated cups, painted vases decorated in the dark-on-light and light-on-dark techniques, amongst which were a few coloured cups with a low foot (egg-cups or goblets), drinking-cups, tripod and other functional vases with incised and barbotine decoration, most of them jugs and cups, which are similar to groups of the MM I A period (c. 2160-2000 B.C.) found in Central Crete, such as the groups from Knossos (Kouloures), Phaistos (Paterikies), Archanes (Phourni) and Pediada (Gournes).

We did not know what was produced in this particular area. Until quite recently, the evidence available made it possible to rule out processing of metals (complete absence of slag and metal objects) and the production of pottery (absence of the features characteristic of a facility of this nature). There was undoubtedly widespread, intensive use of fire. We concluded that the product in question was perishable, and may have been associated with the products attributed to the Minoan city *da-*22-to*, which is placed by most students of Linear B at the site of Chamalevri-Stavromenos, despite the chronological gap separating the MM I A installation (c. 2160-2000 B.C.) and the LM III A (c. 1390-1340 B.C.) tablets. These products are grain, olives, flax, sheep, cattle, wool, aromatic plants and textiles. The discovery of the clay weight with the seal-impressions of a floral motif directed our thoughts provisionally to textiles and flax. We decided to suspend excavation at this particular site, in order to study the data more closely, rather than continue blindly to investigate a highly sensitive area. The finds are almost all from the surface and are badly worn from repeated ploughing of the field.

The results of the analyses of samples from five different vessels (R.M. 15304, 15302, 15312, 15323 and 15521), suggesting that the workshop was engaged in the processing of aromatic plants (such as the iris), while quite unexpected, are very reasonable.

MARIA ANDREADAKI-VLAZAKI
Director 25th Ephorate, Chania, Ministry of Culture

THE ADMONITIONS OF IPW-WER 3
PAPYRUS OF LEIDEN

No-one sails to Byblos today, what shall we do concerning 's-trees' for our mummies?

One used to bury the priests with deliveries of them, one used to embalm the great with oil;

as far as Keftiu they are unable to come and gold is lacking...

We are happy that the oasis-dwellers come with their offerings.

This text was found on a hieratic papyrus dated to the 19th or 20th Dynasties, but is likely to have been first written as early as the end of the Old Kingdom or the beginning of the First Intermediate Period (c. 2200 B.C.).

It deals in part with broken commercial relations with Egypt's northern trading partners, Byblos and the lands of the Keftiu or Crete. Already by the time this text was written, trade relations between Egypt and Byblos were so important, that it has been speculated that Egypt's major trading station in the north was situated there. The fact that the lands of the Keftiu are mentioned means that it may well have been a place sailed to via Byblos.

The commodity referred to, oil or resin from "s-trees" is not known outside Egypt and was especially imported from Byblos for mummification. The reference to the Keftiu lands is a lamentation about a disruption of trade with the island, probably in an exotic commodity, likely to be perfumed oil. Already by the time of the Middle Minoan I A period (c. 2000 B.C.), before the first palaces, there was an established aromatic oil industry at the site of Bolanis, Chamalevri, in Western Crete.

DR. ROBERT ARNOTT
Dept. of Ancient History and Archaeology
University of Birmingham, U.K.

THE PRODUCTION OF AROMATIC AND PHARMACEUTICAL OILS IN MINOAN CRETE: THE CASE OF CHAMALEVRI

The use of pharmaceutical and aromatic oils to clean and beautify the body was widespread in the Eastern Mediterranean during the Bronze Age and is first found in Mesopotamia and Egypt (fig. 1). In cuneiform texts, aromatic oil is counted as one of the three most important items in life, together with food and clothing.

With its long hours of sunshine and temperate climate, the island of Crete is renowned for the abundance of aromatic plants that grow well in its soil. The similarity to the descriptions of oil by Theophrastos, Pliny and Dioscorides in Classical and Roman times, pointing to the long, unchanged history of the techniques used in making ancient perfume.

One of the cities of Minoan Crete mentioned in the Linear B tablets in association with the production of oil and aromatic plants is "*da-22-to*", which students of Linear B place in the region of Chamalevri. The discovery in 1980, in a grave in this area, of two LM II (c. 1425-1390 B.C.) vases apparently associated with

Perfume workshop in ancient Egypt. Scene from a tomb at Egyptian Thebes (1500 B.C.): C. Singer - E. J. Holmyard - A.R. Hall, A History of Tecnhology, Oxford 1954 (3rd ed. 1956).

Minoans realized the value of these plants in everyday life from an early date, and the gathering and processing of them was a vital Minoan occupation. Valuable aromatic and pharmaceutical oils were manufactured for export on a significant scale and formed an important source of revenue. The Mycenaeans are thought to have learned the art of making perfumes from the Minoans, for, according to Marinatos, "olive oil, the noblest of all oils, seems to have been a virtual monopoly first of the Minoan and then of the Mycenaean civilisation".

The Linear B tablets from Knossos (series Fh and Fp), dating from the early 14th c. B.C., and from Pylos (series Fr), dating from 1200 B.C., which presuppose local control and a central authority, afford incontrovertible evidence for aromatic oils. Study of the texts reveals that the ingredients used and the processing of Creto-Mycenaean perfumes bear a striking the making of perfume (the pyxis-strainer R.M. 2337 and the vessel with a fire box lid R.M. 2338), lends further support to the theory that the Minoans of Chamalevri engaged in this activity.

The recent analysis of MM I A (c. 2160-2000 B.C.) vases from the excavation at Bolanis, Chamalevri, which identified traces of olive oil, iris oil, honey and resin, is very revealing, and can hardly be regarded as a fortuitous result. On the basis of this evidence, various structures and features discovered in the Bolanis excavation (pyres, hearths and a pavement), as well as the distinctive clay vessels, may readily be associated with a perfume workshop and the various specialized procedures involved in the technique. The distinct traces of fire on the surface of many of the vases from Bolanis is probably the result of the heating of the olive oil solvent. The miniature phials R.M. 15307 and

15308 were maybe used as measures. The unusually great concentration of obsidian blades on the surface of pyre 3, which were used to cut up soft materials, is perhaps connected with the chopping of aromatic materials, such as the iris rhizome (*wi-ri-za* in Linear B, according to Palmer). Moreover, the most distinct of the imprints taken from the seal on the clay loomweight R.M. 13247 from hearth 3 can probably be interpreted as depictions of the iris flower.

The existence of an advanced perfume industry in Crete as early as 2000 B.C. is not surprising. The well-known Egyptian Medical Papyrus in London (British Museum EA 10059), which, while dating from the 15th c. B.C., is thought to be a copy of a text dating from the end of the 3rd millennium B.C., cites a medical prescription designed to counter "the Asian illness" in the language of the Keftiu. At a period just before the construction of the first palaces on Crete, a craft-industry unit was functioning at Chamalevri that presupposes the development of forms of collective economic activity requiring special organisation, coordination and control. It was, in any case, the contacts of Crete with Egypt and Syria at this period that led to the idea of building the first palaces.

Today, all one has to do is take a walk in the low hills around Chamalevri, in order to encounter several of the indigenous plants of Crete, to breathe in the scent of the characteristic herbs, and to link the rich olive groves of the region with the production of olive oil at Chamalevri in MM I A.

MARIA ANDREADAKI-VLAZAKI
Director 25th Ephorate, Chania
Ministry of Culture

THE LITHIC INDUSTRY AT CHAMALEVRI

The small chipped stone industry of the prepalatial Bolanis settlement MM I A (c. 2160-2000 B.C.) is a typical industry of Bronze Age Greece. Obsidian is grey opaque or grey-black semi-translucent with bands, originating from Melos, whereas flint, probably Cretan, is represented by only two pieces.

The lack of unworked raw material, of cortex removal and core shaping products, as well as the small amount of technical pieces signify that this stage of the reduction sequence took place somewhere in the vicinity. The industry is also characterised by the predominance of blades (mainly micro-blades) produced by pressure, by the limited degree of retouch and the lack of standardised tool types.

The concentration of debitage products around "pyre 3" and "hearth 3" is worth noting: there are debris, technical pieces and quite a few blades, especially micro-blades, entire or fragmentary. Especially in the area of pyre 3, the flint flake bears marginal retouch scars. Many of the blades and micro-blades bear peripheral use scars. During this period the obsidian blades were usually left unretouched because their natural edges were sharp enough. These "*a posteriori*" tools were useful in the manufacture of soft materials. Despite the lack of use- wear analysis, judging by other finds in the same area, it would not seem unreasonable to suggest that these artefacts (in their initial entire state) fulfilled the task of cutting plant stems, leaves or flowers into pieces.

SOPHIA PREVE
Archaeologist

12

12

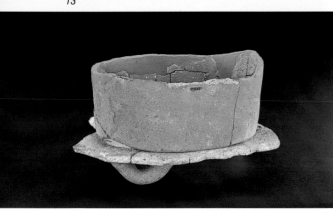

13

14-15

12   INDUSTRIAL VESSEL

R.M. 15312   EUM-105, EUM-33: 2 wall sherds

OIL OF IRIS
A complex preparation for cosmetic use

There were 120 chemical components found in this vessel. In addition to iris oil, olive oil is indicated, and pine resin. Other possible identifications (not confirmed results as the oil of iris) include carnation and anise.

Beck: See method of analysis.

MM I A (c. 2160-2000 B.C.)
Chamalevri, 1992. Bolanis Workshop. North of the stone-paved path; between Hearths Nos 1 and 3. Exc. No 57
H: 21.5 cm.; D: body 21.5 cm., base 13.5 cm.

Only partly preserved and therefore problematic; partly restored. Reddish brown, gritty clay; wet-smoothed. Globular body. Several holes perforate the body and base; the lower backside of the body is depressed. Vertical rim; flat base with relief rope pattern on its contour. Two short feet with central groove fit horizontally at the one side of the base. Plain. Burnt outside. Two sherds were taken for analysis prior to restoration.

M.A.-V.

13   JAR

R.M. 15304   EUM-106: Wall sherd

OIL OF IRIS. OLIVE OIL

Definite confirmed results. What has been found is clearly an aromatic which would be expected to be used in perfume and unguents.

Beck: See method of analysis.

MM I A (c. 2160-2000 B.C.)
Chamalevri, 1992. Bolanis Workshop. SW of Hearth No 1; recess
H: (max. pres.) 14.5 cm.; D: (pres.) body 22 cm., base 14.1 cm.

Only the lower part of the body is preserved; partly restored. Reddish yellow gritty clay. Traces of red paint. Globular body; flat base with incisions and a lump of clay in the exact places where three legs would fit (unsuccessful effort?). Solid paint outside. Heavily burnt in and out. A sherd was taken for analysis prior to restoration (4 to 6 cm. in diameter).

M.A.-V.

14   PITHOID VESSEL

R.M. 15313   EUM-108: Wall sherd

AN ESSENTIAL OIL

Beck: See method of analysis.

MM I A (c. 2160-2000 B.C.)
Chamalevri, 1992. Bolanis Workshop. Construction NW of Hearths Nos 1 and 2. Exc. No 62
H: (pres.) 14 cm.; D: 31 cm.

Only the lower part of the body is preserved; partly restored. Reddish brown, gritty clay; wet-smoothed. Cylindrical body. The whole base is missing; intentional flattening of the contour in order to fit well on top of the vase R.M. 15519. Plain. A sherd was taken for analysis prior to restoration (4 to 6 cm in diameter).

M.A.-V.

15   LID

R.M. 15519

MM I A (c. 2160-2000 B.C.)
Chamalevri, 1992. Bolanis Workshop. Construction NW of Hearths Nos 1 and 2. Exc. No 63
D: (max. pres.) 40 cm.; H: 7.5 cm.; Thickness: 1.9 cm.

Partly preserved and restored. Light reddish yellow. Heavily gritty clay. Circular in shape with a cylindrical handle set horizontally on the middle of the upper surface. A large intentional hole on the body, flat underneath in order to fit well on the vase R.M. 15313. Plain.

M.A.-V.

16

18

16 CHANNEL

R.M. 15521 EUM-335: Wall sherd

BEESWAX (HONEY) AND PROBABLY OLIVE OIL
There were 119 components found in this vessel

Beck: See method of analysis.

MM I A (c. 2160-2000 B.C.)
Chamalevri, 1992. Bolanis Workshop. Beside Fireplace No 2. Exc. No 11
L: 8.9 cm.; W: 18-19 cm.

Many fragments are missing; restored. Buff to pink, gritty clay with grey core; whitish and buff wash. Elongated body; upright sides ending to thick, rounded rim; flat base. Trough-shaped at both ends. Plain. A sherd was taken for analysis prior to restoration (4 to 6 cm. in diameter)

M.A.-V.

17 JUG

R.M. 15302

MM I A (c. 2160-2000 B.C.)
Chamalevri, 1992. Bolanis Workshop. Beside Hearth No 3. Exc. No 58
H: 21.5 cm.; D: body 15 cm., base 6.7 cm.

The neck is partly missing; restored. Reddish brown, fine clay. Traces of dark paint. Beaked jug with cutaway neck. Globular-conical body; tall neck; flat base. The roll handle is slightly arched and goes from the rim to the shoulder. Solidly painted outside.

M.A.-V.

18 BOWL (LEKANE)

R.M. 15311

MM I A (c. 2160-2000 B.C.)
Chamalevri, l992. Bolanis Workshop. SW of Hearth No 1; recess
H: 7.6 cm.; D: small rim 24.5 cm., base 9.3 cm.

Big part of the rim is missing; restored. Light reddish brown, gritty clay; buff wash. Shallow bowl or lekane. Conical body; outward-flaring rim; flat base. Plain. Heavily burnt inside and out.

M.A.-V.

19 MINIATURE PHIAL

17

R.M. 15307 EUM-339: Wall/upper base sample

OIL OF IRIS. BEESWAX MIXTURE WITH A STRONG CEREAL PRESENCE

Was this tiny vessel used as a measure?

Evans: See method of analysis.

MM I A (c. 2160-2000 B.C.)
Chamalevri, 1992. Bolanis Workshop. Stone-paved path, south of Fireplace No 3. Exc. No 52
H: 3.9 cm.; D: small rim 3.9 cm., base 3.1 cm.

Almost complete; restored. Brown, gritty clay. Handleless miniature spouted phial; deep conical body; slightly flaring rim; flat base. Plain. Heavily burnt inside and out.

M.A.-V.

19

20 MINIATURE PHIAL

R.M. 15308

MM I A (c. 2160-2000 B.C.)
Chamalevri, 1992. Bolanis Workshop. Close
to Hearth No 3
H: 5 cm.; D: 2.6 cm.

Part of the rim is missing. Buff to reddish
brown clay. Cylindrical body with flat
base. Plain. Heavily burnt inside and out.

M.A.-V.

21 SPINDLE WHORL

R.M. 13247

MM I A (c. 2160-2000 B.C.)
Chamalevri, 1992. Bolanis Workshop.
On Hearth No 3. Exc. No ME 136
H: 3.3 cm.; D: body 4.3 cm.

Completely preserved. Light grey
brownish clay, slightly gritty. Pierced with

20

a vertical hole. The surface is covered by
39 impressions of a seal's edge, but only
a small part of the edge is impressed
each time. The impressions are faint
and badly preserved. They seem to
indicate a more or less circular flat seal
(cylinder?) with an original diameter of
perhaps 1.1 cm. The composite drawing
of the best-preserved impressions suggest
a motif which could be described as
branches with pointed leaves at the end
or a flower (iris?). Seal impressions on
spindle whorls are not common, but
stamped loom weights are well-known
from the pre-palatial period until the
end of LM I (c. 1425 B.C). According to
Poursat, such impressions "suggest some
sort of control and organization of the
production".

M.A.-V.

22 "WHETSTONE"

R.M. 1787

MM I A (c. 2160-2000 B.C.)
Chamalevri, 1992. Bolanis Workshop.
Exc. No ME 100
L: 12.3 cm.; W: 4.4-3.5 cm.; Weight: 215 gm.

Complete. Some concretion on face.
Natural regular form. Enhanced by use.
No scratches, but surface smooth (low
polish visible in places) from use.

D.E.

22

23

23 STONE AXE

R.M. 1788

MM I A (c. 2160-2000 B.C.)
Chamalevri, 1992. Bolanis Workshop.
Exc. No ME 59
L: 7.35 cm.; W: 3.7 cm.; H: 2.85 cm.

Almost completely preserved. Dark green
hard stone. Elongated in shape.

M.A.-V.

21

21

24 CONICAL CUPS, DEEP

R.M. 16000, 16001, 16003, 16005, 16008, 16010, 16011, 16012, 16013, 16014, 16017, 16028, 16030, 16031, 16032, 16034, 16035, 16047

MM I A (c. 2160-2000 B.C.)
Chamalevri, 1992. Bolanis Workshop. Pit O.
Exc. Nos 31-33, 36-47, 49, 51, 53
H: 5.7-7.6 cm.; D: rim 7.5-8.8 cm.,
body 6.3-9.6 cm., base 4.3-5.8 cm.

Complete or almost complete; restored. Reddish brown or buff, slightly gritty clay. Buff wash on a few of them. Deep and wide body; handleless; flat base. A strong carination below the middle of the body. Plain. Two of them are burnt. The cup R.M. 16047 has a piriform body, vertical rim and narrow, flat base; traces of dark wash cover the outside.

M.A.-V.

25 CONICAL CUPS, DEEP

R.M. 16002, 16004, 16006, 16007, 16009, 16015, 16018, 16026

MM I A (c. 2160-2000 B.C.)
Chamalevri, 1992. Bolanis Workshop. Found scattered along the stone-paved path. Exc. Nos 26, 27, 29 (R.M. 16009 which was found in the recess together with R.M. 15304 and R.M. 15311), 34, 35,54, 55, 59.
H: 5-6.2 cm.; D: rim 7.3-9.1 cm.,
body 6.3-7.3 cm., base 4.3 cm.

Complete or almost complete; restored. Reddish brown or buff, slightly gritty clay. Deep and wide body; handleless; flat base. A strong or light carination below the midst of the body.

M.A.-V.

26 OBSIDIAN AND FLINT

MM I A (c. 2160-2000 B.C.)
Chamalevri, 1992, Bolanis Workshop

The majority of the debitage from stone working in Trench I at Bolanis were found in the area of pyre 3. In the main, they consist of partially corticated flakes and a prismatic chip of obsidian (Λ1607-5, 1607-10 to 12, 1607-15 to 16, 1609-7, 1609-10a and 10b), and fragments of pressure blades and micro-blades (Λ1607-3 1607-6, 1607-17, 1607-19, 1607-21, 1609-6). Traces of use probably connected with activities in this area can be detected on a flake (Λ1607-1) and several blades and micro-blades preserved intact or in fragments (Λ1607-4, 1607-7, 1607-9, 1607-13 and 14, 1607-18, 1607-20, 1607-23). Around floor γ were collected a crested chip-blade of 2nd series (Λ1698-2), a blade, a micro-blade and an irregular chip (Λ1609-3 and 4, 1607-24), as well as the unique flint flake, which also shows signs of working (Λ1609-1). From hearth 3 were collected a flake and a chip (Λ1629-7, 1630-3), a crested blade of 3rd series (Λ1631) and rejuvenation flakes of the striking platform (Λ1693-3, 1632), fragments of blades and micro-blades (Λ1629-1, 1629-4, 1629-6, 1630-4), as well as a flake and fragments of blades and micro-blades bearing traces of use (Λ1630-5, 1629-2, 1629-5).

S.P.

24

25

26
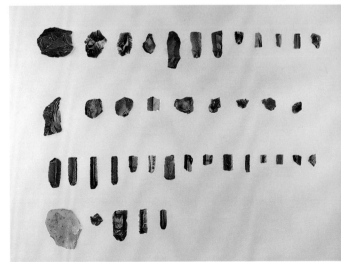

27

27 STRAINER WITH LID

R.M. 2337

LM II (c. 1425-1390 B.C.)
Stavromenos - Chamalevri, 1980.
Rock-cut tomb
H: 31.1/40.8 (with lid) cm.; D: body 26 cm.,
lid 17.1 cm.

Completely preserved. Light brown, fine clay with reddish core; composition typical of Central Crete. Whitish slip; black to brown lustrous paint. Globular-conical body with pierced bottom and cylindrical, hollow base; short, collar rim; two horizontal strap handles with central rib. Semi-globular lid with basket strap handle. The widest part of the belly is accented by a bold running spiral, linked by groups of papyrus flowers. Lilies (lilium candidum), crocuses (crocus carthwrightianus or sativus) and, probably, caper plants spring up around the tapering lower body. Horizontal row of stylised lilies on the lid. Strainers are normally decorated in an elaborate manner, usually with striking floral designs, and these vessels seem to be connected to the production and use of aromatics.

M.A.-V.

28 POT WITH FIRE-BOX LID

R.M. 2338

LM II (c. 1425-1390 B.C.)
Stavromenos - Chamalevri, 1980.
Rock-cut tomb
H: 11.3/14.1 (with lid) cm.; D: base 17 cm.

Completely preserved except for the capsule of the fire-box. Reddish brown, gritty clay; thick, whitish yellow slip; reddish yellow paint. Cylindrical body; short, collar rim with groove to enable the lid to fit well; flat base; two small horizontal, roll handles. The firebox belongs to the flanged type. The body of the pot is decorated by labiate flowers (stylised crocuses) in a horizontal row. Both the strainer R.M. 2337 and the pot with fire-box lid R.M. 2338 were funerary gifts in the LM II period (c. 1425-1390 B.C.). Their function was specialised and connected with the use of aromatics.

M.A.-V.

THE USE OF AROMATICS

Organic residue analysis on potsherds from the Late Minoan Cemetery of Armenoi (c. 1390-1190 B.C.) illustrates the use of aromatics and unguents in the Minoan world.

Particularly note the vessels with iris motifs in the light of what we now know was the use of oil of iris in the production of aromatics and unguents.

Prior to these results' being obtained, oil of iris is not known as a commodity in Minoan Crete from any other source. There is no known Linear B sign for it. All we had were vases decorated with iris motifs, such as those found at the Cemetery of Armenoi, which probably indicates two things: first, the continuity of the use of products that contained oil of iris, since this site dates to the Late Minoan III period, 600 years after Bolanis; and, second, it suggests that these products were used in funerary practice.

DR. HOLLEY MARTLEW

28

ARMENOI, RETHYMNON

The village of Armenoi is situated 10 kilometers south of the town of Rethymnon, on the main road which leads to the south coast of Crete.

One kilometer north of the village, the greatest Late Minoan III A/B (c. 1390-1190 B.C.) necropolis was discovered on a shallow hill called Prinokephalo. The name Prinokephalo means "hill of the wild oaks" and it is the only surviving oak forest in the area of Rethymnon. Systematic excavations started in 1969, and are still continuing. 227 tombs including one tholos (the tholos probably dates to LM II, c. 1425-1390 B.C.), have been uncovered up to the present time. Each tomb represents a family group.

All the tombs were dug into the rock, and each consists of a corridor and a chamber. The corridor is composed either of a staircase or a ramp.

The main characteristics of the Cemetery are that the surface of the rock was levelled in several areas to make the building of, and access to, the tombs easier and roads were constructed. Initially there was an overall plan for the Cemetery which included special areas that were designated for the wealthy tombs and the poor ones, but this plan was abandoned during the Late Minoan III B period (c. 1340-1190 B.C.) and resulted in a mixture of large and small tombs throughout the Cemetery. We believe that there would have been a boundary and a formal entrance, but they have not yet been located.

The wealthier tombs possessed tombstones of different sizes. Eleven of them were collected, but they were not found *in situ*. We believe that these tombstones provided clues for tomb robbers, as it is only the tombs which had tombstones that were robbed. These robberies took place at the end of the Minoan period, after the Cemetery was deserted.

The main finds in the tombs were clay larnakes (sarcophagi); fine decorated pottery; bronze arms, utensils and ornaments; sealstones and necklaces from semi-precious stones. Three important finds are a boars' tusk helmet; a basket made of reeds which was decorated with small bronze pins; and a pendant made of steatite with a Linear A inscription. A fourth significant find was a stirrup jar with a Linear B inscription which gives the name "*wi-na-jo*". This is the only example of an inscription on a vase from a Late Minoan Cemetery. The same scribe did the inscription on a stirrup jar found at Knossos, and the same name appears on a stirrup jar found in Midea.

DR. YANNIS TZEDAKIS

29

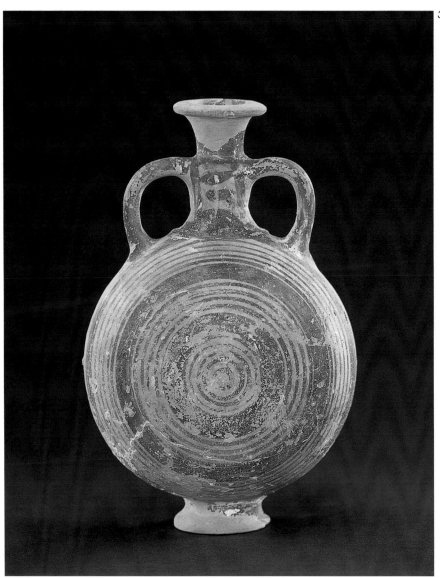

30

29 GLOBULAR FLASK

R.M. 21090 EUM-196: Wall sherd

AN INGREDIENT OF ANIMAL ORIGIN?

The organic residue result indicated the presence of a steroid whose mass spectrum could not be matched to any published compound; it resembles a cholestanone. A cholestanone is a degradation product of cholesterol, and therefore is indicative of any ingredient of animal (not plant) origin. However, the complete absence of any fatty acids calls an animal source into question. This is, therefore, a puzzling result.

Beck: See method of analysis.

LM III A2 (c. 1370-1340 B.C.)
LM Cemetery of Armenoi. Tomb 211
H: 17.75 cm.; D: body 13 cm.

Restored from many fragments. Light brown fabric. Yellowish slip. Brown-red paint. Squat, globular body (FS 188). Narrow neck with angular rim. Flattened handles which start from the middle of the neck and end on the shoulder. Low conical stem. The body on both sides is decorated with concentric circles with a monochrome circle at the centre. A wide zone composed of horizonal zig-zag lines, covers the space below the handles. A wide band runs around the stem and around the neck. The handles, the upper part of the neck and the rim are monochrome. A sherd was taken for analysis prior to restoration.

E.P.

30 GLOBULAR FLASK

EUM-336: Wall sherd

ANIMAL FAT
It can be said with confidence that this vessel never held olive oil

Beck: See method of analysis.

LM III A2 (c. 1370-1340 B.C.)
Chania, Kastelli, pit for 5-002-4
Sherds submitted for analysis averaged between 4 and 6 centimeters in diameter.

The type is similar to R.M. 2356.

R.M. 2356 is a substitute for EUM-336, which only survived in sherd condition and could not be restored.

31

32 SMALL JUG

R.M. 6606

LM III A2 (c. 1370-1340 B.C.)
LM Cemetery of Armenoi. Tomb 199
H: 8.5; D: body 7.8 cm.

Restored at the spout. Off-white fabric, slip of the same colour, brown-red semi-fugitive paint. Squat globular body, tall tubular neck with beak spout. Handle of oval section and oval flat base. The shoulder is decorated with a multi-petal rosette (FM 17), the leaves of which spring from the base of the neck and end on the belly. The spaces between the leaves are filled with stylised irises (FM 10A:5). The vase is encircled by a series of bands from the base to the belly.

E.P

GLOBULAR FLASK

R.M. 2356

LM III A 2 (c. 1370-1340 B.C.)
Vigla Stavromenou, Rethymnon
H: 15.2 cm.; D: (max) 10.1 cm., base 3.55 cm.

Restored. Almost complete. Brown fabric and slip. Brown to orange paint. Globular body (FS 189). Narrow cylindrical neck with wide horizontal rim. Ring at junction of neck and body. Two flattened handles start at the middle of the neck and end on the shoulder. Conical base with concave interior. Concentric circles of varying widths on both sides. The spaces below the two handles are decorated with monochrome elliptical motives filled with angles in a vertical position.

E.P.

31 RING-SHAPED VASE

R.M. 2320

LM III A2 (c. 1370-1340 B.C.)
LM Cemetery of Armenoi. Tomb 119
H: 17.4 cm.; D: body 10.8 cm.

Foot slightly restored. Pink-brown fabric, light brown slip, brown-black, rather fugitive paint. Ritual ring-shaped vase in the form of a flattened flask. Cylindrical body, constricted in the middle by a relief ring, with two flat sides and a hole pierced through the centre. Tall tubular neck with a relief ring below the rim. Horizontal rounded rim. Two vertical handles of circular section. Conical hollow foot. The two faces are decorated with FM19 suspended alternately from the inner and outer band. The edges of the convex side of the cylinder are decorated with zones of chevrons (FM 58:34). The rest of the decoration consists of bands.

E.P.

32

33 STIRRUP JAR

R.M. 2274

LM III B (c. 1340-1190 B.C.)
LM Cemetery of Armenoi. Tomb 115
H.: 17.4 cm.; D: base 6.9 cm., body 19.5 cm.

Intact. Brown-pink fabric, slip of same colour, shiny orange to brown-black paint (FS 173). Narrow closed neck and high, narrow spout with angular rim. Strap handles and flat base. The main decorative motif, on the shoulder of the vase, consists of two elaborate triangles (FM 71), set either side of the mouth and filled with a group of chevrons in each angle. On the other side are four groups of concentric semi-circles (FM 43A) with four stylised irises above them, the stems of which take the form of a series of dots and end inside the semi-circles. Groups of bands encircle the body from the base to the shoulder.

E.P.

34 SMALL JUG

R.M. 2153

LM III A2 (c. 1370-1340 B.C.)
LM Cemetery of Armenoi. Tomb 85
H: 7.7 cm.; D: body 7.14 cm.

Mended and restored on the body and shoulder. Light brown fabric, slip of the same colour, brown to red paint. Squat globular body. Narrow neck with beak spout. Handle of oval section and flat base. The main decorative motif, on the shoulder of the vase, consists of concentric semi-circles (FM43:8) with stylised irises in the spaces between them (FM 10 A:5). The vase is encircled from the base to the belly by a series of bands.

E.P.

33

35 SMALL JUG

R.M. 1757

LM III A2 (c. 1370-1340 B.C.)
LM Cemetery of Armenoi. Tomb 39
H: 5 cm.; D: (max) 5.7 cm.

Mended and restored at the handle. Yellow-grey fabric, slip of same colour, brown-black paint. Squat globular body, low wide neck with beak spout. Strap handle and flat base. The main decorative motif, set on the shoulder of the vase, consists of a zone of stylised irises (FM 10A:5) and a row of dots. The vase is encircled by a series of bands from the base to the belly.

E.P.

36 SMALL JUG

R.M. 1762

LM III A2 (c. 1370-1340 B.C.)
LM Cemetery of Armenoi. Tomb 39
H: 5.3 cm.; D: (max) 5.61 cm.

Part of spout restored. Brown-red fabric, yellow-grey slip, red paint. Squat globular body, high neck with beak spout. Handle of oval section, and flat base. The main decorative motif, on the belly of the vase, consists of a zone of stylised irises (FM 10A:5). A stylised foliate band encircles the shoulder, bordered by a wavy band and dots. The vase is encircled by a series of bands of different widths from the base to the lower part of the body.

E.P.

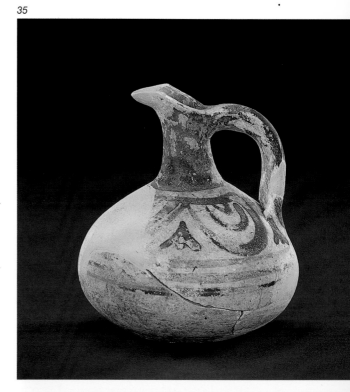

35

34

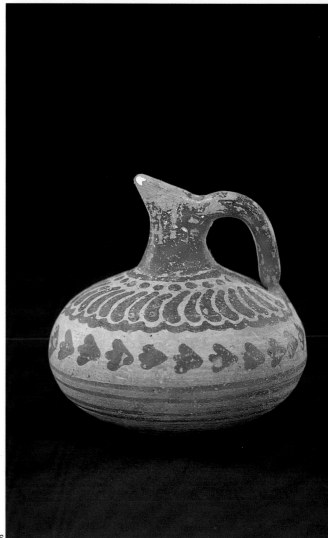

36

CHAMALEVRI ZOOARCHAEOLOGICAL MATERIAL

The zooarchaeological material yielded by the excavations at Chamalevri (1991-1998) have had the good fortune to be studied by two young scholars, Dimitra Mylona (animals) and Frederique Baltzinger (molluscs). The conclusions drawn so far are limited and not based on the entire body of material. They are nonetheless sufficient to form a first, rudimentary picture of the relations between humans and animals in the specific phase of the Minoan period in question.

The material studied comes from a variety of plots of land scattered over the two hills of Tsikouriana and Kakavella. Most of the material comes from the plots on Tsikouriana and dates from the MM I A and B (c. 2160-1900 B.C.) and LM III C periods (c. 1190-1070 B.C.). The plots are owned by Dim. Stratidakis (Bolanis), Mich. Kokolakis (Bolanis), St. and G. Defteraios (Pateras), G. Zacharakis (Tzambakas), and Evang. Psomas (Chatzametis). In contrast, the material from Kakavella goes back to the LM III A and B periods (c. 1390-1190 B.C.). The plots are owned by St. Stratidakis (Kakavella) and El. Chatzidakis (Palaioloutra).

The main bulk of the zooarchaeological material is described as the remains of simple meals, or of their preparation. The group of 66 barnacles found on the floor of a MM I (c. 2160-1900 B.C.) building at Tzambakas, for example, may be interpreted as the remains of one of the last meals before the destruction of the building in MM I B times (c. 2000-1900 B.C.).

An exception to the above rule is formed by the finds from the pits/trenches of the LM III C1 period (c. 1190-1130 B.C.) and the building contemporary with them in the excavation at Chatzamertis, all of them on the Tsikouriana hill. The interpretation of these finds is problematic. The characteristic dark grey soil of the trenches contained, in a uniform, repetitive manner, animal bones, bricks, whole clay vases – often tripod cooking pots, stone tools, mainly grinders and pounders – pieces of pumice, obsidian blades, clay bobbins, figurines, and fallen stones. This circumstance, together with the meticulous cutting of the trenches, readily suggests, that these were something more than ordinary rubbish dumps – possibly structures relating to some specific ritual act.

In general, the pottery contained by the trenches consists of painted sherds, mainly of the plain style, though there were also some examples of the dense style. In a number of cases there were exceptionally fine depictions of birds or animals. An abundance of sherds from cooking vessels was found – mainly tripod cooking pots – as well as from hand-made vases, bowls, baskets, pithoi with bands of incised herring-bone pattern, and stirrup jars used for storage purposes.

The pits/trenches are astonishingly similar to the corresponding pits in the Greek-Italian excavations of Sybrita, Amari, in terms of both construction and content.

MARIA ANDREADAKI-VLAZAKI
Director 25th Ephorate, Chania, Ministry of Culture

ZOOARCHAEOLOGY: AIMS AND METHODS

Zooarchaeology is the study of the past interactions between humans and animals. It is based on animal bones, found during archaeological excavations. It also uses additional data, such as artefacts, documentary sources, art representations, etc.

Animal remains are very common finds in archaeological excavations and they are often accurate witnesses of everyday economic conditions and actions which have passed without leaving any other visible traces.

The zooarchaeological research follows three main steps:

RECOVERY

During the archaeological excavation, many animal remains are collected, including bones of mammals, fish and birds. Hand picking, dry sieving and water flotation are some of the methods employed, each leading to a more or less representative recovery.

RECORDING AND ANALYSIS

Every animal bone found in an excavation bears some information about the animal's physiology as well as on the management of the live animals and the carcasses. Observations on the bone refer to the anatomical part it represents, the animal it belongs to, its sex and maturity, as well as the degree/method of its fragmentation, its preservation state and possible pathologies, cut marks, working evidence, etc. Using a basic statistical analysis all this information elucidates such aspects of elementary human/animal interactions as:

● The range of species exploited by humans in the past (or sharing their living space);

● The age and sex composition of herds or hunted animals;

● The carcass management, i.e. cutting techniques, preference for certain anatomical parts, modes of cooking, etc.

Observations on the preservation of the bones, are used as a guide to the reconstruction of the taphonomic history* of the assemblage and often of the excavated site itself.

INTERPRETATION

The basic information derived from the animal bones is combined with other sets of data, such as related architectural structures and artefacts, written sources, and art representations. They are analysed in the light of ecological observations and ethnographic paradigms. The aim is to build a picture of the past interactions between animals and humans.

Interpretations of animal bone assemblages usually refer to the nature of the environment from which the animals under study originate and the methods developed by humans to manage the animals (hunting, herding, pastoralism, etc.). The socio-economic implications of the above, special uses of animals (e.g. sacrifice), as well as symbolic/ideological values invested on them are also explored.

DIMITRA MYLONA
Archaeologist, Zooarchaeologist
Institute of Mediterranean Studies (ITE), Rethymnon, Crete

* Taphonomic history: refers to the processes which have affected the bones since the moment it ceased being alive to the time of analysis. It involves factors such as crushing, trampling, digesting, and the erosion of bones through weathering.

THE BONES OF SUCKLING ANIMALS

The animal bones collected during the excavation of the Bronze Age settlement at Chamalevri are the remnants of a wide range of activities that linked the inhabitants of Chamalevri with animals.

One of the activities that resulted in the accumulation of bones in this specific area was connected with food. Knife or axe marks, traces of biting, and the association of the bones with other objects connected with the household all demonstrate that the bones found at Chamalevri (or the majority of them, at least), were the remains of meals or of the preparation of meals. The nature of the meals in question, the reasons they were held, and the relationships between those who partook of them are difficult to determine from the archaeological record.

Before the animals found their way into the cooking pot or on to the grill, however, they had already been in contact with human beings through stock-raising or hunting. Some of them supplied food throughout their entire lives in the form of their milk. They also provided wool and fur, and probably also manure for farms, while their muscular power was harnessed for farm work or transportation. Even after they died, animals served as a source of raw materials for craft industries, to which they supplied horn, bone and hide.

For Bronze Age people, however, animals contributed more than their material being. They participated in rituals through sacrifice, or the dedicating of animal models, and were charged with powerful symbolism, as is clear from the rich iconography of the period.

Study of the animal bones from Chamalevri affords only limited evidence for the subjects mentioned above, mainly because of their poor state of preservation.

STOCK-RAISING

The animals reared by the inhabitants of Chamalevri in the Bronze Age (more specifically in the MM I, c. 2160-1900 B.C., and LM III C, c. 1190-1070 B.C., periods) were sheep, goats, pigs and cows. Equines were raised in the settlement during the LM III C period, though it is not impossible that they were also used in earlier periods.

Goats and sheep were the most important animals throughout the entire history of the settlement. Goats appear to have been more numerous. Both goats and sheep were slaughtered before they reached any great age (before their sixth year). It is clear from the deformed teeth and jaw-bones that in some cases the animals slaughtered were not in very good physical condition. It was, of course, their condition that resulted in their being slaughtered and consumed. In addition to meat, goat and sheep provided wool and fur – the presence of which is indicated by the discovery of loomweights in the settlement

– and also horn and bones for the manufacture of tools and other artefacts. It appears that the entire carcass was butchered and consumed in the settlement.

Cows also frequently found their way on to the tables of the inhabitants of Chamalevri. The carcasses were butchered with a sharp, heavy tool – possibly an axe. The significance of cows for the settlement at Chamalevri was probably not confined to the supplying of meat. Cows are known to have been milked on Crete in earlier periods, and this may also have been the case at Chamalevri. They were probably also used for farmwork or transportation.

Pork was also a very common item in the diet of the Bronze Age inhabitants of Chamalevri. The poor state of preservation of the bones makes it impossible to determine the age at which the pigs were slaughtered, or the manner in which the carcass was butchered. However, some specific use of part of the carcass can be discerned, at least in the LM III C period (c. 1190-1070 B.C.). Very few pelvis and thigh bones have been found, and their absence cannot be accounted for by taphonomical considerations. These two bones connect together and bear a large quantity of meat, which is traditionally cured and smoked to make ham. Some such process of preservation, which resulted in these bones being removed from the carcass, is perhaps responsible for the absence of the particular bones in question from the LM III C levels (c. 1190-1070 B.C.) at Chamalevri.

The equines found in the LM III C levels at Chamalevri are small animals, though it is not clear from the surviving bones whether they were donkeys, mules or small horses.

HUNTING

Hunting was evidently a very important pastime of the inhabitants of Chamalevri. Red deer and platoni are the most common wild animals found, and their contribution to the diet was roughly equal to that made by pigs. After the hunt, the entire deer seems to have been taken back to the settlement, where the meat was consumed on the spot and the horns used for the manufacture of tools.

Wild goats were another common prey, though they have been identified at Chamalevri only by their horns.

Hunting on Crete during the Bronze Age, however, was not confined to the animals whose bones have been found at Chamalevri. Hares, badgers, birds, and possibly also wild boar and wild cattle supplemented the range of land animals hunted. The fact that the larger of these have not been found at Chamalevri is perhaps not fortuitous, while the absence of the smaller animals may

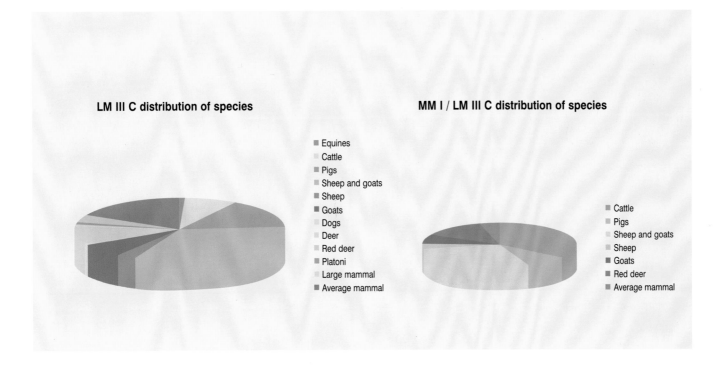

LM III C distribution of species

- Equines
- Cattle
- Pigs
- Sheep and goats
- Sheep
- Goats
- Dogs
- Deer
- Red deer
- Platoni
- Large mammal
- Average mammal

MM I / LM III C distribution of species

- Cattle
- Pigs
- Sheep and goats
- Sheep
- Goats
- Red deer
- Average mammal

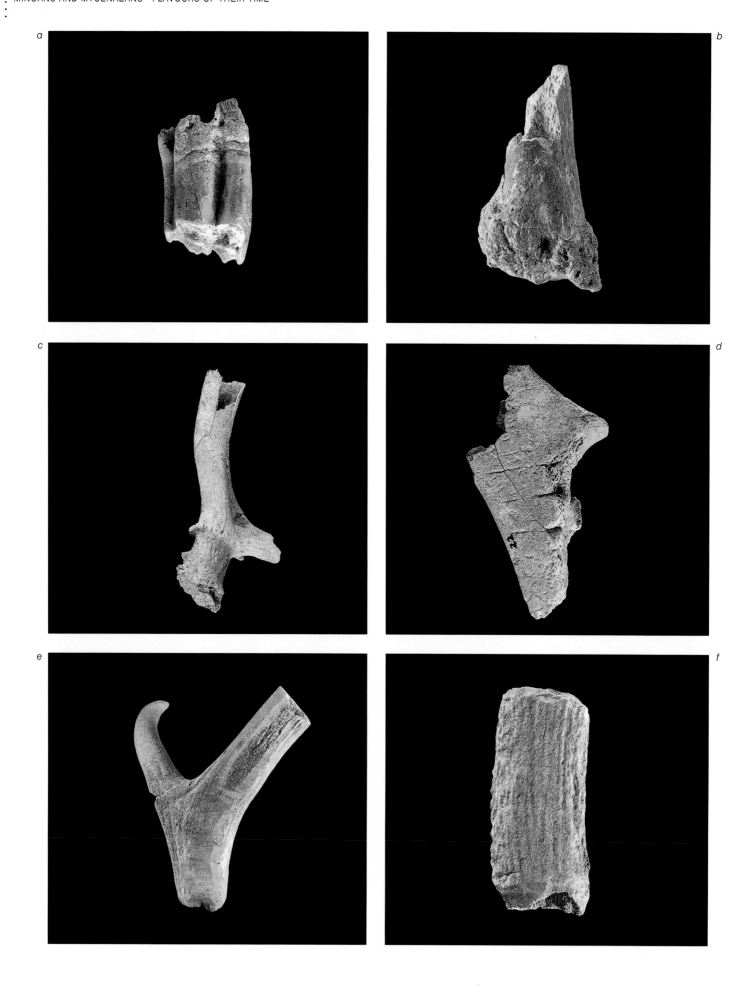

be due to the methods by which bones are collected and their state of preservation in the ground.

In the LM III C levels (c. 1190-1070 B.C) at Chamalevri, bones have been found of dogs, which were associated with hunting in the Bronze Age, as is clear from a large number of both early and later representations in art. Dogs lived in the settlement, alongside humans, and it seems likely from the bite-marks on bones that they were fed on leftovers.

Hunting was a collective activity, though lone hunters are also depicted in artistic representations. One such scene on a sarcophagus from Armenoi, which is several decades earlier in date than the LM III C levels (c. 1190-1070 B.C.) at Chamalevri,

preserves some very vivid details. Three hunters are taking part, with their "weapons" and three dogs. The animals hunted are a deer, a wild goat and a wild (?) cow. The hunters attack, making use simultaneously of their dogs, spears and sword. One of the hunters holds two objects that look like large leaves and is probably attempting to lure the animals into palisades that are indicated by undulating hatched patterns. The double axe held by the man inside the palisade may be a weapon, though it also lends another, ritual or symbolical dimension to the collective hunt.

DIMITRA MYLONA
Archaeologist, Zooarchaeologist
Institute of Mediterranean Studies (ITE), Rethymnon, Crete

a. Tooth with traces of decay.

b. Radius of sheep or goat with traces of disease.

c. Deerhorn.

d. Ulna of cow with cut marks from a heavy tool, possibly an axe (provenance: Chamalevri).

e. Deerhorn.

f. Horn of red deer with traces of working (provenance: Chania, Mathioudakis plot).

g. Anatomical position of bones under-represented in the bone sample from Chamalevri. The absence of thigh and pelvis bones possibly points to the preparation of ham.

g

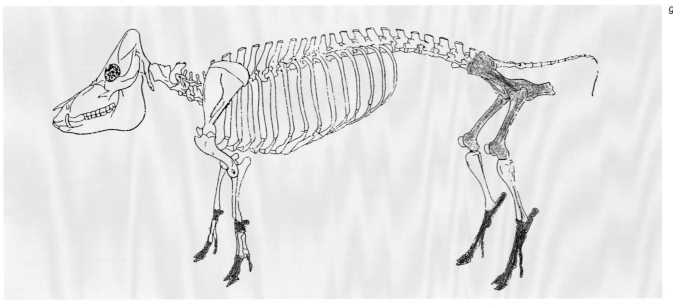

37 ANIMAL BONES

. . . .

MM I A (c. 2160-2000 B.C.),

LM III C (c. 1190-1070 B.C.)
Chamalevri

The animal bones collected during the excavation provide information on the ancient environment and the economy of the site excavated. Amongst the bones recovered at Chamalevri have been recognized cow (Bos taurus), pig (Sus scrota), goat (Capra hircus), sheep (Ovis anes), dog (Canis familiaris) and equines (Equus sp.). Other animals include red deer (Cervus elaphus), platoni (Dama domes) and wild goat (Capra aegagrus). Illustration 37 shows a pair of wild goat horns (Capra aegagrus).

D. M.

38 STAMNOS

. . . .

S.M. 8891

LM I (c. 1600-1425 B.C.)
Zakros
H: 38 cm.; D: rim 28 cm.

Intact. Reddish fabric with slip. Wide flat base. Cylindrical body, mouth with cylindrical lip, two horizontal bridge handles and two smaller vertical ones. Jaw bone of goat inside vessel.

S. Ch.

39 THREE-HANDLED CYLINDRICAL ALABASTRON

. . . .

R.M. 4245

LM III A2 (c. 1370-1340 B.C.)
LM Cemetery of Armenoi. Tomb 175
H: 13.8 cm.; D: body 14.6 cm.

Restored at the rim, neck, shoulder and one handle. Reddish fabric, ochre-brown slip, black paint. Cylindrical body with sloping shoulder. Short, wide neck, with a slightly concave profile ending in a flat, horizontal lip. The three handles have oval sections and are set at right angles to the shoulder. Flat base. Cylindrical body decorated with wild goats (for a similar one, see FM 6:2,3) standing astride, which are placed side by side and separated by antithetic Minoan flowers or by a cross-hatched panel. The scene is enclosed between broad bands, and a floral motif, probably an iris, adorns the zone at the shoulder. The neck, lip, and interior of the vase are painted. The back of the handle is covered with transverse lines and small vertical lines spring from the angle at the shoulder.

E.P.

37

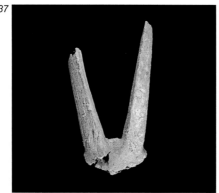

38

38

39

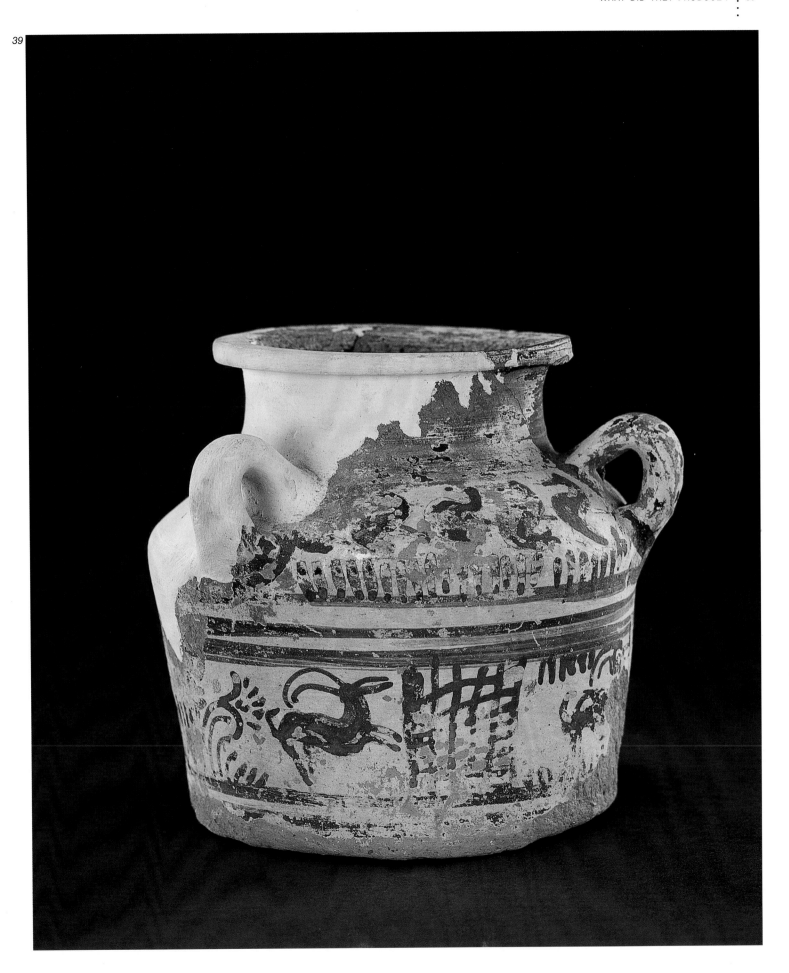

THE STUDY OF SEA-SHELLS

During the last 20 years analysis of faunal and floral remains have assumed an important role in Mediterranean archaeology. More recently studies of animal bones have been systematically carried out, but little attention has been paid to marine molluscs found in archaeological contexts.

NATURE OF THE MESSAGE CARRIED BY THE FAUNAL EVIDENCE

Malacological analysis provides two kinds of data:

a) Intrinsic information through the biology of the animal (its species, state of growth and habitat) and

b) extrinsic information from the interpretation of marks that have been registered after the death of the mollusc (marks on the shell, fragmentation and its position in the site).

The first step of the analysis demands a careful and detailed observation of evidence of the molluscs, so that we can proceed to the interpretation of data. This is followed by collaboration with archaeologists and zooarchaeologists working on the site to position the molluscs in the context of the economic, social and cultural dimension of the site.

COLLECTION OF MATERIAL

Like any faunal analysis, marine mollusc analysis requires a quantity of samples, as well as systematic collection. If possible, the whole quantity of material should be recovered by hand sieving and flotation.

Marine molluscs are resistant to hostile environmental conditions and their presence in archaeological sites is therefore especially reliable, as they are not greatly affected by the soil in which they are buried.

Identification of marine shell species is based on the observation of various morphological features which vary among species. Shape, colour, position and shape of the articulation between the two valves in the case of bivalves, number and configuration of spire in gastropods, configuration of the apex, of the aperture, of the columella: all are indications for the taxonomical classification of material.

QUANTIFICATION OF THE MARINE MALACONFAUNE ASSEMBLAGE

The quantification of the shell assemblage and its statistical analysis provides us with information concerning the frequency of appearance of shell species by chronological period. We will be able to deduce conclusion about taste throughout time or other forms of selectivity in human behaviour, which can be determined by environmental factors.

INFORMATION GAINED FROM A STUDY OF MARINE MOLLUSCS

a) Reconstitution of the palaeogeography (species living in lake, sea or river), of the palaeoenvironment and, more specifically, of the palaeolittoral, where the molluscs used to live, based on the ecological balance of marine molluscs, and

b) the utilisation of molluscs: i) as food, ii) as utensils, iii) as ornaments, iv) as objects of symbolic value, widening our knowledge of diet, the technological and material aspect of ancient communities, as well as their cultural and spiritual dimensions.

The exact provenance of sea-shells in archaeological excavations and their chronostratigraphic position in the site make possible interpretation of their use.

FREDERIQUE BALTZINGER
Archaeologist

CHAMALEVRI   THE SEA-SHELLS

Shellfish are known to have made a contribution to various aspects of human life from the very beginnings of Antiquity, ranging from the most simple aspects, such as diet, to highly complex, socio-economic and cultural expressions. The malacological material from Chamalevri confirms the importance of marine molluscs to the diet of the inhabitants from the Early to the Late Bronze Age on Crete.

Although fairly limited in number, the remains of sea-shells collected from a series of excavations on farms in the region of Chamalevri have made it possible to identify some species of gastropods (Patella caerulea, Patella ulyssiponensis, Patella rustica, monodonta (Osilinus turbinata) and bivalves (Cerastoderma edule), that were widely consumed in the Minoan period, and which also served as food at Chamalevri. Fragments of other species (Spondylus gaederopus, Glycymeris glycymeris, Arca noae) were probably also food remains, though their context is not clear enough for us to determine their use with any certainty.

The consumption of Patellidae is confirmed at Chamalevri from MM I A to MM I B (c. 2160-1900 B.C.): this is indicated by the discovery of a total of 320 Patellae sp., either intact or ring-shaped, in a rubbish pit of MM I A (c. 2160-2000 B.C.) on the Stratidakis property at Bolanis, together with a few bone remains and a large quantity of functional pottery; by the assembly of approximately 60 Patellae that were food remains, found next to a few fragments of the species Cerastoderma edule and Monodonta turbinata collected from a MM I B (c. 2000-1900 B.C.) destruction level in a room of the MM I A period (c. 2160-2000 B.C.) on the Zacharakis property at Tzambakas; and by the few examples of patellae found in habitation levels antedating the destruction. Three known species of patellae common to the shores of the Mediterranean are represented by the archaeological population of Chamalevri: Patella rustica, Patella caerulea and Patella ulyssiponensis shared the rocks of the upper and lower level. These species of gastropods live in very dense populations and are to be found attached to the rocky infrastructure of the rising coastline. That they were collected by the inhabitants on the nearby coastal rocks is a ready hypothesis.

In the Late Minoan period, the evidence for the consumption of molluscs is less secure. The few fragments of Spondylus gaederopus and Arca noae in a LM III A1 (c. 1390-1370 B.C.) habitation level on the Stratidakis property at Kakavella, and the rather scattered remains of sea-shells (a fragment of Spondylus gaederopus and a valve of a Glycymeris glycymeris) found in LM III C1 (c. 1190-1130 B.C.) rubbish pits alongside other food remains on the St. and G. Defteraios property at Pateras and on the Ev. Psomas property at Chatsametis, or one thrown away in a LM III C1

(c. 1190-1130 B.C.) habitation level on the St. and G. Defteraios property at Pateras, could have been collected with a view to consumption. The very small quantity of these remains means that the possibility cannot be precluded that they were trapped in the sediment, or that their valves were brought empty from the shore. The species Spondylus gaederopus, Glycymeris glycymeris and Arca noae live in the subshore belt; Arca noae uses its powerful sucker to attach itself to the rocky infrastructure, making it more difficult to approach than the species collected in the MM I period (c. 2160-1900 B.C.).

No signs have been found of the valves of bivalves being broken, or of the shell of gastropods being pierced, which might indicate the use of some special technique to extract the mollusc. Bivalves could be opened by simply placing the shellfish on a source of heat or by breaking the valve with a pointed object.

The discovery of sea-shells in ritual deposits going back to LM III C1 (c. 1190-1130 B.C.) on the Stratidakis property at Bolanis might indicate that the molluscs formed as a special kind of offering. A small Conus mediterraneus, a Monodonta turbinata and a fragment of a Charonia tritonis variegata, known to have been used traditionally as a conch horn or a drinking vessel in the Mediterranean, were found near finds that give them a ritual significance.

That so few shells were found at Chamalevri is a matter of curiosity, especially when account is taken of the factor of archaeological chance, which is of increased importance in rescue excavations. Sea-shells apparently formed only an occasional supplement to the diet and the "fruits of the sea" do not seem to have been a substantial food resource on which the inhabitants drew regularly.

FREDERIQUE BALTZINGER

Archaeologist

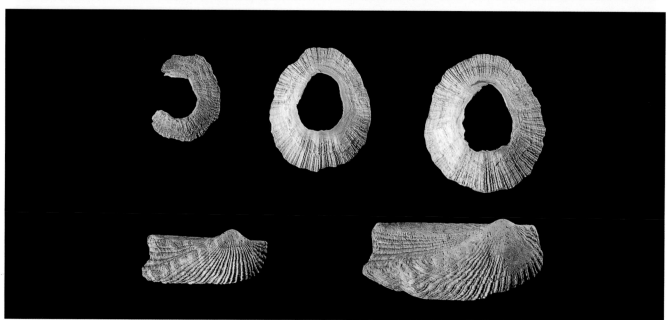

40 SEA-SHELLS

MM I A (c. 2160-2000 B.C.)

Chamalevri, 1992. Bolanis Workshop. Pits
H: (max) 3.54 mm.; D: (max) 21.72 mm.

Three species of limpets, common to the
Mediterranean coast, are represented
here. These species are distributed on
the rocks of the upper and the lower
middle-coastal areas. They are found
stuck to the rocky substata of the raised
coastal zone. Consequently, collecting
them is an easy task.

F.B.

40

41

41 KAMARES WARE CUP

H.M. 5797

MM II B (c. 1700 B.C.)
Phaistos Palace, Room XIX
H: 7 cm.; D: rim 11.5 cm.

Mended from a large number of fragments and restored. Pink-red pure fabric.
Eggshell cup with vertical walls and a
vertical handle. The larger part of the
surface of the vase is decorated with
relief shells. White bands around the
base and rim and parallel white lines
on the handle. Repeated floral motif
(double semi-circle with petals), also in
white, beneath the rim, and an imitation of polished stone with orange paint
and white outline. Antithetic band decoration in white paint on the interior of
the vase and the base.

A.K. - E.K.

42

42 STIRRUP JAR

. . . .

R.M. 2216

LM III B1 (c. 1340-1250 B.C.)
LM Cemetery of Armenoi. Tomb 107
H: 12 cm.; D: body 11.4 cm.

Intact. Pink-red fabric, light brown slip, shiny brown to black paint. Squat biconical body with an almost flat shoulder (FS 179). Closed, tubular neck, set lower than the height of the handles, and spout ending in angular rim. Vertical strap handles and ring base. The zone at the shoulder is decorated with a sea-shell (FM 11) set freely in the space and the body and base are encircled by bands. Product of a Kydonia workshop.

E.P.

43 STIRRUP JAR

. . . .

R.M. 1579

LM III B1 (c. 1340-1250 B.C.)
LM Cemetery of Armenoi. Tomb 8
H: 15 cm.; D: body 18 cm.

Intact. Brown-yellow fabric, orange-yellow slip, red to black paint. Squat, bi-conical body (FM 179). Closed tubular neck and spout with funnel mouth. Handles of oval section and ring base. The zone at the shoulder is decorated with a chain of stylised shells (FM 25) and supplementary motifs consisting of concentric U-shapes (FM 43). The body and base of the vase are encircled by bands and the handle disc is decorated with a spiral.

E.P.

43

44 STIRRUP JAR

. . . .

R.M. 2649

LM III B (c. 1340-1190 B.C.)
LM Cemetery of Armenoi. Tomb 125
H: 8.4 cm.; D: body 10.5 cm.

Mended from two pieces and slightly restored. Brown-orange fabric, light brown slip, brown paint. Squat conical body (FS 180). Tubular false neck and spout with angular rim. Handles of oval section and flat base. The zone of the shoulder is adorned with eight stylised sea-shells, and the body and base are encircled by bands. The handle disc is adorned with two antithetic semi-circles.

E.P.

44

44

What did they cook?

The Tests
Infra-red Spectroscopy,
Gas Chromatography,
Mass Spectroscopy,
High Performance
Liquid Chromatography,
Wet Chemical Spot Tests.

The Time
One sherd: One week's work
One sherd: The amount of
computerised data produced
can be up to 100 pages.

The Interpretation
The most time-consuming part,
it includes:
- Searching databases
- Searching the literature
- Identifying constituents
- Searching constituents
- Identifyng botanical sources

The Results - The Alternatives Are:

1 Conclusions can be proposed: see presentation in the Exhibition, site by site.

2 Chemical compounds were detected, but no further conclusions can be drawn.

3 No organic signals detected in the potsherd.

4 The full story can never be known because chemical compounds, when detected,
may not be the same, nor are they equally distributed, throughout a vessel.
Also it can never be known if all the chemical compounds to which the pot
had been exposed, were retained in the fabric of the vessel.

What did they cook?

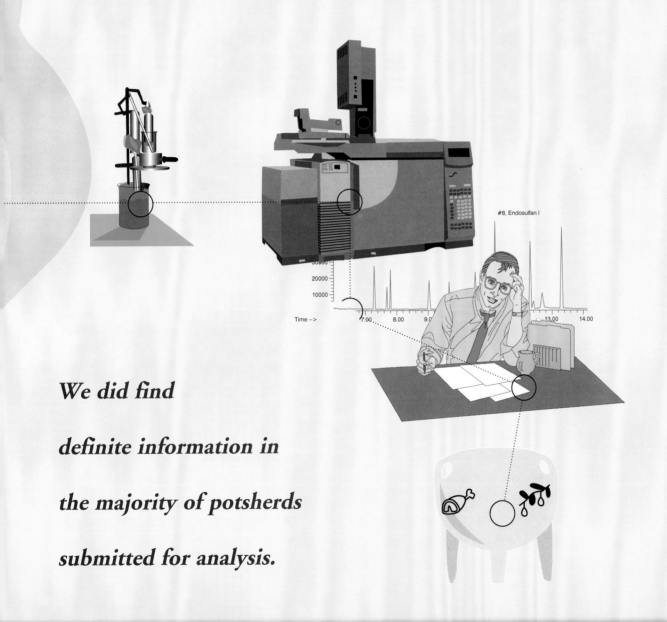

#8, Endosulfan I

We did find

definite information in

the majority of potsherds

submitted for analysis.

VEGETABLE STEW IN THE NEOLITHIC CAVE
OF GERANI, RETHYMNON (c. 6000-3800 B.C.)

The cave dwellers of Gerani were indulging in vegetable stews that contained a lot of olive oil (R.M. 960/EUM-146). They also might have been eating foods which contained marine animal oil (R.M. 1003/EUM-138). The latter is one of only two organic residue results in the project which indicated the possibility of marine food/oil. The other is from the hearth deposit in the Room with the Fresco at the Mainland palace site of Mycenae (EUM-164). The two finds could not be much further apart for this project: the Neolithic result dates to c. 3800 B.C., and the Mycenaean, to c. 1250 B.C.

The possibility of marine foods is worth noting, in view of the results achieved on skeletal material. It will be shown in Section V: You Are What You Eat, that only in Grave Circles A and B were there indications of the consumption of fish. Although by no means exhaustive, the meagre results for fish (2 potsherds out of 300+ tested) corroborate the skeletal material results that a significant number of Minoans and Mycenaeans were not fish eaters.

DR. HOLLEY MARTLEW

THE EXCAVATION

The Cave of Gerani is situated 7 kilometers west of Rethymnon, on the north coast of Crete, in an area called Kyani Akti. The cave was found by chance during the construction of the new national road in 1969. The entrance to the cave today is not the original one, but was opened by explosives used during the road construction. The original entrance was located during the course of the excavation. It had been blocked by rocks before the end of the Late Neolithic period. For this reason, unlike other caves in Crete, the Final and Transitional Neolithic as well as the Minoan, are not represented. The final event gives us the terminus post quem for the use of the cave. Because the cave was sealed and therefore unknown between the demise of its use and the excavation, the stratification of Early Neolithic II, Middle Neolithic and Late Neolithic was excellent. Hearths from all three periods were found and they were surrounded by pottery, implements, and animal bones. Shells were also abundant. Three human skeletons were found at the far end of the cave. These people had apparently been trapped and died of suffocation.

The cave was only used for habitation sporadically during the year. This would have been connected to cultivation, animal husbandry and possibly fishing. The work also extended to the production of stone, but mainly bone, implements. These tools were identified as coming mainly from bones of hare, rabbit, pig, and goat.

The organisers of the Exhibition decided to submit pottery samples from the Cave of Gerani for organic residue analysis as an experiment. Because of the importance of the results that were obtained, they are presented in the Exhibition as an introduction to the Minoan/Mycenaean world.

DR. YANNIS TZEDAKIS

BOWL

R.M. 830

Middle Neolithic (c. 4500 B.C.)
Cave of Gerani
H: 9 cm.; D: 19.7 cm.

Mended from a large number of sherds and mostly restored. Hemispherical body. Above the middle of the belly there is a relief knot with incisions. Black-painted, burnished surface.

E.P.

46 BOWL

R.M. 1003   EUM-138: Wall sherd

OLIVE OIL. PLANT WAX FROM LEAVES AND FRUIT

These results are definite. Other possible constituents: milk fat or depositional fat from sheep and goats; and/or marine animal oil.

Beck: See method of analysis

Middle Neolithic (c. 4500 B.C.)
Cave of Gerani, West Crete
Sherds submitted for analysis averaged between 4 and 6 centimeters in diameter.

46

45

45 BOWL

R.M. 1045A   EUM-145: Wall sherd

ANIMAL/VEGETABLE FATS
No particular food source can be assigned.

Beck: See method of analysis.

Middle Neolithic (c. 4500 B.C.)
Cave of Gerani, West Crete
Sherds submitted for analysis averaged between 4 and 6 centimeters in diameter.

Part of a large globular vase, of which part of the globular body and the slightly everted rim are preserved. The black-painted surface is burnished. The type is similar to R.M. 830.

Bowl R.M. 830 is a substitute for R.M. 1045A/EUM 145, which only survived in sherd condition and could not be restored.

47

Only the base and a small part of the body survive. The type is similar to R.M. 827.

R.M. 827 is a substitute for R.M. 1003/ EUM-138, which only survived in sherd condition and could not be restored.

BOWL
R.M. 827

Middle Neolithic (c. 4500 B.C.)
Cave of Gerani, West Crete
H: 6.4 cm.; D: 13.2 cm.

Mended from a large number of sherds and about half-restored. Shallow bowl with conical body ending in a rounded rim. Two pierced lug handles beneath the rim. Black-painted, burnished surface.

E.P.

47 BOWL
R.M. 960   EUM-146: Wall sherd

VEGETABLE STEW
A preparation using leafy vegetables and a copious amount of olive oil

Beck: See method of analysis.

Late Neolithic (c. 3800 B.C.)
Cave of Gerani, West Crete
Sherds submitted for analysis averaged between 4 and 6 centimeters in diameter.

Only part of the globular body and the rim survive. The type is similar to R.M. 824.

R.M. 824 is a substitute for R.M. 960/ EUM-146, which only survived in sherd condition and could not be restored.

BOWL
R.M. 824

Late Neolithic (c. 3800 B.C.)
Cave of Gerani, West Crete
H: 6.5. cm.; D: 12 cm.

Mended and almost half-restored. Handleless semi-globular skyphos, with no base and with inward-sloping walls. Black-painted, burnished surface.

E.P.

48 CONICAL CUP
R.M. 828

Early Neolithic (c. 6000 B.C.)
Cave of Gerani
H: 8.1 cm.; D: rim 11.6 cm.

Mended and almost half-restored. Conical body ending in a straight rim. Black-painted, burnished surface.

E.P.

49 BOWL
R.M. 837

Early Neolithic (c. 6000 B.C.)
Cave of Gerani
H: 7.3 cm.; D: 17.5 cm.

Mended and almost half-restored. Semi-globular body with circular base, bulging at the belly, creating a depression below the rim. Black-painted, burnished body.

E.P.

48

49

50

50 SHALLOW SKYPHOS WITH RAISED HANDLE

R.M. 834

Middle Neolithic (c. 4500 B.C.)
Cave of Gerani
H: 5.5 cm.; D: (with handle) 8.4 cm.

Mended and restored. Shallow body with circular bottom and raised handle set obliquely on the rim. Black-painted, burnished surface.

E.P.

51

51 BOWL

R.M. 835

Middle Neolithic (c. 4500 B.C.)
Cave of Gerani
H: 2.3 cm.; D: rim 4.8 cm.

Almost half-restored. Semi-globular body with conical lug on the rim in place of a handle. Straight, rounded rim.

E.P.

52

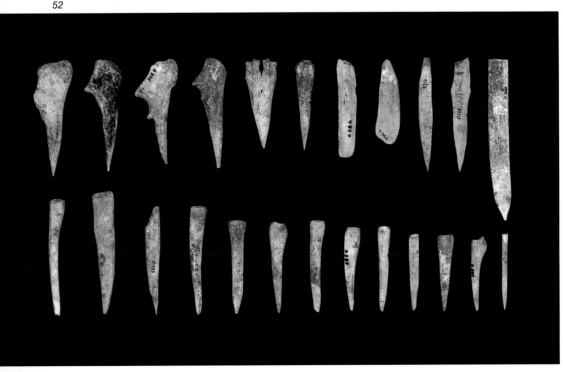

52 BONE TOOLS

(R.M. 448-358-359-557-330-361-384-410-360-376-447-391-389-374-495-383-375-380-416-387-418-385-390-556.)

Neolithic (c. 6000-3800 B.C.)
Cave of Gerani
Length: (max) 8.4 cm.

Bone tools, the shape of which varies according to the bone of which it is made.

E.P.

THEY ATE MEAT AND LEAFY VEGETABLES
AT APODOULOU, RETHYMNON (c. 1900-1700 B.C.)

Different shapes of tripod cooking pot gave results that included olive oil, vegetables (possibly the sweet courgette of Crete: EUM-21), fruit waxes, and meat (EUM-19; EUM-20; EUM-21; EUM-27; EUM-28; EUM-221/224; EUM-225/229).

Two of these tripods gave what the organic chemist thought was a very unusual result: no fats or oils at all (EUM-220; EUM-221/224).

The Minoan baking basin has always been viewed as an enigmatic vessel. The results on one baking basin (EUM-24) indicated the possibility of olive oil, and the other (EUM-19) gave a result of ruminants (sheep; cows; goats).

DR. HOLLEY MARTLEW

APODOULOU

THE SITE

The modern village of Apodoulou lies in the district of Amari (Rethymnon, Crete), roughly 20 km northwest of Phaistos. The Minoan settlement is located on a low hill, called "Tou Digeni to Chalkoma" or "Gournies", 1 km to the northwest of the modern village. The site was inhabited during several Minoan periods.

The main occupation occurred during the Middle Minoan II period (c. 1900-1700 B.C.). The area excavated so far covers 625 square meters and has c. 30 ident-ifiable rooms. The Middle Minoan building complex (houses A, B, C, D and E) has more than one building phase and was destroyed at the end of Middle Minoan II B (c. 1700 B.C.).

House A is the only house that has been completely excavated. It measures 220 square meters. If the first floor was of a comparable size, it would indicate that the building was an important one.

Possible functions of the rooms of House A can be supported by the finds. In discussing House A, those rooms from which material was submitted for organic residue analysis, will be pointed out. A double staircase belonging to House A, gave evidence that its western "leg", which was a pottery store under the stairs (sottoscala), also functioned as a hearth, because in it were found burned earth, charcoal, a lot of bones and sherds mostly from cups.

Room 9 had a double function as a pottery store-room and staircase, as is shown on the isometric plan. 116 vases were found, all of which had originally been placed on wooden shelves. Very important organic residue results came from two tripod vessels found in this room.

Several rooms functioned as storerooms. Rooms 2, 3 and possibly 4, comprise a complex of interconnecting large storerooms and workshops. Numerous polishers and other stone tools found in this room gave evidence for household activities. Room 2 contained a store of small vases which were found *in situ*, along with fragments of pithoi. Sherds from vases found in Room 2 were submitted for analysis. The large room 3 had 16 pithoi arranged in two rows on the southwest side. The first row of pithoi had been placed on a bench. The second row was at a lower level.

In Room 32 a stamped loomweight and 5 seals were found. Room 32 also contained pounders and mortars.

Houses A, B and C were divided by a corridor. Houses B and C were built on a more or less flat part of the hill on its upper slope. House A is on the downward slope and the rooms were built into the hillside. Houses D and E are on the lower slope.

Room 15 in House B may have had a combined function as a workshop and storeroom. This is indicated by the contents. In an earlier building phase Room 15 and Room 14 were part of the same big room which was subsequently divided. Sherds from vessels from the earlier building phase of Room 15 were submitted for analysis.

At the southeast of Houses A and B, there was a quadrangular space, Room 22. Three of the walls came from earlier building phases. A conical cup and a tripod cooking pot as well as blue-painted stucco were found in one area. In another area, which must have been a hearth, charcoal and many bones were found, and on top of them were two tripod cooking pots *in situ*. Sherds from both these tripods were submitted for analysis. Below the pots were small pebbles and schist fragments.

At the settlement of Apodoulou we can see the main characteristics of Middle Minoan architecture: on the ground floor are storerooms, workshops, hearths, staircases, pottery stores under the stairs (sottoscalas), and on the first floor the main habitation quarters, as well as a common facade joining what were originally individual houses. Typically in front of the facade parts of a paved road were also found. The presence of a stamped loomweight, together with five seals, in Room 32, provides evidence for the existence of administrative control in the settlement.

Apodoulou was on a road, which ran from Phaistos to the north coast of the island. The existence of a road which connected a number of sites (including the palatial centre at Monastiraki and Kavousi near the Monastery of Arkadi) before terminating at the Minoan site of Chamalevri (near Rethymnon), the study of pottery, of architecture, and the other finds, lead us to the conclusion that Apodoulou was under the overall control of the palace of Phaistos.

ANASTASIA TSIGOUNAKI
Curator of Antiquities, Ministry of Culture

Plan of the excavation site.

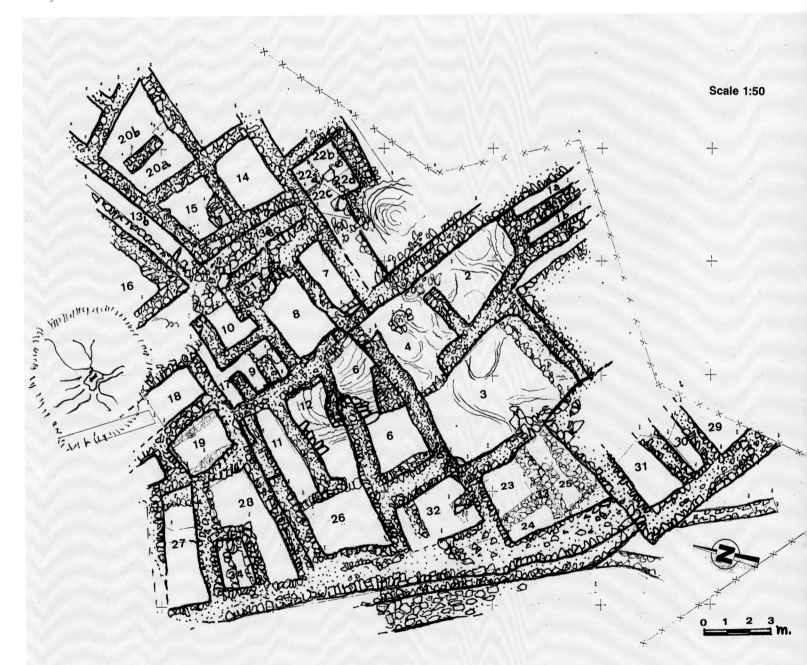

Scale 1:50

0 1 2 3 m.

53 TRIPOD COOKING POT

. . . .

EUM-20: Base/leg junction sherd

OLIVE OIL

Beck: See method of analysis.

MM II B (c. 1700 B.C.)
Apodoulou, Room 9, a storage area under the stairs

Sherds submitted for analysis averaged between 4 and 6 centimeters in diameter.

Box-shaped vessel. The type normally had a small, pulled-out spout. It is known to have been in use between MM II and LM III A/B (c. 1900-1190 B.C.).

H.M. F 65 5027a is a substitute for EUM-20, which only survived in sherd condition and could not be restored.

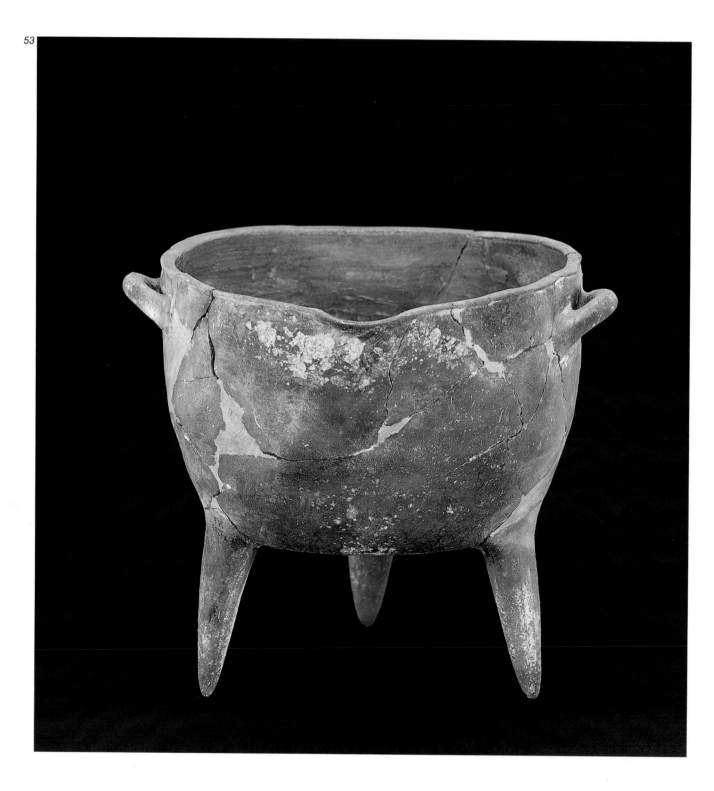

53

TRIPOD COOKING POT

H.M. F 65 5027a

MM II-III (c. 1900-1600 B.C.)
Phaistos
H: 24 cm.; D: rim 28 cm.

Restored. Reddish brown fabric. Box-shaped vessel. Two horizontal/coil in section handles set below the flat rim. The rim has a small pulled-out spout. The base is flat and the legs are oval in section.

A.K.- E.K.

54   TRIPOD COOKING POT

EUM-21: Base sherd

THE SWEET COURGETTE OF CRETE?

Beck: See method of analysis.

MM II B (c. 1700 B.C.)
Apodoulou, Room 9, a storage area under the stairs
Sherds submitted for analysis averaged between 4 and 6 centimeters in diameter.

Elliptical vessel. The type normally had an incurving mouth and no spout. It is known to have been in use at the palace site of Phaistos between MM I B and MM III A (c. 2000-1640 B.C.)

R.M. 4747 is a substitute for EUM-21, which only survived in sherd condition and could not be restored.

TRIPOD COOKING POT

R.M. 4747

MM II B (c. 1700 B.C.)
Palatial centre at Monastiraki, Amari, Room 3-84
H: 32.7 cm.; D: rim 14-14.5 cm.

Restored. Coarse orange clay with dark and white grit. Thin brown wash. Elliptical body with two horizontal handles under the low collar rim. The base is flat. There are three legs with a flattened oval section. There are traces of burning on the exterior of the vase.

Ath.K.

55   BAKING BASIN

EUM-18: Wall/base sherd

RUMINANT ANIMALS (COWS; SHEEP; GOATS)
The components could also be the product of bacterial metabolism

Beck: See method of analysis.

MM II B (c. 1700 B.C.)
Apodoulou, Room 9, a storage area under the stairs

Sherds submitted for analysis averaged between 4 and 6 centimeters in diameter.

The type is similar to R.M. 22914.

R.M. 22914 is a substitute for EUM-18, which only survived in sherd condition and could not be restored.

54

BAKING BASIN

R.M. 22914

MM I (c. 2160-1900 B.C.)
Chamalevri, 1995. Pateras field. Pits A and M
H: 12.3 cm.; D: 50.3cm.

Almost the whole base is missing; restored. Reddish brown to light brown, gritty clay. Light reddish brown slip. Large semi-globular body. Vertical rim with broad spout; wall opposite is inverted. Convex base. Plain.

M.A.-V.

56   BAKING BASIN

EUM-24: Wall/base sherd

OLIVE OIL?

Beck: See method of analysis.

MM II B (c. 1700 B.C.)
Apodoulou, Room 9, a storage area under the stairs
Sherds submitted for analysis averaged between 4 and 6 centimeters in diameter.

The type is similar to R.M. 22914 for description. See above.

57   TRIPOD COOKING POT

EUM-19: Wall/base sherd

RUMINANT ANIMALS (COWS; SHEEP; GOATS)
(The components could also be the product of bacterial metabolism)

Beck: See method of analysis.

MM II (c. 1900-1700 B.C.)
Apodoulou, Room 2
Sherds submitted for analysis averaged between 4 and 6 centimeters in diameter.

Elliptical vessel. The type normally had an incurving mouth and no spout. It is known to have been in use at the palace site of Phaistos between MM I B and MM III A (c. 2000-1640 B.C.). The type is similar to R.M. 21189.

R.M. 21189 is a substitute for EUM-19, which only survived in sherd condition and could not be restored.

TRIPOD COOKING POT

R.M. 21189

MM II (c. 1900-1700 B.C.)
Apodoulou, trench 2 to the west of the complex (trial trench next to wall 61)
H: 38.5 cm.; D: base 15.5 cm.

Mended and restored in places. Brown/ brown-red coarse fabric with inclusions. Elliptical body ending in a rounded inverted rim. Two horizontal handles of circular section. Flat base, legs of oval section, with rope decoration running along the centre.

A.T.

58   TRIPOD COOKING POT

EUM-27: Wall sherd

OLIVE OIL. ANIMAL FAT

Beck: See method of analysis.

MM II (c. 1900-1700 B.C.)
Apodoulou, sector 5, level 4
Sherds submitted for analysis averaged between 4 and 6 centimeters in diameter.

Type unknown. Not Illustrated.

59   TRIPOD COOKING POT

EUM-28: Wall sherd

INGREDIENT OF PLANT ORIGIN

Beck: See method of analysis.

MM II (c. 1900-1700 B.C.)
Apodoulou, sector 5, level 3
Sherds submitted for analysis averaged between 4 and 6 centimeters in diameter.

Type unknown. Not Illustrated.

55

Elliptical vessel. The type normally had an incurving mouth and no spout. It is known to have been in use at the palace site of Phaistos between MM I B and MM III A (c. 2000-1640 B.C.).

A.T.

57

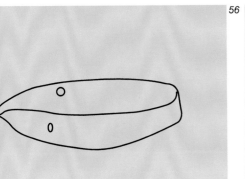

61 TRIPOD COOKING POT

EUM-221/224: Profile sherds

THE MOST WIDELY DISTRIBUTED SESQUITERPENE IN PLANTS
No fats or oils found in this vessel

Beck: See method of analysis.

MM II (c. 1900-1700 B.C.)
Apodoulou, Room 22, level 3
Sherds submitted for analysis averaged between 4 and 6 centimeters in diameter.

Box-shaped vessel. The type normally had a small, pulled-out spout. It is known to have been in use between MM II and LM III A/B (c. 1900-1190 B.C.).

A.T.

62 TRIPOD COOKING POT

EUM-225/229: Profile sherds

WAXES FROM FRUIT AND LEAFY VEGETABLES

Beck: See method of analysis.

MM II (c. 1900-1700 B.C.)
Apodoulou, Room 22, level 3
Sherds submitted for analysis averaged between 4 and 6 centimeters in diameter.

Box-shaped vessel. The type normally had a small, pulled-out spout. It is known to have been in use between MM II and LM III A/B (c. 1900-1190 B.C.).

A.T.

63 CONICAL BOWL

R.M. 7620

MM II B (c. 1700 B.C.)
Apodoulou, Room 9
H: 4.1-3.4 cm.; D: rim 17.7 cm.

Mended and restored. Orange fabric with inclusions, beige slip, brown-red paint. Distinctly conical body, straight rim, flat, not smooth base. Two concave bands around the exterior lower body. Traces of paint on the interior.

A.T.

56

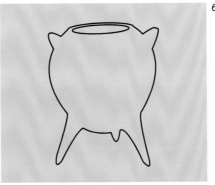

60

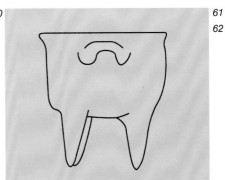

61
62

60 TRIPOD COOKING POT

EUM-220: Base/leg sherd

PINE OR OTHER PLANTS
No fats or oils found in the vessel

Beck: See method of analysis.

MM II (c. 1900-1700 B.C.)
Apodoulou, Room 22, level 3
Sherds submitted for analysis averaged between 4 and 6 centimeters in diameter.

63

64 JUG

R.M. 7619

MM II B (c. 1700 B.C.)
Apodoulou, Room 9
H: (pres.) 16.8 cm.; D: body 12.8 cm.

Mended and restored. Beige coarse fabric with inclusions, off-white matt slip, black, matt, fugitive paint. The neck is of a different fabric which is pure with only a few inclusions. Oval body, slightly conical neck, vertical handle of circular section, springing from the top of the neck and ending at the top of the body. Flat base. Decorated with a horizontal band at the base of the neck, from which spring groups (3?) of pairs of lanceolate, slightly convex bands, with the pairs converging just above the base. Band around the base of the handle.

A.T.

65 LARGE CARINATED CUP

R.M. 7632

MM II B (c. 1700 B.C.)
Apodoulou, Room 9
H: 7.5 cm.; D: rim 12 cm.

Mended and the larger part restored. Orange fabric with a few inclusions, beige slip and traces of dark brown paint. Carinated body, the upper part biconcave and the lower distinctly conical. Vertical, proportionately very small handle, flat base. Exterior probably originally painted solid.

A.T.

66 JUG

R.M. 7633

MM II B (c. 1700 B.C.)
Apodoulou, Room 9
H: 9.7 cm.; D: rim 3.4 cm., base 6.8 cm.

Complete except for a few chips on the rim. Brown buff to orange gritty clay. No spout. An elliptical mouth is set onto a high collar. The body is globular and the base is flat. A vertical coil handle extends from the top of the rim to the shoulder. Traces of black paint survive on the collar and on the base of the handle.

E.P.

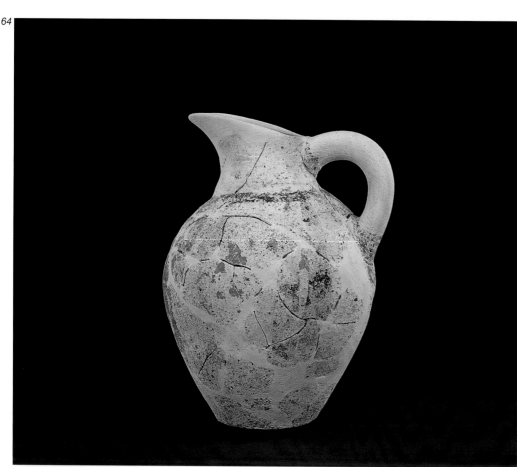

64

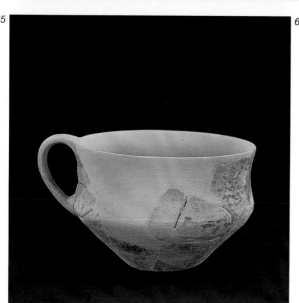

65

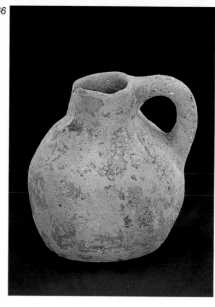

66

FRUIT, VEGETABLES AND OLIVE OIL
AT THE PALATIAL CENTRE AT MONASTIRAKI, RETHYMNON
(c. 1900-1700 B.C.)

The most significant result came from a "grater", named by the Italians in the early part of the 20th century because it reminded them of a cheese grater. "Graters" have only been found at two sites, and all found so far are dated between 1800 and 1500 B.C. The two sites are the major palace site at Phaistos and the smaller palatial centre at Monastiraki. In the majority of cases at Phaistos the graters were found in cult contexts. The grater from Monastiraki came from a storeroom that did contain artefacts with cult connections.

The sherd EUM-242 submitted for analysis was located on the base of the vessel R.M. 23125 just below the grating platform. The organic residue result was olive or plant oil.

DR. HOLLEY MARTLEW

THE EXCAVATION

The Palatial Centre at Monastiraki in the Amari valley lies between the west side of Mound Ida and the hill of Samitos, by the east side of Mount Kedros. The site controls the natural road from the north coast to the south coast of Crete and it probably can be indentified with Suqirita–Sybrita of Linear A and B texts.

A very large complex of buildings dating from the Protopalatial period has been uncovered. They comprised, or have given indications as to, all the basic components of the palatial centres of the period. Extensive storerooms have been uncovered in all the four areas tested so far. Official quarters can be identified in a monumental building with a recessed facade which, in the Protopalatial period, is a palatial characteristic. This building has a hall with a column base which has produced evidence for ritual use. It was associated with pen areas, courts, and massive,

Room 3, pithoi.

extensive retaining walls which are still under investigation. The religious element present in the centres of this period is represented at Monastiraki, among other religious traits, by the clay model of a shrine with horns of consecration on its wall. The palatial character of the Monastiraki complex of buildings is mainly established by the great number of sealings which have been found in three different parts of the site stressing the centrally organized administration which controlled access to the produce and its distribution. There is evidence that the centre was a dependant of the palace of Phaistos in the Mesara plain and an outpost of the state of Phaistos in the Amari valley. It finally was destroyed by fire and perhaps earthquake at the end of the Protopalatial period–MM II B, c. 1700 B.C.

The material presented in this Exhibition comes from the Monastiraki storerooms. The number of storerooms discovered at the centre is impressive, larger than any other site in Crete, including the great Minoan palaces. The produce was stored in large storage jars –pithoi– which were standing along the walls of the storerooms, sometimes even in the doorways, together with other smaller storage vessels such as amphorae of various sizes, pithoid jars, tubs etc. as well as other specialized shapes such as tripodic cauldrons, graters, "milk jugs", hole mouthed-bridge spouted jars etc. The use of these vases is studied in detail in the forthcoming publication of the site. Specialized cooking areas including ovens and probable open air hearths have benn identified. The remains of a pottery kiln show that a part at least of the Phaistian type ceramics of the centre were made *in situ*.

One of the largest storerooms found at Monastiraki, which has produced material included in the Exhibition, is room 3. The areas adjacent to it have produced interesting remnants of ritual and cultic activities. The axonometric plan of the room gives an impression of the finds found *in situ*.

In the last ten years a large flotation program of the burnt soil from the destruction level of the centre has been undertaken, which has yielded very rich results. Together with the animal bones which have been collected in large numbers from the various rooms, they give us a very detailed picture of the economy of the centre and the dietary habits of its inhabitants. Cereals and pulses of various types were common and so were the olive and olive oil, the vine and wine and the fig. Residues of olive oil and wine have been found within the large pithoi of the site. The type of wine is not known, but some of it may perhaps have been resinated, as discovered in other areas of the Mediterranean, a practice which goes back to much earlier times than those of Monastiraki. A large program of testing the contents of various containers is currently under way and will produce interesting results in the future. As in Crete today, sheep and goats were the main species bred, although there is a high percentage of pigs and even cows. The wild species which are well represented among the assemblage: beer, ibex, wild cattle and hare suggest that hunting was a well established occupation at Monastiraki. The presence of fish at this inland site is another testimony not only to trade and communication but to the food preserving skills of this early society as well. The discovery of equid bones at a site of such an early date brings new evidence to bear on the established view that the horse was brought to Crete in the Neopalatial period probably from the Mycenaean Mainland. The faunal and floral evidence from the site will be published in detail shortly.

PROF. ATHANASIA KANTA
University of Rethymnon, Crete

Storeroom with pithoi.

67   TRIPOD COOKING POT

EUM-31: Base/leg sherd

WAXES FROM FRUIT AND LEAFY VEGETABLES

Beck: See method of analysis.

MM II B (c. 1700 B.C.)
Palatial centre at Monastiraki, Amari, Room 3-82
Sherds submitted for analysis averaged between 4 and 6 centimeters in diameter.

Elliptical vessel. It normally had an incurving mouth and no spout. The type is known to have been used at the palace site of Phaistos between MM I B and MM III A (c. 2000-1640 B.C.).

R.M. 3651 is a substitute for EUM-31, which only survived in sherd condition and could not be restored.

TRIPOD COOKING POT

R.M. 3651

MM II B (c. 1700 B.C.)
Palatial centre at Monastiraki, Amari, Room 35 A-85
H: 29 cm.; D: rim 15.5-16.5 cm.

Mended from many fragments and restored in parts of the body, handles and rim. Coarse buff clay with dark and white grit. Thin brown wash. Elliptical body with two horizontal handles under the rim which forms a low ring. The base is flat and the three legs have a flattened oval section. Traces of burning on the exterior.

Ath.K.

68   GRATER

R.M. 23125   EUM-242: Base sherd

OLIVE OIL/PLANT OIL

Beck: See method of analysis.

MM II B (c. 1700 B.C.)
Palatial centre at Monastiraki, Amari, Room 3-82
Length: 8.5 cm.,
D: (max. pres.) 17.5 cm.
Sherds submitted for analysis averaged between 4 and 6 centimeters in diameter.

Coarse orange-buff clay with dark and white grit. Black, worn paint. Part of the base and body of the vase is preserved. Mended from many sherds. The base of the bowl is flat. There is a hole in the preserved part of the body of the vase, which acted as a handle. A grater has been attached in the interior of the bowl. Three rows of low ridges with indentations are preserved on the grating surface. There are traces of paint around the base of the grater inside the bowl.

Ath.K.

67

69 GRATER

H.M. 5825

MM II B (c. 1700 B.C.)
First Palace of Phaistos, Room 22
H: 9 cm.; D: 21 cm.

Restored. The medium coarse fabric is yellowish in colour. The walls are thick, and the vessel has a pulled-out spout. The horizontal handle is restored, and the base of the vessel is flat. Inside, on the same line as the spout, there is a triangular platform which has parallel rows of notched ridges formed out of soft clay. Brown painted bands decorate the inside.

A.K.-E.K.

68

69

COOKING AT MINOAN KYDONIA

The globular tripod pot CH.M. 3788 (LM I B, c. 1480-1425 B.C.) contained peas, shown in a dish next to it. If eaten in sufficient quantity, these peas cause a disease called lathyrism.

The cooking jar CH.M. 4485, found in Chania Kastelli, dates to a later time, LM III C1, c. 1190-1130 B.C. It is interesting not only because it was found with a cooking stand (CH.M. 4486), which is the only one found to date in Minoan Crete. It is significant as an example of Mycenaean influence in the island. This type of cooking jar was the most popular cooking utensil on the Mycenaean Mainland from at least LH III A (c.1390 B.C.) until the demise of the civilisation (c. 1070 B.C.). At the present time there are no examples from Crete that date to a time earlier than c. 1250 B.C. (the middle of the 13th century B.C.).

DR. HOLLEY MARTLEW

EXCAVATIONS AT CHANIA
MINOAN KYDONIA. THE HILL OF KASTELLI

THE SITE

The site occupied by the modern town of Chania was in all probability also the site of ancient Kydonia, the *ku-do-ni-ja* of the Linear B tablets. Excavations over the last 30 years have brought to light considerable remains of the Minoan settlement on the nearby Kastelli hill and the neighbouring district of Splanzia, two sites in the heart of the Old Town. The excavations on Kastelli are conducted by the Greek Archaeological Service, with the exception of the joint Greek-Swedish excavation in Ayias Ekaterinis Square directed by Dr. Yannis Tzedakis.

All archaeological phases of Minoan civilisation are represented in the finds from the hill, beginning with EM I (c. 3650-3000 B.C.) and ending in LM III C (c. 1190 B.C.). The discovery of both Linear A and Linear B tablets points to the existence of a palace complex in the surrounding area.

The unbroken occupation of the site from Geometric times to the present, and particularly the multi-storey Venetian buildings with their deep foundations, have caused extensive destruction to the Minoan architectural remains. The best-preserved phase goes back to the New Palace period, and is sealed beneath a thick layer of fire destruction dating from the end of this period (c. 1425 B.C.) – a destruction contemporary with that of other Minoan centres, with the exception of Knossos.

In Ayias Ekaterinis Square was discovered one complete house plan of this period (house I), and parts of three others (II-IV), together with narrow streets and a small square. The building had isodomic facades, monumental thresholds, painted wall-surfaces, a "Minoan hall", a lightwell, a staircase and an upper storey, a kitchen with a hearth and a loom, storerooms, and a drainage system. There was clear evidence in some cases for workshops and artistic and religious activities. The excavation yielded a large number of both clay and stone, functional and storage vases, as well as some pottery of fine art, clay sealings, parts of clay Linear A tablets, a few bronze tools and weapons, the remains of a piece of burnt woven fabric, microlithic and stone tools (rubbers, grinders, whetstones), and a small quantity of jewellery and seals. A pithos contained grains and the large tripod vase CH.M. 3788 held carbonised peas. This vase was found amongst several other pots in the storeroom E next to the kitchen M of House I.

The final destruction of the complex occurred in the LM III C period (c. 1190-1070 B.C.). A group consisting of the clay cooking vessels CH.M. 4485 and CH.M. 4486, a cooking-pot and a stand, were found *in situ* in the middle of Room O of House I of the Greek-Swedish excavations, along with a pithos and a millstone. The group dates to LM III C (c. 1190-1070 B.C.)

The carbonised figs came from the LM III B (c. 1340-1190 B.C.) farmhouse at Sternes Akrotiri, near Chania. The excavation, which was carried out in 1972, revealed buildings consisting of two rooms, in one of which there was a small, destroyed oven with carbonised figs inside it. Other finds from this excavation included two pithoi and a bronze axe.

MARIA ANDREADAKI-VLAZAKI
Director 25th Ephorate, Chania
Ministry of Culture

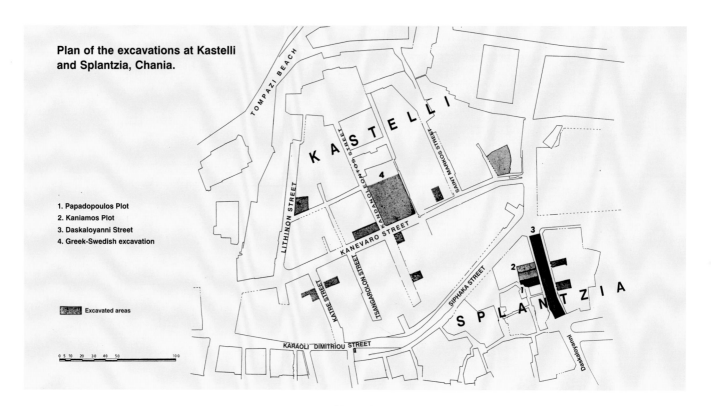

Plan of the excavations at Kastelli and Splantzia, Chania.

1. Papadopoulos Plot
2. Kaniamos Plot
3. Daskaloyanni Street
4. Greek-Swedish excavation

Excavated areas

0 5 10 20 30 40 50 ... 100

LATHYRISM

A potential toxic hazard in antiquity was the extensive consumption of the grass pea or bread made from a flour, produced by milling them. The grass pea **Lathyrus sativus L.** or its variants, such as **Lathyrus cicerus L.** found in a cooking pot in the Late Minoan I B (c. 1480-1425 B.C.) levels at Chania-Kastelli and exhibited here, was cultivated throughout Europe and the Eastern Mediterranean in the Bronze Age and earlier. It often appears by itself, or is grown together with another leguminous crop, particularly the broad or fava bean, **Vicia faba L.** The seeds of **Lathyrus sativus L.** contain a toxic alkaloid, and if not carefully boiled before eating, they can lead to a disease known as lathyrism. Lathyrism is characterised by a spastic paralysis of the lower limbs, and occurs as a result of regular consumption. Those affected present a characteristically scissoring gait in which the balls of the feet take most of the weight.

It is an irreversible condition. Once it develops, neuro-lathyrism is usually not progressive, but little or no recovery occurs even if grass pea consumption ceases. Localised aneurysms may also occur.

Lathyrism develops when the grass pea comprises 30% of the diet or more. This seems a lot, but the over-consumption of the grass pea could easily have been prevalent during famine, for example in soups, and as a vegetable supplementary protein supply. Those suffering from the genetic disorder Glucose-6-phosphate dehydrogenase (G6PD) deficiency are particularly susceptible to lathyrism, although an advantage of this condition is that, as with thalassaemia and sickle-cell anaemia, a hostile environment for the Plasmodium or malaria parasite is created.

Protection against lathyrism may be behind the Pythagorean prohibition of the consumption of κύαμος, now identified as the broad or fava bean. This bean was also well-known in the Eastern Mediterranean, having been reported as having been found in Mycenaean chamber tombs.

The Romans made porridge for sacrificial purposes from fava beans. Bread was also made from fava bean flour, and Pliny knew it had a dulling effect on the senses, and an ability to cause sleeplessness.

DR. ROBERT ARNOTT
Dept. of Ancient History and Archaeology
University of Birmingham, U.K.

70 TRIPOD COOKING POT

CH.M. 3788

LM I B (c. 1480-1425 B.C.)
Chania, 1977. Kastelli hill - Greek-Swedish
Excavations. LM I House I - Room E
(storeroom)
H: 30 cm.; D: body 37 cm.

Almost complete; restored. Light brown,
gritty clay; white, chalky slip; red paint.
Globular body; short collar rim; flat
base; short legs, elliptical in section. Six
roll handles: four vertical on the
shoulder and two horizontal on the
belly. Traces of horizontal bands of paint
on the body and handles. "Peas" were
found inside the vessel.

M. A.-V.

71 DISH OF PEAS

LM I B (c. 1480-1425 B.C.)

Found in CH.M. 3788 (Cat. No 71)

Lathyrus cicera/sativus, grass peas. The
sample also contains other pulses in
small numbers such as **Vicia faba,**
horsebean and lentil, **Lens esculentus L.**

A.S.

71

70

72-73

72 COOKING POT

CH.M. 4485

LM III C1 (c. 1190-1130 B.C.)
Chania, 1977. Kastelli hill-Greek-Swedish
Excavations. LM III House I - Room O
H: 21 cm.; D: rim 19.3 cm., body 23.5 cm.,
base 13 cm.

Almost complete; restored. Light reddish
brown, very gritty clay. Conical-globular
body; narrow flat base. High, flaring rim
with rolled lip. On the shoulder, two
vertical strap handles. Plain. Heavily
burnt inside and out.

M.A.-V.

73 COOKING STAND

CH.M. 4486

LM III C1 (c. 1190-1130 B.C.)
Chania, 1977. Kastelli hill-Greek-Swedish
Excavations. LM III House I - Room O
H: 19.5 cm.; D: rim 22.5 cm., base 21.5 cm.

Completely preserved; restored. Reddish
brown, very gritty clay. Wheel ridges
inside. Cylindrical body with a rectangular opening. The rim is crudely
moulded. Plain. Burnt.

M.A.-V.

74  74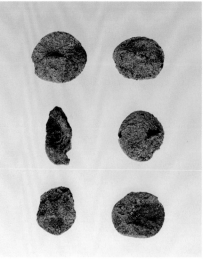

74 FIGS

LM III B (c. 1340-1190 B.C.)
Sternes, Akrotiri, Chania. Amygdalokefali

A fairly large quantity of figs, **Ficus carica**,
were found during the excavation of a
Minoan villa. The figs were found on
stone slabs which belonged either to the
roof or the floor of the second storey. It
is important to note that the figs were
dried prior to charring, and therefore,
they provide us with the earliest evidence
to date for dried figs in Minoan Crete.

A.S.

THEY ATE STEW AT MINOAN KYDONIA

Meat and vegetable stews were definitely part of the diet in Chania c. 1480-1425 B.C. Tripod vessel CH.M. 6975/EUM-165 which was used to boil meat and leafy vegetables, is cylindrical with a small spout, a shape that was typical of West Crete from Middle Minoan III period (c. 1700-1600 B.C.). This particular tripod was the subject of a special series of organic residue tests: several sherds down the profile of the vessel were tested.

DR. HOLLEY MARTLEW

MINOAN KYDONIA
TOWN OF CHANIA. EXCAVATION OF THE SPLANZIA

SACRED AREA

The excavation covered a large part of Daskaloyanni Street (90 m. long) and two adjoining private properties owned by N. Papadopoulos and N. Kaniamos. In these areas part of an extensive building complex of the city of Chania (Kydonia) was uncovered, dating from the New Palace period and with an area of over 750 square m. The complex comprised a large number of rooms, lightwells, an adyton or lustral basin, a large courtyard, an impressive open-air stone exedra, the site of a pyre with slaughtered animals and a grille-bothros, and a row of underground rooms. To the above should be added an unusual drainage system that starts inside the building, runs into the court, and encircles the

a. Reconstruction of the adyton (drawing by G. Christodoulakos).

b. Chania town, 1997. Splantzia. Excavation in Daskaloyianni street and the N. Papadopoulos and N. Kaniamos plots. LM I A complex (drawing by G. Christodoulakos).

c. Excavation in Daskaloyianni street. Part of the LM I complex.

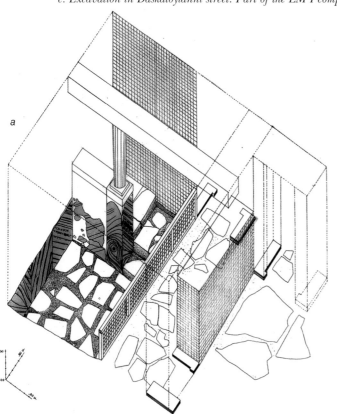

a

exedra, and is associated with a large number of conical cups. Similarly, a very large number of conical cups were deposited at various points of the court and in the area of the pyre. The fill of the underground rooms to the north of the drain, one of which was a hypostyle room, was also full of conical cups, a few tripod cooking pots and other functional vases.

The above finds indicate that the building was a sacred area - that is, an urban sanctuary, and possibly a palace sanctuary if it belongs to the palace complex of Kydonia dating from 1600 B.C. All the indications are that the rituals conducted at particular points of time followed a fixed route from the interior of the main building complex to the open-air spaces or vice versa, and linked the "lustral basin" with the open-air exedra, the initiates with the crowd of people attending.

The sanctuary continued to function in the LM I B period (c. 1480-1425 B.C.), but its architecture and the mode of worship exhibit some differences. The rituals were of limited extent, the adyton had already been converted into a groundfloor room, though with larger dimensions, before the end of the LM I A phase (c. 1600-1480 B.C.), and there were fewer conical cups. The rooms to the south of the adyton were used for collecting and preparing food. In one of these rooms, three cooking pots were found *in situ* with the remains of the final meal.

The final destruction of the building took place at the end of the LM I B period (c. 1425 B.C.), when the other centres on the island were also destroyed. It was accompanied by an extensive fire, as was also the case with the excavations on the nearby Kastelli hill. This important building finally ceased to function and was buried beneath the rubble from its superstructure. It was remorselessly destroyed over the following centuries by quarrying for building material.

MARIA ANDREADAKI-VLAZAKI

Director 25th Ephorate, Chania,
Ministry of Culture

b *c*

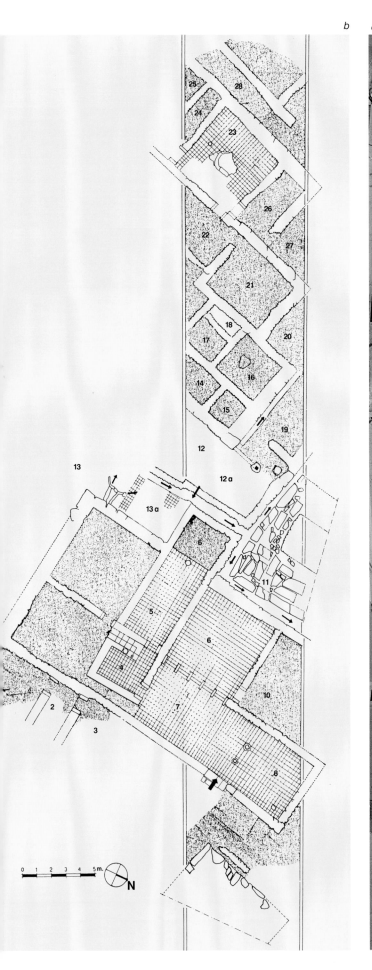

EXCAVATION AT SPLANZIA - SACRED AREA

THE SLAUGHTERED ANIMALS ASSOCIATED WITH THE PYRE

It is clear from the area in which this particular group of bones was found (in a pyre on the floor of a LM I, c. 1600-1425 B.C., courtyard), and the circumstances in which it became part of the archaeological level (as a result of a destruction) that it represents activities which took place at a single point in time, or over a very brief period. The association of the bones with other finds of a "ritual" nature makes it possible to investigate the role played by animals in cult practices.

The most common animal in the group is the pig. The remains of at least six beasts have been found. Most of them are young animals that were slaughtered before the end of their first year of life, while one, probably male, was 2 1/2 - 3 1/2 years old. The carcasses of pigs were butchered with a knife used at the joints, as is clear from the knife marks. In addition to the pigs, at least two female, mature sheep were slaughtered. The bones of at least two goats, in contrast, do not represent the complete carcass: evidently only the hind legs were proffered for the activities that took place in this particular area. There were at least three cows, and similarly only parts of the fore and hind legs were found. In addition to the main farm animals, the bones of a male dog were found. Its body does not appear to have been butchered in the same way as the other animals, for many of the bones connect together.

In addition to the bones of domestic species, the bones of a platoni were found, as well as the horns of two male wild goats and a bone of a bird.

Animals are known to have played a role in the cult practices of Minoan Crete, attested by the discovery of bones, both burned and unburned, near altars, by the dedication of models of animals in temples, and also by the iconography. There is a large number of scenes depicting animal sacrifices. The animal may be shown on the altar, or being carried to it. On the Ayia Triada sarcophagus, two animals beneath the altar are apparently waiting their turn to be sacrificed. It is highly likely that the sacrificial animals, or at least parts of them, were consumed by the worshippers after the sacrifice.

REMAINS OF THE "FINAL MEAL"

Bones from at least three sheep and a goat, and at least one cow and a platoni were found on the floor of rooms D and E. From the distribution of the anatomical parts of the animals, it appears that the carcasses of goats and sheep were completely used up, whereas in the case of the cow, only part of the hind leg and the skull, and of the platoni part of the foreleg and the head were used.

DIMITRA MYLONA
Archaeologist, Zooarchaeologist
Institute of Mediterranean Studies (ITE), Rethymnon, Crete

Splantzia. Papadopoulos plot. Room E. Cooking pots nos. 92-93 on the floor.

Animal bones from the pyre. Excavation at Splantzia. Sacred Area.

75   TRIPOD COOKING POT

EUM-40: Wall/base sherd

OLIVE OIL

Beck: See method of analysis.

LM I (c. 1600-1425 B.C.)
Chania, Splanzia, Room ST with pillar base
Sherds submitted for analysis averaged
between 4 and 6 centimeters in diameter.

Cylindrical vessel. The type normally had
a small, pulled-out spout. It is known to
have been in use in West Crete between
MM III and LM III A (c. 1700-1340
B.C.).

CH.M. 6944 is a substitute for EUM-40,
which only survived in sherd condition
and could not be restored.

TRIPOD COOKING POT

CH.M. 6944

LM I B (c. 1480-1425 B.C.).
Chania, 1989. Splanzia - Papadopoulos plot.
Room 2
H: 29 cm.; D: rim 21 cm., base 18 cm.

Restored. Reddish brown, very gritty
clay. Cylindrical body. Everted rim;
small, pulled-out spout. Two small,
horizontal roll handles just below rim.
Legs ovoid in section. Plain. Strong
traces of burning inside and out.

M.A.-V.

76   CONICAL CUP

EUM-34: Wall/base sherd

PROBABLY OLIVE OIL AND OTHER FAT(S)

Beck: See method of analysis.

LM I A (c. 1600-1480 B.C.)
Chania, 1997. Splanzia - Daskaloyiannis St.
Room ST with pillar base
Sherds submitted for analysis averaged
between 4 and 6 centimeters in diameter.

The type is similar to CH.M. 9398.

CH.M. 9398 is a substitute for EUM-34,
which only survived in sherd condition
and could not be restored.

CONICAL CUP

CH.M. 9398

LM I A (c. 1600-1480 B.C.)
Chania, 1997. Splanzia - Daskaloyiannis St.
Room ST. Exc. No 624
H: 3.9 cm.; D: rim 8,6 cm., base 4.4 cm.

Almost complete; restored. Reddish brown,
very gritty clay; wet-smoothed. Conical
body; broad rounded rim; narrow, flat
base. Strong wheel ridges inside. Plain.

M.A.-V.

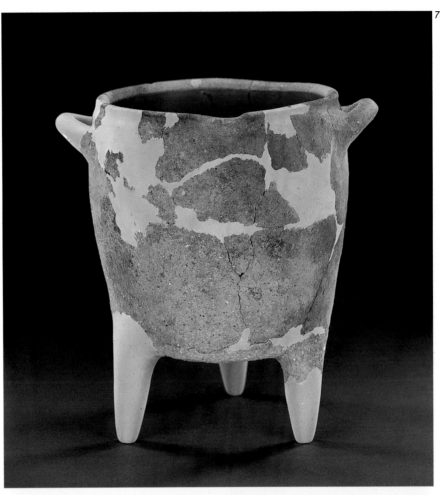

75

76

77 TRIPOD COOKING POT

. . . .

CH.M. 6975   EUM-165: Profile sherds

MINOAN STEW: THE RESULTS ARE CONSISTENT WITH BOILING MEAT AND LEAFY VEGETABLES IN A POT, WITH OLIVE OIL AS AN INGREDIENT. GRAPES COULD ALSO HAVE BEEN ADDED TO THE STEW.

The profile of this vessel was tested to see if there would be different results down the vertical of the vessel. This is the first time, to our knowledge, that this method has been successfully tested on Bronze Age material.

Beck: See method of analysis.

LM I B (c. 1480-1425 B.C.)
Chania, 1989. Splanzia - Papadopoulos plot.
Room 2
H: 33.5 cm.; D: rim 20 cm., base 16 cm.

Restored. Reddish brown, gritty clay. Cylindrical body; rim slightly incurving; flat base; horizontal, roll handle, just below rim. Plain. Burnt outside. A sherd was taken for analysis prior to restoration. The type is similar to CH.M. 9398 above.

M.A.-V.

77

A SUMMARY OF ORGANIC RESIDUE RESULTS FOR TRIPOD COOKING POT CH.M. 6975

Rim/wall sherd was large enough to extend well down into the pot. It was broken into 3 pieces to ascertain differences of distribution of organic material in 3 areas, filed by Beck under the names RIM, UP (the upper part of the wall immediately below the rim), and DOWN (the lowest part of the sherd not at base level).

DOWN

produced the fewest organic components: it produced less than 1/2 than the rim did, and slightly more than 1/7 in the UP fragment. The level at which the greatest concentration of organic material will be found must, of course, depend on the level to which the pot was filled when in use.

It is interesting to note that a rim sherd of a tripod from Monastiraki, of the elliptical type, yielded nothing. Presumably this vessel was not filled "to the top".

OLIVE OIL: methyl pelargonate, a degradation product of oleic acid, the principal fatty acid of olive oil.

EPICUTICULAR WAXES: fruit waxes: 2 hydrocarbons, heptadecane and octadecane.

METHYL PALMITATE (HEXADECONOATE): in most sherds the predominant fatty acid.

RIM and UP

Both rich in organic constituents, but there were significant differences between the two.

OLIVE OIL: pelargonic acid: see above.

LAURIC (Dodecanoic) acid

ANIMAL FATS/PLANT OILS: FATTY ACIDS with 14, 16, 18, and 24 carbon atoms: common to both fragments.

Waxy coatings of leaves and fruit, including bergamot and grape (Vitis vinifera): This is the most unusual: C 24 lignoceric acid.

UP

Richest of all the sherds in saturated hydrocarbons.

Vegetable origin: Leafy vegetables or fruit: alkanes with 27, 29, and 31 carbon atoms are the principal components of epicuticular waxes.

PROF. DR. CURT W. BECK
Vassar College, Poughkeepsie,
N.Y., U.S.A.

78

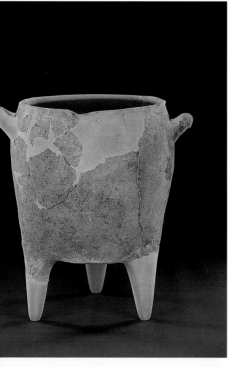

78 TRIPOD COOKING POT

CH.M. 6948

LM I B (c. 1480-1425 B.C.)
Chania, 1989. Splanzia - Papadopoulos plot.
Room 2. Exc. No 92
H: 30 cm.; D: rim 20-23 cm., base 18.5 cm.

Restored. Brown, gritty clay. Cylindrical
body; broad, incurving rim with a small,
pulled-out spout; two roll handles set
horizontally on the shoulder; flat base.
Plain. Traces of burning.

M.A.-V.

79 TRIPOD COOKING POT

CH.M. 6968

LM I B (c. 1480-1425 B.C.)
Chania, 1989. Splanzia - Papadopoulos plot.
Room 2. Exc. No 93
H: 27 cm.; D: rim 19.5 cm., base 18 cm.

Half of the body is missing; restored.
Reddish yellow, gritty clay. Cylindrical
body; incurving rounded rim; flat base;
legs ovoid in section. Plain. Heavily
burnt outside; traces of burning inside.

M.A.-V.

79

80-81 CONICAL CUPS

(68 in number)

CH.M. 9362, 9364, 9366-7, 9369-71, 9375-97,
9399-9415, 9416 (2), 9417-19, 9421-25, 9427-37

LM I A (c. 1600-1480 B.C.)
Chania, 1997. Splanzia - Daskaloyiannis St.
Sacral area (generally)
H: 2.9-4.5 cm.; D: rim 6.8-8.9 cm.,
base 3.3-4.8 cm.

Complete or almost complete; restored.
Some of them are crooked. Reddish
brown to yellow clay. CH.M. 9430 is
covered by white chalky slip. Conical
body; rounded or slightly outward
flaring rim; narrow flat base, pierced in
two of them. Some have strong wheel
ridges inside and others bear traces of
burning. Plain.

M.A.-V.

80

81

THEY ATE MEAT AND LENTILS AT THE LATE MINOAN CEMETERY OF ARMENOI, RETHYMNON

The LM I B-LM III A1 (c. 1480-1390 B.C.) Settlement:

According to the organic chemist, the fact that one tripod vessel (EUM-202) held only two organic compounds (decalins), was a unique result.

The LM III (c. 1390-1190 B.C.) Cemetery:

Sherds from a broken tripod cooking pot (R.M. 17313/2 EUM-294) found in the dromos of a chamber tomb gave an organic residue result of meat and olive oil. Results from a tripod pot (EUM-302) found in a ceremonial pit, included olive oil, cereal, meat, and pulses, possibly lentils (Evans).

An unusual result was that a decorated juglet (R.M. 22855/ EUM-170) and a decorated alabastron (R.M. 22857/EUM-171), both found inside chamber tombs, were deemed never to have held any fats or oils. Also interesting is that large amounts of plant waxes were present in both vessels (Beck).

DR. HOLLEY MARTLEW

THE EXCAVATION

A cemetery of the size and importance of Armenoi would belong to a large community. Over the years there has been a systematic investigation of the surrounding countryside in order to try to locate this settlement. This investigation which has met with varying degrees of success, is still continuing. The results obtained have been affected by deep cultivation that has been carried out in the area in recent years, as well as destructions that were carried out in the Roman period.

We believe that the settlement of Armenoi was founded at a time when trade in copper with the island of Cyprus became problematic. A copper mine has been located at a distance of about 4 kilometers south of the cemetery. It is therefore more than likely that the main purpose of the town was industrial. This would also provide an explanation for the large number, and the quality, of the bronzes found in the cemetery. In the cemetery itself, dromoi and ceremonial pits yielded coarse cooking ware, sherds of which were submitted for organic residue analysis.

A small area of habitation 500 meters northeast of the cemetery, yielded some domestic pottery, sherds of which were submitted for organic residue analysis. The date of painted pottery is LM I B to early LM II (c. 1425 B.C.). One tripod cooking pot (EUM-338) is LM III A1, c. 1390 B.C.

DR. YANNIS TZEDAKIS

82 TRIPOD COOKING POT

EUM-202: Wall/base sherd

A UNIQUE FIND: ONLY TWO ORGANIC COMPOUNDS, DECALINS, WHICH ARE DEGRADATION PRODUCTS OF SESQUITERPENES COMMON TO MOST FLOWERING PLANTS

Beck: See method of analysis.

LM I B / LM II (c. 1480-1390 B.C.)
Armenoi, settlement, sector 11, surface
Sherds submitted for analysis averaged between 4 and 6 centimeters in diameter.

Cylindrical vessel. The type normally had a small, pulled-out spout. It is known to have been in use in West Crete between MM III and LM III A (c. 1700-1340 B.C.).

CH.M. 3811 is a substitute for EUM-202, which only survived in sherd condition and could not be restored.

TRIPOD COOKING POT

CH.M. 3811

LM I B (c. 1480-1425 B.C.)
Chania, 1973. Kastelli hill - Greek-Swedish Excavations. Pit B
H: 28.3 cm.; D: rim 19.3 cm., body 27.5 cm.

One quarter of the body is missing; restored. Reddish, brown, gritty clay; buff slip. Cylindrical body; vertical, incurving rim with a small, pulled-out spout; roll handles put horizontally just below rim; convex base; legs ovoid in section. Plain. Traces of burning inside and out.

M.A.-V.

83 TRIPOD COOKING POT

EUM-200: Wall/base sherd

PLANT MATERIAL

Beck: See method of analysis.

LM I B/LM II? (c. 1480-1390 B.C.)
Armenoi, settlement, sector 11, extension north
Sherds submitted for analysis averaged between 4 and 6 centimeters in diameter.

Cylindrical vessel. The type normally had a small, pulled-out spout. It is known to have been in use in West Crete between MM III and LM III A (c. 1700-1340 B.C.).

E.P.

84 TRIPOD COOKING POT

EUM-338: Wall/base sherd

OLIVE OIL. OTHER COMPONENTS

Evans: See method of analysis.

LM III A1 (c. 1390-1370 B.C.)
Armenoi, settlement, sector 11, extension north
Sherds submitted for analysis averaged between 4 and 6 centimeters in diameter.

Convex vessel. Legs extend from body, and are nearly round in section. The type shows Mainland/Mycenaean influence and at present has not been found in a Minoan context prior to LM III A1.

85 CUP WITH SOIL INSIDE

EUM-241: Wall/base sherd - Soil sample

A LACTONE OF UNKNOWN BOTANICAL ORIGIN

SOIL: PLANT MATERIAL

Soil sample taken within 2 weeks of excavation

Beck: See method of analysis.

LM I B/LM II (c. 1480-1390 B.C.)
Armenoi, settlement, sector 13, level 2
Sherds submitted for analysis averaged between 4 and 6 centimeters in diameter.

CH.M. 7015 is a substitute for EUM-241, which only survived in sherd condition and could not be restored.

82

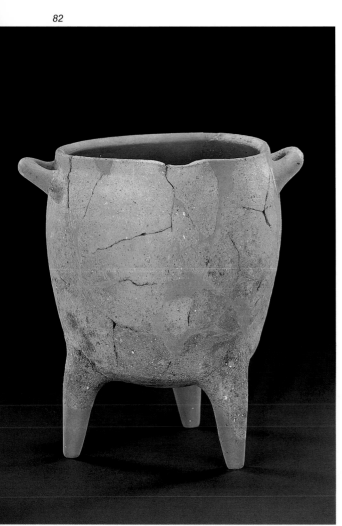

83

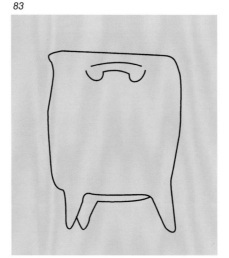

84

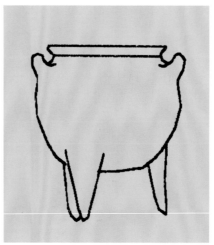

CUP

CH.M. 7015

LM I B (c. 1480-1425 B.C.)

Chania, 1989. Splanzia-Papadopoulos plot Room Δ. Floor 8. Exc. No 77

H: 4 cm.; D: rim: 8 cm., base: 3.3 cm.

Complete. Reddish-brown to orange, fine clay. Conical body; rounded rim; narrow, flat base. Wheel marks on the outside of the vessel.

M.A.-V.

86 JUGLET

R.M. 22855   EUM-170: Soil Sample

COPIOUS AMOUNTS OF PLANT WAXES. NO FATS OR OILS WERE EVER HELD IN THIS VESSEL

Beck: See method of analysis.

LM III A2 (c. 1370-1340 B.C.)

LM Cemetery of Armenoi. Tomb 226

H: 4.9 cm.; D: body 5.3 cm.

Almost complete. Restored at the handle and rim. Light brown fabric and pale yellow slip. The orange paint is badly flaked all over the body. Squat globular body (FS 112) with sloping shoulders. Low, wide neck with concave profile. Horizontal flared rim. Vertical handle from rim to belly. Flat base. Quirk motif (FM 48) decorates the shoulder. Two wide bands border the motif. Thinner bands run around the body and the base. The neck is monochrome inside. A soil sample was submitted for analysis within two weeks of the excavation.

E.P.

87 AMPHORA WITH SOIL INSIDE

R.M. 22852   EUM-172: Soil Sample

OLIVE OIL OR A PLANT OIL

Beck: See method of analysis.

LM III A2 (c. 1370-1340 B.C.)

LM Cemetery of Armenoi. Tomb 227

H: 12.6 cm.; D: 14.4 cm.

Almost complete. One handle restored. Gritty brown fabric. Yellow brown slip. Badly flaked black paint. Squat conical body. Wide low neck ends in a rounded horizontal rim. Two handles round in section, are horizontally placed on the shoulder. Flat base. Triglyph motifs (FM 27) filled with concentric semi-circles and multiple wavy lines decorate the shoulder zone between the handles. Bands run around the belly, the neck, and the rim. The neck and rim are monochrome inside. A soil sample was submitted for analysis within two weeks of the excavation.

E.P.

85

87

86

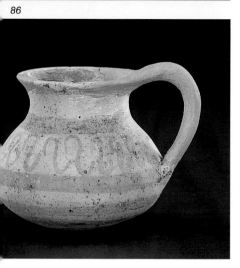

88   ALABASTRON

R.M. 22857   EUM-171: Soil Sample

THE WAXY COATINGS OF FRUITS, PETALS, OR LEAVES, BUT NO PARTICULAR PLANT CAN BE IDENTIFIED. NO FATS OR OILS WERE EVER HELD IN THIS VESSEL

Beck: See method of analysis.

LM III A2 (c. 1370-1340 B.C.)
LM Cemetery of Armenoi. Tomb 227
H: 7 cm.; D: body 6.15 cm.

Almost complete. Restored slightly at the rim. Light brown fabric. Slip and decoration do not survive. Traces of black paint. Very small and squat, globular, baggy alabastron. High cylindrical neck with concave profile. Ledge rim rounded at the edge.

E.P.

88

89   CYLINDRICAL ALABASTRON

R.M. 2676   EUM-305: Soil Sample

OIL. PULSES/LENTILS

Evans: See method of analysis.

LM Cemetery of Armenoi. Tomb 132, the tomb of the Minoan couple whose skulls have been reconstructed for the Exhibition. See Cat. No 215.

R.M. 1585 is a substitute for R.M. 2676/EUM-305, which is on display with the Minoan couple of Tomb 132.

ALABASTRON

R.M. 1585

LM III B (c. 1340-1190 B.C.)
LM Cemetery of Armenoi. Tomb 10
H: 15.5 cm.; D: base 8.4 cm.

Complete. Light brown fabric. Shiny yellowish to brown slip. Brown-orange paint. Convex body, with a low cylindrical neck. Flaring rim. Two horizontal handles on the shoulder. Flat base. A double zig-zag line (FM 61), the ends of which are filled with concentric arcs (FM 44), decorates the shoulder zone between the handles. Bands run around the vessel from the belly to the base. The neck and the rim are monochrome.

E.P.

89

90 TRIPOD COOKING POT

R.M. 17313/2 EUM-294: Soil Sample

MEAT. OLIVE OIL. A COMPLEX MIXTURE

Evans: See method of analysis.

LM III B (c. 1340-1190 B.C.)
LM Cemetery of Armenoi. Tomb 177, dromos
Sherds submitted for analysis averaged between 4 and 6 centimeters in diameter.

Only fragments of the legs of the pot survive. The type is similar to R.M. 13284.

R.M. 13284 is a substitute for R.M. 17313/ EUM-294, which only survived in sherd condition and could not be restored.

TRIPOD COOKING POT

R.M. 13284

LM III A1 (c. 1390-1370 B.C.)
Chamalevri, 1993. Kakavella hill.
St. Stratidakis field
H: 27.8 cm.; D: rim 19. 5 cm., base 17 cm.

Many fragments are missing; restored. Red, very gritty clay; wet-smoothed. Quite deep body with curved sides; almost flat base. Short everted rim; two horizontal roll handles set at an oblique angle below the rim on either side. Flattened feet. Plain. Badly burnt.

M.A.-V.

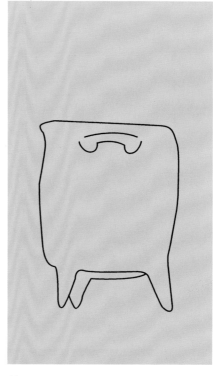

91

91 TRIPOD COOKING POT

R.M. 17322/1 EUM-299: Wall sherd

OLIVE OIL. MILK?

Evans: See method of analysis.

LM III B (c. 1340-1190 B.C.)
LM Cemetery of Armenoi. Southwest of Tombs 177 and 178
Sherds submitted for analysis averaged between 4 and 6 centimeters in diameter.

Fragments of the flat base, the flaring rim, and a part of the horizontal coil handle, and fragments of the body survive.

E.P.

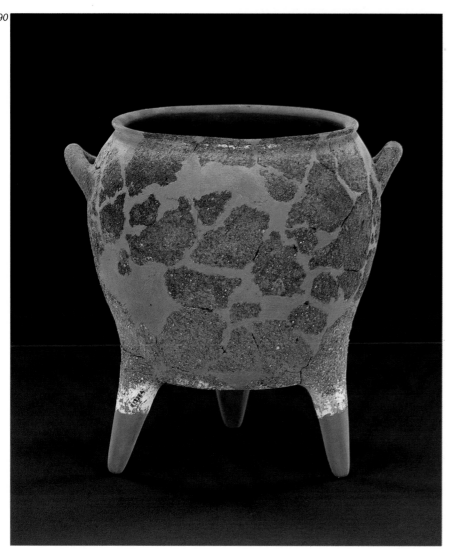

90

92

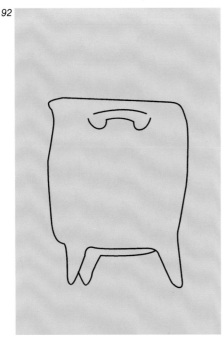

92 TRIPOD COOKING POT

R.M. 17326/14 EUM-295: Wall sherd

OLIVE OIL. A COMPLEX MIXTURE

Evans: See method of analysis.

LM III B (c. 1340-1190 B.C.)
LM Cemetery of Armenoi, southwest of
Tomb 178
Sherds submitted for analysis averaged
between 4 and 6 centimeters in diameter.

Parts of a horizontal coil handle and
body fragments survive.

E.P.

93 TRIPOD COOKING POT

EUM-302: Wall sherd

**TRACES OF OLIVE OIL. CEREAL.
MEAT. PULSES/LENTILS?**

Evans: See method of analysis.

LM III B (c. 1340-1190 B.C.)
LM Cemetery of Armenoi. Ceremonial pit
southwest of Tomb 178
Sherds submitted for analysis averaged
between 4 and 6 centimeters in diameter.

The type is similar to R.M. 13281.

R.M. 13281 is a substitute for EUM-302,
which only survived in sherd condition
and could not be restored.

93

TRIPOD COOKING POT

R.M. 13281

LM III A 1 (c. 1390-1370 B.C.)
Chamalevri, 1993. Kakavella hill. St.
Stratidakis field
H: 20.1 cm.; D: rim 19.7 cm., base 13.7 cm.

Many fragments are missing; restored.
Red, very gritty clay; wet-smoothed.
Rather cylindrical shape with curved
sides and flat base. Vertical rounded rim,
slightly pulled out to form a pouring
spout, just opposite the handle. One
vertical, flattened handle set below the
rim with an attached knob on its upper
end; a double knob on either side,
below the rim. Triangular, flattened feet.
Plain. Partly burnt.

M.A.-V.

94 TRIPOD COOKING POT

EUM-303: Wall sherd

OLIVE OIL. A COMPLEX MIXTURE

Evans: See method of analysis.

LM III B (c. 1340-1190 B.C.)
LM Cemetery of Armenoi. Ceremonial pit
southwest of Tomb 178
Sherds submitted for analysis averaged
between 4 and 6 centimeters in diameter.

Type unknown. Not illustrated.

THEY ATE PORK, CEREALS, PULSES AND HONEY
AT MYCENAEAN THEBES

There were two outstanding results from Thebes (c. 1380-1130 B.C.). One result was a cooking pot (T.M. 24432/EUM-312) which held a complex mixture that included pork. The second was a result from a decorated vessel, a skyphos (T.M. 27426/EUM-323) that appeared to have held pulses or cereal.

There was a cooking jar (EUM-309) that contained beeswax, an almost certain indication of honey. Honey is a very difficult commodity to trace as the water in it evaporates and the sugar degrades.

DR. HOLLEY MARTLEW

THE EXCAVATION

Thebes was one of the greatest Mycenaean centres according to ancient tradition, and this has been confirmed by archaeological research. The glory and the misfortunes of the House of Lavdakides, and especially of King Oedipus, inspired the tragic poets of classical times. The Mycenaean palace, the Kadmeion, has been located in the centre of the modern city of Thebes. As it is presently revealed, it had two building phases which have been called the Old Kadmeion (site 1) and the New Kadmeion (site 2). Parts of the palace itself or palace annexes have been excavated in different areas of the Mycenaean acropolis, the Kadmeia. Most important is the "Arsenal" where a few Linear B tablets have been found (site 3); magazines of agricultural products (sites 4, 5); workshops of jewellery (sites 2, 6, 7) and of ivory artefacts (site 8), a number of clay sealings which bear Linear B letters (site 9); and a Linear B tablet archive (site 10).

The material in the Exhibition was found in the Mycenaean/Late Helladic (LH) levels (14th-12th centuries B.C.), which have been recently excavated in three sites: two of them are in the eastern part (sites 11, 12) and the third is in the northwestern part of the Kadmeia (site 13). In these three sites, as usually in Thebes, habitation has been continuous from the Early Bronze Age, until modern times. Consequently, the archaeological strata are often disturbed and the buildings have suffered a lot of damage.

In site 11, the Mycenaean habitation was marked by two successive disasters caused by fire. In the first case, a storeroom of agricultural products, most probably part of a larger building, was burnt down. The destruction deposit, 0.50 m. thick, was rich in pottery (EUM-79 and EUM- 80) that dated to LH III A2 (c. 1370-1340 B.C.). A century later (at the end of LH III B, c. 1185 B.C.) another fire caused the destruction of the building and baked the clay tablets inscribed in Linear B, which were kept in it. In the vicinity of the Linear B archive, storerooms must have existed, as indicated by burnt fruits and seeds. This important find of the archive testifies to the palatial character of the building. In the next period, Late Helladic III C Early (c. 1185-1130 B.C.), the area was occupied by houses, of which only the clay floors with their hearths were preserved. The layer above produced a great deal of pottery (EUM-82) dated to the Late Helladic III C Middle period (c. 1130-1090 B.C.).

In site 12, habitation debris has been recovered, belonging probably to houses. The cooking pots EUM-306 and EUM-318 (T.M. 27117 and T.M. 28949) come from a layer with LH III B pottery (c. 1340-1185 B.C.).

The sherds of the vase EUM-319 (T.M. 28950) were deposited on the bottom of a hearth coated with clay. This vase, hand-made, burnished and decorated with a cordon-like stripe, belongs to a special category of pottery completely different from the Mycenaean vases and it dates to the LH III C Early period (c. 1185-1130 B.C.). The presence of this pottery in Mycenaean layers has prompted several interpretations.

In site 13, a very small part of a room, that is presumed to have been a storage area has been excavated. It revealed rich finds, including a seal; large lead and bronze sheets; LH III B1 (c. 1340-1185 B.C.) storage and fine vases (EUM-307, 308, 309, 310, 311, 322/ T.M. 27426, and T.M. 27425). In the centre of the excavated area was a large rectangular building, partially preserved and comprising at least two rooms. The function of the larger one, probably the main room of the building (EUM-312, 314, 316, 320) seems to be composite, since there was found evidence for ceremonial activities and also for procedures to obtain boars' tusks from animal mandibles, perhaps to be used in constructing boars' tusk helmets. Ceremonial activities in the area are indicated as well by other finds from the area around the building (examples are the krater with sphinx representation, female clay figurines, and a vase in the shape of a human being). The building was destroyed at the very end of LH III B (c. 1185 B.C.) at the same time when the Linear B tablets in sites 10 and 11 were baked by the disastrous fire. Beneath this building was an earlier destruction layer caused by a fire in the LH III A2 (c. 1370-1340 B.C.) period (EUM-313 and EUM-321). EUM-323 (T.M. 27426) and EUM-317 (T.M. 26990) came from Mycenaean deposits in site 13, disturbed by the continuous use of the area until Byzantine times.

DR. ELENI ANDRIKOU
Curator of Antiquities, Ministry of Culture

KADMEIA

1. Old Kadmeion
2. New Kadmeion
3. "Arsenal"

4, 5. Magazines
6, 7. Jewellery workshop
8. Ivory workshop

9. Group of clay sealings
10, 11. Linear B tablets archives

12. Habitation debris
13. Ivory workshop, habitation debris

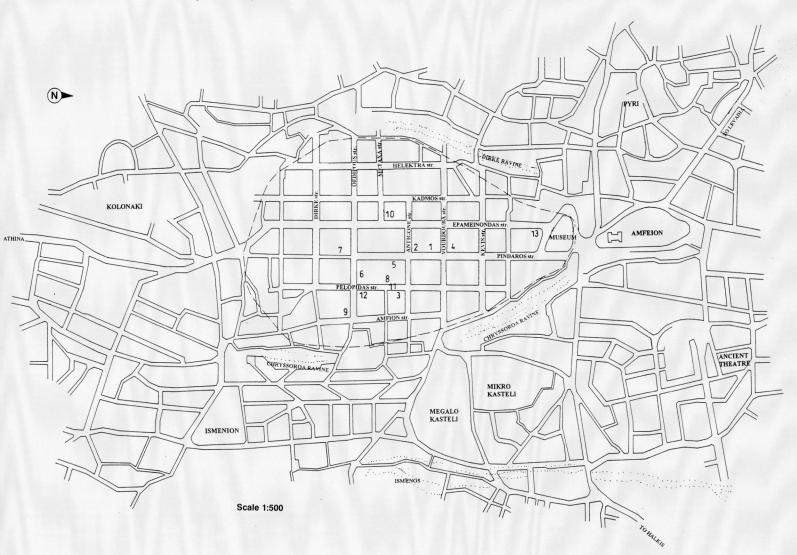

Scale 1:500

95 97

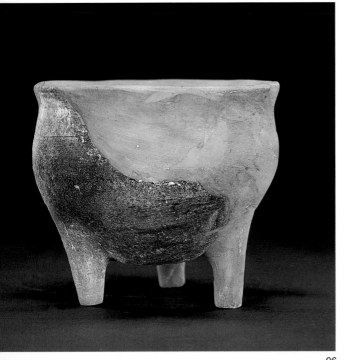

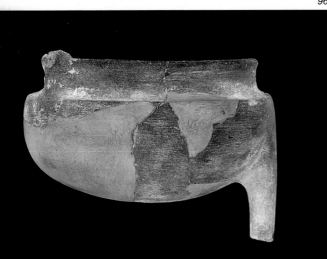

96

96 TRIPOD COOKING POT

T.M. 27117 EUM-306: Wall sherd

MEAT PRODUCTS. OLIVE OIL. CEREAL? A FERMENTED SYSTEM. RESIN

Evans: See method of analysis.

LH III B (c. 1340-1185 B.C.)
Thebes, probably a house, site 12
H: (pres.) 14.5 cm.; D: rim 17 cm.
Coarse red fabric. Self slip. Nearly 1/3 of the pot exists, preserving one of the three cylindrical legs; its tip is missing. The body is hemispherical, and is carinated below the rim. On the outside of the rim the stub of the handle survives. It was horizontal and raised. There are clear traces of burning. A sherd was taken for analysis prior to the restoration that was possible.

E.A.

97 TRIPOD COOKING POT

EUM-80: Base/leg sherd

WAXY COATINGS OF FRUIT (SUCH AS APPLES) LEAVES, OR PETALS
No fats or oils

Beck: See method of analysis.

LH III A2 (c. 1370-1340 B.C.)
Thebes, storeroom, site 11
Sherds submitted for analysis averaged between 4 and 6 centimeters in diameter.

Coarse red fabric. The vessel appeared to be similar to M.M. 24327. Only part of the leg and a small area of the base survived.

E.A.

M.M. 24327 is a substitute for EUM-80, which only survived in sherd condition and could not be restored.

TRIPOD COOKING POT

M.M. 24327 Exc. No 66-413

LH III C Early (c. 1185-1130 B.C.)
Mycenae, Cult Centre, Area 36
H: total 13.1 cm., bowl 5.4 cm.; D: rim 18 cm., base 16.3 cm.

Shallow cylindrical vessel. No spout.

E.B.F.

95 TRIPOD COOKING POT

T.M. 28949 EUM-318: Wall sherd

OLIVE OIL. CEREAL. COMPLEX MIXTURE

Evans: See method of analysis.

LH III B (c. 1340-1185 B.C.)
Thebes, probably a house, site 12
H: (pres.) 8.7 cm.; D: rim 10.8 cm.

Brownish red fabric. Two thirds of the tripod survives. It is hemispherical and has a spreading lip. There are clear traces of burning. A sherd was taken for analysis prior to the restoration that was possible.

E.A.

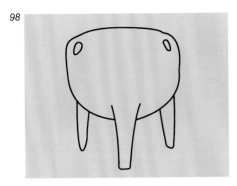

98

99

98 TRIPOD COOKING POT

EUM-307: Base/leg sherd

A COMPLEX MIXTURE

Evans: See method of analysis.

LH III B (c. 1340-1185 B.C.)
Thebes, habitation deposit, site 13
Sherds submitted for analysis averaged
between 4 and 6 centimeters in diameter.

Only part of one leg and a small area of
the base survived. The leg is elliptical in
section. On the outside, there is a cut
and two holes for better firing.

E.A.

99 COOKING JAR

EUM-79: Base sherd

**WAXY COATINGS OF FRUIT (SUCH
AS APPLES) LEAVES, OR PETALS**
No fats or oils

Beck: See method of analysis.

LH III A 2 (c. 1370-1340 B.C.)
Thebes, storeroom, site 11
Sherds submitted for analysis averaged
between 4 and 6 centimeters in diameter.

The base was that of a typical ovoid
cooking jar that would have had a
collar neck and two handles.

E.A.

100 COOKING JAR

T.M. 24432   EUM 312: Wall/rim sherd

PORK. A COMPLEX MIXTURE

Evans: See method of analysis.

LH III B/C (c. 1200 B.C.)
Thebes, room with evidence for ceremonial
and working activities, site 13
Sherds submitted for analysis averaged
between 4 and 6 centimeters in diameter.

Area of wall and rim, and one handle
survive. The vessel has a globular body
and a deep collar neck.

E.A.

M.M. 6978 is a substitute for EUM-312,
which only survived in sherd condition
and could not be restored.

COOKING JUG

M.M. 6978

LH III B (c. 1340-1185 B.C.)
Mycenae 1963. House of Sphinxes
H:18.6 cm.; D: mouth 14 cm., belly 18.1 cm.,
base 7 cm.

Mended and completed. Reddish clay.
Cooking vessel, with one vertical handle
from the junction of the almost vertical
rim to the belly. Discoid raised base.

EL.P.

100

101, 103

102

101 COOKING JAR

EUM-309: Wall/rim sherd

BEESWAX (HONEY?) OLIVE OIL?

Evans: See method of analysis.

LH III B1 (c. 1340-1250 B.C.)
Thebes, storeroom, site 13
Sherds submitted for analysis averaged
between 4 and 6 centimeters in diameter.

An area of wall and rim survived. The
vessel appeared to be a typical ovoid
cooking jar with upstanding rim.

E.A.

102 STORAGE JAR

EUM-310: Wall fragment

OLIVE OIL. PULSES?

Evans: See method of analysis.

LH III B1 (c. 1340-1250 B.C.)
Thebes, storeroom, site 13
Sherds submitted for analysis averaged
between 4 and 6 centimeters in diameter.

Wall area with the stub of a handle
survive.

E.A.

103 COOKING JAR

EUM-314: Wall/rim sherd

MEAT. PULSES? OLIVE OIL

Evans: See method of analysis.

LH III B/C (c. 1200 B.C.)
Thebes, room with evidence for ceremonial
and working activities, site 13
H: (pres.) 9.3 cm.; D: rim 14-15 cm.
Sherds submitted for analysis averaged
between 4 and 6 centimeters in diameter.

Area of wall and rim with the stub of a
handle survive.

E.A.

104 SKYPHOS

T.M. 27426 EUM-323: Wall/rim sherd

PULSES? CEREAL?

Evans: See method of analysis.

LH III B (c. 1340-1185 B.C.)
Thebes, habitation deposit, site 13
H: (pres.) 10 cm.; D: rim 15 cm.

Decoration in brown-red paint on light
brown slip. Semi-globular bowl with
a slightly flaring rim. Stub of one of
the two handles is preserved, and is
horizontal/cylindrical. There is a band
around the rim. Outside, a band
borders the decorative zone beneath
vertical narrow triglyphs: straight lines
on both sides of a zig-zag alternating
with a simple group of straight lines.
There is a blob on the inside edge of the
handle. Inside there is a band below the
lip. A sherd was taken for analysis prior
to the restoration that was possible.

E.A.

104

CEREALS, CHICK PEAS AND MEAT
AT MIDEA IN THE ARGOLID (c. 1340-1100 B.C.)

The result was cereal and oil for a "griddle tray" (M.N. 28090/EUM-87). This is a shallow round tray that is punched with holes on the internal surface. The fact that these "holes" are only on the upper surface gives the impression that they might have been used to keep food from adhering to the surface. Was this to keep Midean pancakes from sticking?

A bridge-spouted cooking jar (EUM-88) was found, which contained chick peas, oil, and meat, at Midea in a cult area, and other traditionally shaped cooking jars (without spouts) from domestic areas, gave results of oil and meat (EUM-89 and M.N. 28094/EUM-91). Another interesting sample came from a Mycenaean ladle (M.N. 28091/EUM-92), the only ladle from which a sample was submitted for analysis. It gave a result of oil and meat.

DR. HOLLEY MARTLEW

THE EXCAVATION

THE SITE

The Midea material comes from the Lower Terraces, northwest of the summit of the acropolis and inside the fortification wall. Two different areas were excavated there on two different terraces made in recent times.

On the terrace furthest to the southeast, a group of rooms built up against the fortification wall in LH III B (13th century B.C.) appeared. In three of these rooms, Room II, VIII an IX was a thick ash layer covering a LH III B floor. On the floor and in the ashes were a number of objects including a griddle tray EUM-87, which is on display, a stone tripod vessel and a collection of blue glass jewellery. Organic remains such as carbonized figs, olive cores, grape seeds, and lentils were still recognizable among the ashes. A neck of a large female terracotta figure and the fragment of a bovine terracotta decorated with a four-leaf clover pattern as well as a stirrup jar decorated with a number of cult symbols, birds, flowers, double axes and horns of consecration were also found here. The 1997 excavations of Room XXXIII revealed three subsequent LH III B floors and brought to light a terracotta "offering table" of coarseware, decorated with thumb impressions along the rim, a "naturalistic" female terracotta figurine of much earlier date than the floors, an agate bead from a necklace and a miniature terracotta model of a tripod "offering table". On the lowest floor of Room XXXII was a hearth which contained charcoal, ashes, a bronze arrowhead and small fragments of animal bones. It seems possible that all five rooms formed part of a Mycenaean sanctuary and that the hearth played a role in ritual. However, no altar was found and no finds appeared to be in their original place.

On the terrace further to the north was a large building of "megaron" type, which measured 14 x 7.50 m. It was originally built in the 13th century B.C. while pottery that belonged to the LH III B (c. 1250 B.C.) phase was in use, and it had a back area with two rooms separated from a main hall by a transverse wall. At some time during the 13th century while LH III B pottery was still in use, a new floor was laid down, and a hearth surrounded by four columns or roof supports was placed in the middle of the room. The main room was made larger by the construction of a new transverse wall further to the east. A platform with a smaller block in front was placed outside the building. It is similar to a block found in the Cult Centre at Mycenae which has sometimes been interpreted as an altar.

The building was damaged by an earthquake, indicated by curved and tilted walls and rock-falls on the LH III B floor later in the 13th century. In the 12th century substantial repairs were made. An exterior wall was built to shore up the northwest part of the megaron. A long wall was also built inside the megaron along the south side, ending at some distance from the transverse wall and forming a niche, in which three large sword pommels (of ivory, alabaster and green lapis lacedaemonicus) and the beads of a faience necklace were found. A row of three columns in the middle of the main room replaced the hearth. Among the finds in the megaron on the 12th century floor was the ladle or scoop EUM-92 (on display). A relatively large room (Room XVII) built in the 13th century was found opposite the entrance to the megaron. Outside the room was a niche of the same type as the niche with the sword pommels. It contained fragments of large storage vessels and coarse ware vessels. A room further to the east (Room XVIII) contained a 13th-12th century B.C. bench and next to it a shaft surrounded by parapet walls. The walls framed the opening of a shaft, which led down to a cistern. The cistern was fed by water channels, and near to one of these was a coarseware vessel which seemed to have been used for the collection of water. One of the finds from this room was a small terracotta snake, reminiscent of the terracotta snakes from the Cult Centre at Mycenae. In the nearby Room XX was a semi-circular stone formation, possibly an altar or a platform for the deposition of offerings.

The zoological remains from these excavations have been studied by David S. Reese and the botanical remains by J. and T. C. Shay. Their analyses have shown that beef and pork were important items on the menu at Midea in the Bronze Age. Some remains of sheep and goats were also found as well as of wild boar, deer and hare. The finds also included fish bones and shells. The cattle and deer bones showed signs of butchering. Many bones showed signs of burning and could have been burnt in connection with destructions of the site or as part of food preparation.

The botanical remains revealed a decline in the frequency of most seed types from the 13th to the 12th century B.C. Traces of termites were found in a 12th century B.C. floor and a large, charred weevil appeared in the 13th century B.C. destruction debris which was disturbed in the following century as a preparation for repairs and rebuilding. Cereals and legumes, such as chick peas, lentils, bitter vetch, grass peas, common vetch, fava beans and broad beans seem to have played a role in Late Bronze Age diet. According to J. and T. C. Shay, the chick peas may have been used as a "swing crop" which could produce yields when other crops failed. The assemblage from the Lower Terraces at Midea is the most diverse Late Bronze Age assemblage of legumes found to date.

PROF. GISELA WALBERG
University of Cincinnati, Ohio, U.S.A.

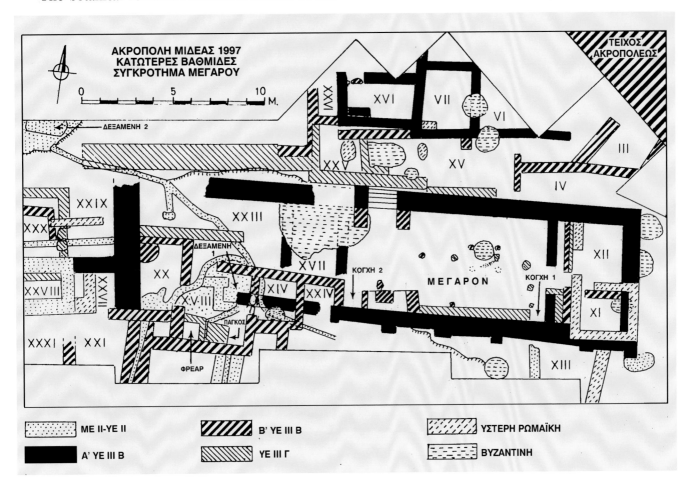

105

106

107

105 GRIDDLE TRAY

M.N. 28090 EUM-87: Base sherd

CEREAL. OIL
Did Mideans make pancakes in 1250 B.C.?

Evans: See method of analysis.

LH III B (c. 1340-1250 B.C.)
Midea, Sanctuary area
H: 3.9 cm.; D: 35 cm.

Coarse red fabric. Circular tray. The interior surface is punched with holes at irregular intervals. Badly burnt on underside of base, outside wall, and on the rim. A sherd was taken for analysis prior to the restoration that was possible.

G.W.

106 COOKING JUG

M.N. 28089 EUM-86: Wall sherd

WHEAT, OIL +

Evans: See method of analysis.

LH III C (c. 1185-1065 B.C.)
Midea, West of Megaron
H: 16.7 cm.; D: rim 11.5 cm. (across handles)

Coarse red fabric. Ovoid jug with deep collar neck and one handle. Ring base. Burning on body except in area of handle and under base. A sherd was taken for analysis prior to restoration.

G.W.

107 BRIDGE-SPOUTED JAR

EUM-88: Wall sherd

CHICK PEAS. OIL. MEAT?

Evans: See method of analysis.

LH III B (c. 1340-1185 B.C.)
Midea, Room I, Sanctuary area, Lower Terraces
H: 23 cm.; D: rim 22.4 cm.
Sherds submitted for analysis averaged between 4 and 6 centimeters in diameter.

Fine red cooking fabric. Deep incurving bowl with offset lip and two horizontal handles (FS 282). Marks of burning on outside.

G.W.

M.M. 24331 (Exc. No 66-1522) is a substitute for EUM-88, which only survived in sherd condition (rim, body, and base fragments) and could not be restored.

108

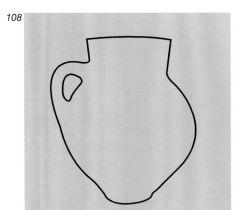

BRIDGE-SPOUTED JAR

M.M. 24331 Exc. No 66-1522

Mid LH III B (c. 1340-1250 B.C.)
Mycenae, Cult Centre, Area 36
H: 14 cm.; D: rim 14.4-5 cm.

Fine red clay. Deep incurving bowl with offset lip and two horizontal handles (FS 282). Lower body slightly burnt below handles.

E.B.F.

108 COOKING JUG

EUM-89: Wall sherd

OIL. MEAT. VERY COMPLEX

Evans: See method of analysis.

LH III B (c. 1340-1250 B.C.)
Midea, Sanctuary area
H: (ex.) 14.5 cm.
Sherds submitted for analysis averaged between 4 and 6 centimeters in diameter.

Coarse red fabric. Ovoid jug with deep collar neck.

G.W.

109 COOKING JAR

M.N. 28094 EUM-91: Base sherd

OIL. MEAT. VERY COMPLEX

Evans: See method of analysis.

LH III B (c. 1340-1185 B.C.)
Midea, West of Megaron
H: 34 cm.; D: rim 15 cm., body 31 cm.

Coarse red fabric. Globular jar with deep collar neck. Burning marks on body below handles, on top of the rim and on one handle. None under base. A sherd was taken for analysis prior to restoration.

G.W.

109

110

110 LADLE

M.N. 28091 EUM-92: Bowl sherd

OIL. MEAT

Evans: See method of analysis.

LH III C (c. 1185-1065 B.C.)
Midea, on the floor near the centre of the main room, the Megaron

Length: 6.7 cm.; W: 17 cm.; D: 12.7 cm.

Coarse red fabric. Ladle with ring base and a short strap handle, curving downward, and indented along the upper surface. Plain rim. Burning all over. A sherd was taken for analysis prior to restoration.

G.W.

MYCENAE, CULT CENTRE AND VICINITY

The artefacts date to the 13th-12th centuries B.C.

A cooking jar (EUM-156) found in the fill of the Room with the Fresco in the Cult Centre of Mycenae gave an important result. The organic residues were the same as those from the large tripod pot (M.M. 24353/EUM-152) which was in use at the time of the destruction of the cult room: meat, oil, and possibly lentils.

A bowl (M.M. 24343/EUM-158) from the room behind the Room with the Fresco held the remains of beeswax (honey).

A Mycenaean shape which is commonly referred to as a "souvlaki tray" (M.M. 24351/EUM-77) gave a result that indicated it probably was used for cooking meat.

A sherd from a vessel normally referred to as a Mycenaean "brazier" (Exc. No 66-1546/EUM-74) held an oil. The "pierced neck jar", a small, flattish coarse jar (M.M. 24322/EUM-78) which had burning marks around the rows of holes which were on one side of the collar, contained animal fat.

DR. HOLLEY MARTLEW

THE EXCAVATION

THE SITE

The Cult Centre of Mycenae, a complex of temples, shrines and annexes, was built in the early 13th century B.C. on the southwest slope of the citadel in the middle of the residential area, at a considerable distance from the palace and at a much lower level. It was excavated by the Archaeological Society of Athens (Tsountas, 1866), the British School of Archaeology (Wace, l950, 1953, 1954; Lord William Taylour, 1959-1969) and again by the Archaeological Society (Mylonas, l968-1975). Access to the sanctuaries was provided by a processional road leading to a temple with altars, a slaughtering stone and an inner sanctum. Stairs and ramps led down to a building known as Tsountas House and to a still lower level occupied by another temple with an altar, stepped platforms, an alcove and a cache of terracotta cult idols. In front of these rooms was a small court with another large circular altar in the middle, and next to them were more rooms, one of which was decorated with a fresco. The idols and the fresco show that the cult buildings were dedicated to the worship of the deities of war, fertility and, probably, the Netherworld, to whom sacrifices and libations were offered. The buildings were severely damaged in the late 13th century B.C. by a strong earthquake and were then repaired and reused on a reduced scale. A little later they were destroyed by a locally confined conflagration and abandoned. In the 12th century B.C. during the gradual decline of the citadel, the area was occupied by houses which were inhabited until the end of the Mycenaean era.

S.E. IAKOVIDIS, HON. FSA
Prof. Em. of Archaeology
Member of the Academy of Athens

ARCHAEOLOGICAL EVIDENCE FOR FOOD STUFFS AT MYCENAE

Two deposits of grain and seeds from quite distinct periods, burnt and thus preserved in the destruction of the buildings where they were stored, have been studied. Another from the Middle Helladic period (c. 2090-1600 B.C.) awaits study.

Deposit 1: House of Sphinxes, Mid LH III B (c. 1250 B.C.) from material fallen into the basement Room 8. Here the material was studied by Dr. Hans Helbaek of Copenhagen who identified seeds of Bitter Vetch, Lentils and a few Grass Peas.

Deposit 2: The Granary, LH III C Middle (c. 1100 B.C.) from material fallen into the East Basement: The building takes its name from this find, though the quantity of grain stored makes it unlikely that this was a central granary, but rather supplies for a small group of people. This material has been studied by Dr. Gordon Hillman of the University of London. It comprised five main components: Emmer Wheat, Einkorn Wheat, Barley, Bitter Vetch and Fava Beans.

Finds such as these can give us important information about the methods of agriculture used during the Bronze Age and the methods by which cereals were stored. They can also suggest some components of the diet when the evidence is related to ancient written sources and modern rural practices.

All three of the grains, the two types of wheat and the barley, are most likely to have been used as the base for a porridge of some kind though Emmer Wheat can be roasted and mixed with things like nuts to make a "snack food" that could be taken with one. Barley also can be used as a thickener for soups and stews or as the basis for beer. The Fava Beans could also have been used in stews or perhaps as a Bronze Age version of the modern meze.

The usage of the Bitter Vetch is more problematic as this plant requires pre-boiling to remove its toxicity to both humans and oxen. It may perhaps have had a medicinal or folk usage that we can no longer trace.

It is likely that these basic dishes were both supplemented nutritionally and made more attractive by the addition of flavourings like onion and the range of wild herbs still popular in Greece today.

The list of flavourings on the so-called "Spice" tablets, which like the seeds were found in the House of Sphinxes at Mycenae, includes cardamon, celery, coriander, cumin, fennel, mint, safflower and sesame. Not only would a range of condiments like these add flavour to rather bland concoctions but, as Dr. Hillman has pointed out, several of them would be of considerable value in reducing the flatulence which that basic diet would otherwise cause.

The Linear B texts indicate that a day's ration of cereal grains was 3 of the smallest measure "Z". This measure is represented by an ideogram resembling the handleless or conical cup. On the mainland the largest of these cups measures c. 300 ml (like the European cup measure), a suitable size for a single meal of this type of food. A day's ration would thus be for 3 light meals or 2 bulkier ones.

DR. ELIZABETH B. FRENCH
Former Director, British School at Athens

111 SEEDS

LH III C middle (c. 1100 B.C.)
Seed material that fell into the East Basement of "The Granary"

1) 2 grains of wild or domestic einkorn. This could have been cultivated or it could be a contaminent.
2) Domestic emmer or einkorn. The state of preservation makes it impossible to distinguish.
3) Latex cast of a sherd that was impressed with one grain of 6-row barley: Hordeum vulgare.
4) Triticum diococum.
5) Bitter vetch: small grain.
6) Bitter vetch: larger grain.
The bitter vetch, Vicia avillia, was found in two sizes, with no weeds mixed with it. The smaller grained one appears to be a specific small variety, much smaller than any variety known today. Therefore, these two (5 and 6 above) represent two separate, different, assemblages.

G.H.

112 COOKING JAR

M.M. 24344   EUM-154: Wall sherd   Exc. No 69-675

OLIVE OIL. WINE. COMPLEX

Evans: See method of analysis.

Mid LH III B (c. 1250 B.C.)
Mycenae, Cult Centre, Room 3l, the Room with the Fresco, destruction level
H: 22.4 cm.; D: 21.6 cm.

Red sandy clay. Typical example of this shape though only half-preserved; heavily burnt from use, as if left sitting next to the fire. The surviving handle has burning marks below it and smudges on one side. A sherd was taken for analysis prior to restoration.

E.B.F.

113 COOKING JAR

EUM-156: Wall/base sherd   Exc No 69-673

OLIVE OIL. MEAT. LENTILS?

The results of organic residue analysis were exactly the same as for the large tripod cooking pot found near the altar in the destruction level (EUM-152)

Evans: See method of analysis.

Mid LH III B (c. 1250 B.C.)
Mycenae, Cult Centre, fill placed in Room 31, the Room with the Fresco
H: 19 cm.; D: rim 26 cm.
Sherds submitted for analysis averaged 3 centimeters in diameter.

An unusual example of this shape in fine pale red micaceous clay. Krater with short flaring rim. Traces of burning inside and outside from use notably on the rim and with a very burnt area near the base.

E.B.F.

M.M. 24326 is a substitute for EUM-156, Exc. No 69-673, which only survived in sherd condition and could not be restored.

COOKING JAR

M.M. 24326   Exc No 66-1518

LH III C early (c. 1185-1130 B.C.)
Citadel House Area, Room 34
H: 18.8 cm.; D: rim 12.8 cm.

Restored. Red slighty sandy clay. Ovoid jar with two handles and a low flaring rim. Typical of the shape which was in use at Mycenae from at least the late 13th until the middle of the 11th century B.C.

E.B.F.

112

113

114 ANTHROPOMORPHIC FIGURE, TYPE A

M.N. 17180   Exc. No 69-1221

Mid LH III B (c. 1250 B.C.)

Mycenae, Cult Centre, Room 32, "The Shrine". Found *in situ* on a small dias in the SW corner of the sanctuary store behind the Room with the Fresco

H: 29 cm.; D: base 8 cm., W: shoulders 9 cm., head: 6.5 cm.

Fine buff clay with pink core. Complete except for upper part of right arm. Roughly cylindrical apparently coil-made hollow body, pinched together across to form shoulders and flaring slightly at the base; paring on internal surface, external surface smoothed; applied breast; hollow head and neck applied over shoulders; small curled coils applied for ears; incised line over each eye; applied, pinched nose; applied coil around top of head for polos headdress; applied plait from centre of top of head which trails down back of head and body; hollow arms applied over shoulders; both arms raised in "Psi" pose; terminus of left arm flattened and tilted back slightly. Three band groups on lower body which consist of two broad bands with three or four lines between; group of lozenges (FM 73:aa) under each arm and further two on either side of plait at back; monochrome breast; bands around arms; band around base of neck with double row of dots above and single row below; double row of dots droop from this between the breasts, which indicates a necklace; band around neck below chin with double row of dots below and row of six lozenges (FM 73:b) above at back; wavy band around back of head between ears; monochrome plait and polos; polos with wavy edge, deeper at back than at front; lozenge (FM 73:aa) on each cheek; lines over eyebrows, down nose and double line for mouth; monochrome eyes with lines above and below; foliate line for each eyelash.

E.B.F.

114

115   SHALLOW ANGULAR BOWL

M.M. 24343 EUM-158: Wall sherd Exc. No 69-1430

BEESWAX (HONEY)
Honey is a very difficult commodity to trace. It is mostly water, which evaporates, and the sugar in honey degrades. Traces of beeswax therefore are one of the only reliable indications for honey

Evans: See method of analysis.

Mid LH III B (c. 1250 B.C.)

Mycenae, Cult Centre, Room 32, "The Shrine" /sanctuary store behind the Room with the Fresco

H: 5.5 cm.; D: rim 14 cm., base 9.5 cm.

Buff clay with pink tinge. Complete profile of well-finished example of a shape (FS 295) which formed one of the basic repertoire of unpainted vessels in use at Mycenae from the late 13th at least until the end of the 12th century B.C. This example has only a few small impurities in the clay and is fairly well smoothed on the surface, thus assignable to the "standard" category of unpainted ware. It is sharply carinated and has a raised base. A sherd was taken for analysis. The vessel could not be restored from the few surviving sherds.

E.B.F.

116   SHALLOW ANGULAR BOWL

M.M. 24336 EUM-160: Wall sherd Exc. No 69-666

TRACES OF FAT, IDENTITY UNCERTAIN

Evans: See method of analysis.

Mid LH III B (c. 1250 B.C.)

Mycenae, Cult Centre, Room 32 "The Shrine"/ sanctuary store behind the Room with the Fresco

H: 5.6 cm.; D: 16.7 cm.

Pinkish buff clay. Well-finished example of a shape (FS 295) which formed one of the basic repertoire of unpainted vessels in use at Mycenae from the late 13th at least until the end of the 12th century B.C. This example has only a few small impurities in the clay and is fairly well smoothed on the surface, thus assignable to the "standard" category of unpainted ware. It is sharply carinated and has a raised base. A sherd was taken for analysis prior to restoration.

E.B.F.

115

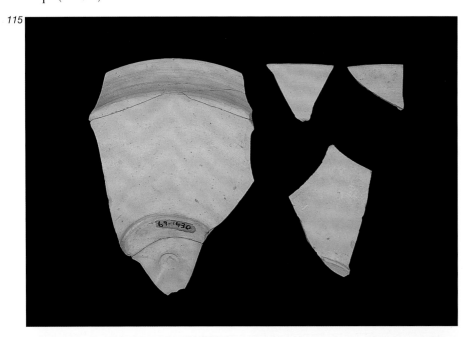

116

117   SOUVLAKI TRAY

M.M. 24351   EUM-77: Base sherd   Exc. No 62-464

COOKING MEAT CANNOT BE EXCLUDED

Beck/Kouzeli: See method of analysis.

LH III B1 (c. 1340-1250 B.C.)
Mycenae, rubbish thrown into Passage 3, between the South House Annex and the Cult Centre
H: (with legs) 11.6 cm.; Length: 52.9 cm.; W: 47.1 cm.

Sun-dried pale buff clay with straw fill. Undecorated. Rectangular tray with 3 low sides: one short side and two long sides. Stands on low feet placed at either end of long sides. Small notches in the rim on long sides. Round horizontal handle on either side. A sherd was taken for analysis prior to restoration.

E.B.F.

118   BRAZIER

EUM-74: Wall/base sherd   Exc. No 66-1546

OILS OF PLANT ORIGIN. PROBABLY OLIVE OIL IS ONE OF THESE

Beck: See method of analysis.

Mid LH III B (c. 1250 B.C.)
Mycenae, Cult Centre, Area 36
H: unknown; D: c. 21 cm.
Sherds submitted for analysis averaged between 4 and 6 centimeters in diameter.

Sandy reddish clay with red wash inside and perhaps outside. Brazier or lamp, burnt and shattered; no handle preserved. Typical example of shape FS 311. The type is similar to M.M. 24332.

E.B.F.

M.M. 24332 is a substitute for EUM-74/ Exc. No 66-1546, which only survived in sherd condition and could not be restored.

BRAZIER

M.M. 24332   Exc. No 66-1506

LH III C early (c. 1185-1130 B.C.)
Mycenae, Citadel House Area, Room 34
H: 4.3 cm.; W: 20.3 cm.;
Length: handle 12 cm.

Restored. Red gritty clay. Lamp or brazier, almost complete but with ancient crack. Typical example of FS 311.

E.B.F.

119   PIERCED NECK JAR

M.M. 24322   EUM-78: Wall sherd   Exc. No 64-917

A FAT FROM SHEEP OR GOAT

Beck: See method of analysis.

LH III B (c. 1340-1185 B.C.)
Mycenae, debris over South House, Room 22
H: 7 cm.; D: (largest sherd) 12.5 cm.
Sherds submitted for analysis averaged between 4 and 6 centimeters in diameter.

Red gritty coarse clay, but purpose unknown and not from a functional context. Enigmatic vessel with elliptical neck pierced by holes on one side only. The vessel could not be restored, and although other vessels of this type are known from the palace site of Mycenae, none in sufficient quantity to be restored.

E.B.F.

117

118

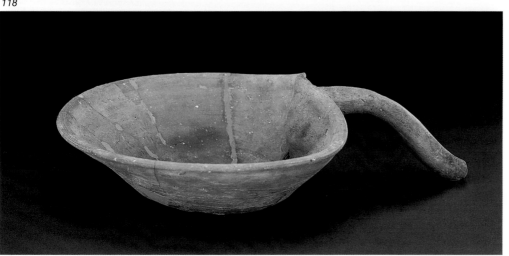

11

120 COOKING JUG

M.M. 24325 EUM-71 Exc. No 66-1523

FATTY ACIDS OF ANIMAL ORIGIN?

Beck: See method of analysis.

Mid LH III B (c. 1250 B.C.)
Mycenae, Cult Centre, Area 36. Probably from storage context related to Cult Centre activities
H: 22.5 cm.; D: 19 cm.

Red sandy clay. Typical ovoid cooking jug with tall collar neck and single handle from the base of the neck to the greatest diameter. Heavily burnt outside on side away from handle; whole surface in very poor condition in this area, presumably from usage. A sherd was taken for analysis prior to restoration.

E.B.F.

121 COOKING JUG

M.M. 24333 EUM-70 Exc. No 66-1519

THE COMPONENTS ARE MORE LIKELY TO BE OF PLANT, THAN OF ANIMAL, ORIGIN

Beck: See method of analysis.

LH III C early (c. 1185-1130 B.C.)
Mycenae, Citadel House Area, Room 34
H: 15.2 cm.; D: 14.5 cm.

Grey gritty clay, fired reddish buff. Small ovoid vessel with flaring collar neck and single handle from rim to shoulder; raised base. Burnt in patches. Typical of domestic wares from at least the late 13th to the early 11th century B.C. at Mycenae. A sherd was taken for analysis prior to restoration.

E.B.F.

120

121

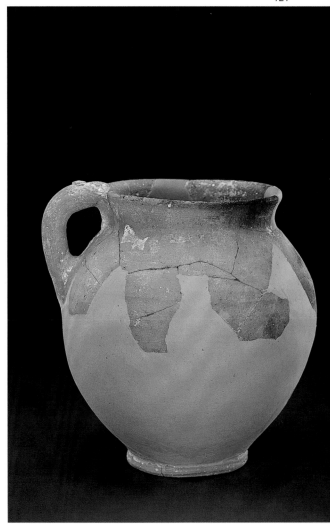

TRANSPORT STIRRUP JARS

A number of stirrup jars with Linear B inscriptions and dating from the LH III B1 period (c. 1340-1300 B.C.) have been found at Thebes, Orchomenos, Mycenae and Eleusis. The texts of the inscriptions contain a series of place-names in West Crete and the adjective *wa-na-ka-te-ro*, which means "belonging to the king". The inscriptions on these vases come from the same hands as those on similar vases found at the palatial centre of Kydonia. Recent analysis has shown, moreover, that the clay used in all these vases comes from the Chania area. Clearly the inscribed stirrup jars found in the Mycenaean palaces of Mainland Greece were imported from a region in West Crete, namely from *ku-do-ni-ja*, Kydonia, where during the LH III B1 period there was still a king who continued to control at least the trade in liquid goods. This appears to confirm the theory that after the final destruction of the palace at Knossos Minoan production and trade continued to be practiced under a king based at Kydonia.

PROF. LOUIS GODART

University of Naples, Italy
Academia dei Lincei

122 TRANSPORT STIRRUP JAR

M.M. 9224 Exc. No 50-205

Mid LH III B (c. 1250 B.C.)
Mycenae, House of the Oil Merchant, north
end of basement corridor
H: 41 cm.; D: (max) 29 cm.

Reddish black heavy clay. Light-on-dark
jar of West Cretan provenance with clay
stopper and cap sealed with Hounds
and Genius ring.

E.B.F.

123 TRANSPORT STIRRUP JAR

M.M. 9236 Exc. No 60-299

Mid LH III B (c. 1250 B.C.)
Mycenae, House of the Oil Merchant, north
end of basement corridor
H: 44.5 cm.; D: (max) 28 cm.

Reddish brown heavy clay. Light-on-
dark jar of West Cretan provenance
with clay stopper and cap sealed with
Hounds and Genius ring; when found,
the jar showed clear signs of oil
impregnation.

E.B.F.

122

123

What did they drink ?

The Tests

Infra-red Spectroscopy,
Gas Chromatography,
Mass Spectroscopy,
High Performance
Liquid Chromatography,
Wet Chemical Spot Tests.

The Time

One sherd: One week's work
One sherd: The amount of
computerised data produced
can be up to 100 pages.

The Interpretation

The most time-consuming part,
it includes:
- Searching databases
- Searching the literature
- Identifying constituents
- Searching constituents
- Identifyng botanical sources

The Results - The Alternatives Are:

1 Conclusions can be proposed: see presentation in the Exhibition, site by site.

2 Chemical compounds were detected, but no further conclusions can be drawn.

3 No organic signals detected in the potsherd.

4 The full story can never be known because chemical compounds, when detected,
may not be the same, nor are they equally distributed, throughout a vessel.
Also it can never be known if all the chemical compounds to which the pot
had been exposed, were retained in the fabric of the vessel.

What did they drink?

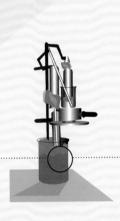

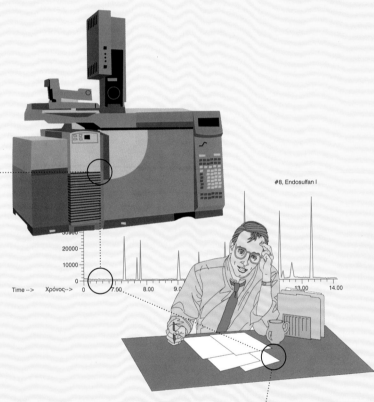

We did find

definite information in

the majority of potsherds

submitted for analysis.

WINE WITH RESIN IN EARLY MINOAN CRETE

All the samples of pithoi which were submitted for analysis from this small settlement (population estimated by the excavator as about 50), produced positive results for wine. This gives an indication of the importance of wine production to Minoans who lived in the third millennnium B.C.

The special significance of the results presented here is that samples from two pithoi (A.N.M. 13101/EUM-97; EUM-99) produced the possibility of resinated wine. The organic signals were such that the result is qualified, but the clear indication is for resination.

This is the earliest scientific proof of wine in the Greek Bronze Age, and the fact that at this date resinated wine appears to have been produced, makes the Myrtos Phournou Koryphe results even more significant.

DR. HOLLEY MARTLEW

THE EARLY MINOAN SETTLEMENT
OF MYRTOS-PHOURNOU KORYPHE (c. 2900-2200 B.C.)

The settlement on the hilltop above the sea at Phournou Koryphe, east of Myrtos on the south coast of Crete, was built and occupied within 2900-2200 B.C. (Early Minoan II). It was a very small village, c. 0.125 ha. in extent, and consisted of about one hundred closely packed rooms, passages and open areas protected by a continuous outside wall, with two main entrances preserved. The rooms formed six or seven contiguous houses, single-storied and flat-roofed. Each house usually had a kitchen or cooking place, working and storage areas, the latter with large store jars (pithoi). Groups of loomweights indicated the presence of wooden upright looms and large terracotta tubs with spouts were for grape-pressing and olive oil manufacture. The many querns and rubbing stones were for grinding grain. All areas contained large numbers of pots of many shapes, often finely decorated with dark patterns on a buff surface or in red-brown-black paint all over. There were many pieces of mottled red-yellow-black Vasilike Ware. Fine grey burnished pottery was used in the first period of occupation. At the time of destruction, by fire around 2200-2150 B.C., there were a few pots with white-on-dark painted patterns alongside the other wares. Specialist activities included pottery-making (a potter's workshop with eight turntables still on the floor) and the carving of stone seals.

In the southwest area was a sanctuary, with many vessels for food and drink offerings set in front of a low bench or altar on which had stood a female terracotta figure (height 21.1 cms.), a statuette of the Minoan female divinity who was holding a small jug, symbolic protection of the supply of wine, oil or water.

Phournou Koryphe was a typical prepalatial village, though smaller than many others. Its population, estimated at around fifty persons, farmed the surrounding land with olive trees, vines and cereals; they grazed sheep, goats, pigs and cattle and they surely used wild plants and herbs for food, medicines and dyes, and probably also for perfumes and incense. They enjoyed trade or exchange contacts, acquiring Melian obsidian and a few Cretan stone vessels perhaps from Mochlos on the north coast. As well as producing their own pottery, they brought in significant amounts from the Mirabello district to the northeast.

Of the pithoi exhibited A.N.M. 13101/Myrtos P. 600 (EUM-97) came from Area 26, a storage area or room on the west edge of the settlement. It was one of four large storage vessels lying broken against the inside face of the outer wall of the village, together with a fine bowl, jugs and teapots for pouring liquids. The fire destruction was very clear here. Interior red staining was noted when the pithos was first published. The two pithoi (not exhibited) Myrtos P. 605 (EUM-95) and P. 623 (EUM-100) were among the magnificent collection of fifty-three vessels found in the burnt destruction level in Room 80, the largest room in the village, located in the southwest area. They had stood beside each other at the centre of the south side of the

thought that this might have been caused by acids from liquid contents. The pithos had a small hole at the base for the egress of liquid contents or to assist cleaning. Pithos P. 604 (EUM-99) was in the southeast corner of the room, along with large amphoras and a fine jug decorated with the fan pattern called Myrtos Ware. Similarly a dark-painted jug was found with P. 605 (EUM-95) and P. 623 (EUM-100).

Myrtos P. 616 is a pithos from Room 82, immediately northwest of Room 80 and reached by doorways from that room and from Room 81. Although very small, Room 82 contained another magnificent pottery collection, forty-four vessels of all shapes and sizes. These had stood on benches round the walls and the room seems to have been a workplace, the fine small vessels used for pouring and transferring substances to and from the large storage vessels such as P. 616 in the north corner. It too had a small hole just above the base.

The dark trickle decoration on these pithoi, and

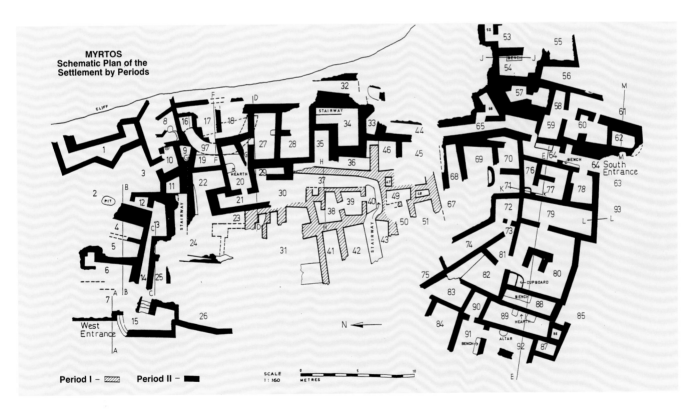

room, against the outer wall and with other large storage jars ranged alongside them. P. 605 (EUM-95) contained pips, stalks and skins of grapes, suggesting that the vessel had contained wine. The lower half of the interior of P. 623 (EUM-100) was rotted away; it was

on many others, has often been thought to have been painted, conventionally or even with a touch of humour, to symbolize liquid contents.

PROF. PETER WARREN
University of Bristol, U.K.

124 PITHOS

A.N.M. 13101 EUM-97: Wall sherd Pub. No 600

WINE. POSSIBLY IT WAS RESINATED

Mc Govern: See method of analysis.

EM II B (c. 2200 B.C.)
Myrtos Phournou Koryphe,
Room 26, the "Area of the Fallen Pithoi"
H: 77 cm.; D: rim 35-37 cm., body 55.8 cm.,
base 25 cm.

Coarse fabric with dark, also occasionally white grits, firing from grey to pink or buff. Buff slip and dark painted trickle decoration. Warren's type (1) with band of applied thumb-impressed decoration on the shoulder, producing a deep collar. Ovoid/barrel shaped. Everted rim. Parts of body missing. Interior, especially lower part, stained red. A sherd was taken for analysis prior to restoration.

P.W.

125 PITHOS

EUM-99: Wall sherd Pub. No 604

WINE. POSSIBLY IT WAS RESINATED

Mc Govern: See method of analysis.

EM II B (c. 2200 B.C.)
Myrtos Phournou Koryphe, Room 80, the largest room in the settlement, used for living and working
H: c. 60 cm.; D: rim 32.7 cm., body 54.3 cm.,
base 26 cm.
Sherds submitted for analysis averaged between 4 and 6 centimeters in diameter.

Coarse fabric with dark, also occasionally white grits, firing from grey to pink or buff. Buff slip and dark painted trickle decoration. Warren's type (1) with band of applied thumb-impressed decoration on the shoulder, producing a deep collar. Everted rim. Four vertical handles on body.

P.W.

126 PITHOS

EUM-98: Wall sherd Pub. No 611

WINE

Mc Govern: See method of analysis.

EM II B (c. 2200 B.C.)
Myrtos Phournou Koryphe, Room 53,
southeast Magazine A
H: c. 75 cm.; D: rim 32.5 cm., body 46 cm.,
base 25 cm.
Sherds submitted for analysis averaged between 4 and 6 centimeters in diameter.

Coarse fabric with dark, also occasionally white grits, firing from grey to pink or buff. Buff slip and dark painted trickle decoration. Warren's type (2) with band of applied thumb-impressed decoration high on the shoulder, producing a small collar. Everted rim. Small hole just above base. Most of inside much rotted.

P.W.

124

127 PITHOS

EUM-95: Wall sherd   Pub. No 605

WINE
The remains of pressed grapes, pips, stalks and skins were recovered from the original vessel. Tests confirmed a grape/wine product.

Mc Govern. See method of analysis.

EM II B (c. 2200 B.C.)

Myrtos Phournou Koryphe, Room 80, the largest room in the settlement, used for living and working

H: 63.8 cm.; D: rim 23.6 cm., body 47 cm., base 22.6 cm.

Sherds submitted for analysis averaged between 4 and 6 centimeters in diameter.

Coarse fabric with dark, also occasionally white grits, firing from grey to pink or

125

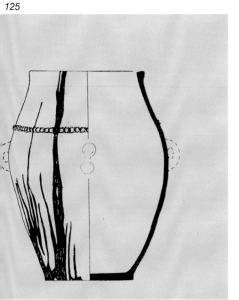

126

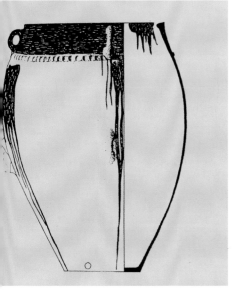

buff. Buff slip and dark painted trickle decoration. Warren's type (1) but without a band of applied, thumb-impressed decoration on the shoulder. Ovoid shape. Everted rim. Two horizontal handles on the body.

P.W.

A.N.M. 13099 is a substitute for pithoi EUM-95 and EUM-98, both of which only survived in sherd condition and could not be restored.

PITHOS

A.N.M. 13099   Pub. No 616

EM II B (c. 2200 B.C.)

Myrtos Phournou Koryphe, Room 82

H: 80.7 cm.; D: rim 43.3-46.8 cm., body 59.5-62 cm., base 25.4 cm.

Coarse fabric with dark, also occasionally white grits, firing from grey to pink or buff. Buff slip and dark painted trickle decoration. Warren's type (2) with band of applied, thumb-impressed decoration high on the shoulder, producing a small collar. Three small vertical handles on collar, three larger on body. Small hole just above base. Burnt. Elliptical vessel rather than circular, from above, through manufacture or firing.

P.W.

127

RESINATED WINE IN AN OAK BARREL AT MONASTIRAKI, RETHYMNON (c. 1900-1700 B.C.)

A tripod cooking pot (EUM-30) has given the most unusual result of the project: resinated wine stored in a toasted oak barrel, or with toasted oak chips in the barrel.

To be able to obtain such information indicates the detail that modern scientific methods are capable of producing. The circumstances should be taken into account: EUM-30 was a small, diagnostic sherd from a tripod cooking pot that had been buried in mid-western Crete for nearly 4,000 years. The possibility that the Minoans of 1900-1700 B.C. appear to have had such sophisticated taste, is surprising and important. It also must serve as a lesson: not to underestimate the capabilities of people who lived in prehistoric times.

DR. HOLLEY MARTLEW

128

128 TRIPOD COOKING POT

EUM-30: Base/leg sherd

RESINATED WINE THAT WAS STORED IN AN OAK BARREL
It may well have been a toasted oak barrel, because although oak lactones are present in any case, the number of oak lactones would increase with charring, and therefore the likelihood of their being detected would increase. Also, toasting would add to the flavour. The other possibility is that toasted oak chips were added to the resinated wine. In either case, oak, especially toasted oak, would have been used in order to give the wine a distinctive taste, such as enjoyed by Scotch whisky drinkers today. Ancient ship-building technology probably also involved toasting oak timbers.

Beck & Mc Govern: see methods of analysis.

This is an organic residue result of great significance.
It is important to note the use of resinated wine in Crete just after 2000 B.C., and also that it was present in a storage area that included material that had been used for ritual purposes.
The find marks the continuation of the use of resinated wine, first identified at the village of Myrtos Phournou Koryphe in southern Crete, c. 2200 B.C., into the first palatial period, and in a different part of the island, the Amari Valley in the southwest, which was an area under the influence nominally, if not directly, of the major palace site of Phaistos.
To find evidence that wine had either been stored in toasted oak barrels, or that toasted oak chips had been added to the wine, is an astonishing discovery. It gives us an insight into the drinking habits of the Minoans, like none other we have ever had.

MM II (c. 1900-1700 B.C.)
Palatial centre at Monastiraki, Amari,
Room 3-82
Sherds submitted for analysis averaged
between 4 and 6 centimeters in diameter.

Elliptical vessel. The type normally had
an incurving mouth and no spout. It is
known to have been in use at the palace
site of Phaistos between MM I B and MM
III A (c. 2000-1640 B.C.).

R.M. 3650 is a substitute for EUM-30, which
only survived in sherd condition and
could not be restored.

TRIPOD COOKING POT

R.M. 3650

MM II B (c. 1700 B.C.)
Palatial centre at Monastiraki, Amari,
Room 35 A-85.
H: 32 cm.; D: rim 15.2-17.2 cm.

Coarse orange clay with dark and white
grit. Thin brown wash. Mended from
many fragments and restored in parts
of the body and rim. Elliptical body with
two horizontal handles under the rim
which forms a low collar rim. The base
is flat and there are three legs with a
flattened oval section. One side of the
vase has strong traces of burning.

A. K.

129 PITHOS

EUM-136: Wall sherd   Exc. No 8

RESINATED WINE

McGovern: See method of analysis.

MM II (c. 1900-1700 B.C.)
Palatial centre at Monastiraki, Amari,
Room 70, a storeroom
Sherds submitted for analysis averaged
between 4 and 6 centimeters in diameter.

The type is similar to R.M. 22835.

R.M. 22835 is a substitute for EUM-136,
which only survived in sherd condition
and could not be restored.

PITHOS

R.M. 22835

MM II B (c. 1700 B.C.)
Palatial centre of Monastiraki, Amari,
Room 67-93
H: 90.5 cm.; D: rim 50.3 cm.

Coarse orange-buff fabric with black
and white grit. Black paint. Intact, but
small pieces of the rim are chipped off,
one handle is mended and one is missing.
It has an elongated oval body, everted
rim with rounded profile, four thick
handles below the rim and two above the
base. It is decorated with trickle pattern
dripping from the rim to the body.

A.K.

129

WINE WITH TEREBINTH RESIN
AT THE SETTLEMENT OF APODOULOU (c. 1900-1700 B.C.)

Two vessels (EUM 148 and 149) found at Apodoulou, Rethymnon held the remains of resinated wine. It was a wind-swept and exposed settlement situated on the brow of a hill, inland from the sea. Its importance is presumed to have been as a staging and look-out post en route from the palace of Phaistos, in the south of Crete, to a port on the north coast, but it was a rather small settlement, and the physical circumstances as well as the artefactual remains found to date, indicate that the residents were not the upper echelons of Minoan society, but were hard-working, ordinary people living in the most basic housing facilities of the time. Yet they consumed resinated wine with the best of them. Once more we have an indication of the generally high standard of eating and drinking that Minoans enjoyed.

DR. HOLLEY MARTLEW

130 CONICAL SMALL BOWL

EUM-148: Base sherd

TEREBINTH RESIN
The result is identical to sample KW 165 from the Ulu Burun shipwreck.

Mills and White (1989) have convincingly shown that the Ulu Burun resin is terebinth resin produced by Pistacia atlantica (turpentine tree). These authors did not identify this compound; the reference spectrum was obtained at Vassar College from sample KW165 from the Ulu Burun wreck... Both EUM-148 and EUM-149 contained terebinth resin and no additional compounds other than the identifiable contaminants.

Terebinth resin has been widely used in medicine and as an additive to wine. In its medicinal uses, as an antiseptic dressing of wounds, it was compounded with many other ingredients, including pine resins. The conical cups of Apodoulou contain no other ingredients and specifically no pine resins, whose diterpenoid resin acids are easily identified. We therefore conclude that these (bowl EUM-148; cup EUM-149: see below) were used to drink wine flavored with terebinth resin.

PROF. DR. CURT W. BECK

Beck: See method of analysis.

MM II (c. 1900-1700 B.C.)
Apodoulou, Room 15, level 5
Sherds submitted for analysis averaged between 4 and 6 centimeters in diameter.

The type is similar to that of R.M. 6615.

R.M. 6615 is a substitute for EUM-148, which only survived in sherd condition and could not be restored.

SMALL BOWL

R.M. 6615

MM II B (c. 1700 B.C.)
Apodoulou, Room 9
H: 4.74 cm.; D: rim 12.1 cm., base 3.8-3.57 cm.

Light brown coarse fabric. Light slip. Trickle pattern on the outside, in brown-reddish to black paint. Conical body, rounded rim. Flat, slightly raised base.

E.P.

131 CONICAL CUP

EUM-149: Base sherd

A DECIDUOUS RESIN, ALMOST CERTAINLY TEREBINTH

The absence of other ingredients indicates that these (bowl EUM-148; cup EUM-149) contained wine flavored with terebinth.

Beck: See method of analysis.

MM II (c. 1900-1700 B.C.).
Apodoulou, Room 15, level 5
Sherds submitted for analysis averaged between 4 and 6 centimeters in diameter.

The type is similar to that of R.M. 6613.

R.M. 6613 is a substitute for EUM-149, which only survived in sherd condition and could not be restored.

CONICAL CUP

R.M. 6613

MM II B (c. 1700 B.C.)
Apodoulou, Room 9
H: 4.19 cm.; D: rim 6.92-6.54 cm., base 5 cm.

Restored at the rim. Light brown fabric. Conical body. Flaring rim. The lower part of the cup is conical and the upper is cylindrical. Irregular flat base.

E.P.

130

131
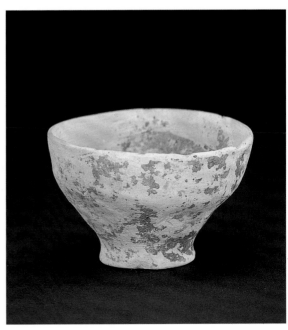

THE ULU BURUN SHIPWRECK

Between 1984 and 1994, the Institute of Nautical Archaeology of The Texas A&M University, under the direction of George F. Bass and Çemal Puluk, excavated a shipwreck off the coast of Ulu Burun, near Kas on Turkey's southern coast. In doing so, they brought to light one of the wealthiest and largest known assemblages of Late Bronze Age objects ever found in the Mediterranean. Dendrochronological dating of a small piece of firewood found on the wreck suggests a date of 1306 B.C., or at most a very few years later, for the sinking of the ship.

The ship's cargo was comprised of around ten tons of what appears to be primarily Cypriot copper in the form of a great number of oxhide or bun ingots, and a ton of tin ingots in similar shapes. Of particular interest is the approximately one ton of terebinth resin

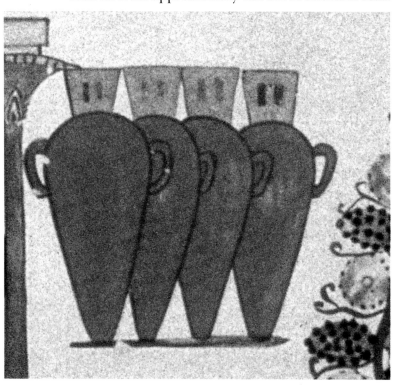

found in most of the nearly one hundred and fifty Canaanite jars from the site. Also found were the earliest known intact ingots of glass, coloured cobalt blue, turquoise, or lavender; logs of Egyptian ebony; ostrich eggshells; elephant tusks; a number of hippopotamus teeth; opercula from murex sea-shells; and modified tortoise shells, likely to have become sound-boxes for stringed musical instruments. Some large storage jars contained pomegranates, and possibly olive oil.

Manufactured goods found on the shipwreck included Cypriot fine and coarseware ceramics, faience drinking cups, bronze and copper cauldrons and bowls. The overall wealth of the cargo is clearly indicated by the Canaanite jewellery, scrap gold and silver, Egyptian objects of gold, electrum, silver, and stone, including a scarab bearing the cartouche of Queen Nefertiti. Other finds included ivory cosmetic containers, and a number of tin vessels and jewellery. Amongst the tools and weapons were awls, drills, chisels, axes, adzes, a saw, and bronze spearheads, arrowheads, daggers, swords, and stone maceheads. There were two wooden writing boards or diptychs, each consisting of a pair of leaves joined with an ivory hinge, and slightly recessed to receive wax writing surfaces.

The majority of the crew was Canaanite or Cypriot, as indicated by the anchors, tools, and oil lamps. However, the presence on board of at least two Mycenaeans is revealed by, amongst others, a pair of lentoid seals, two bronze swords, amber beads and a number of pieces of fine and coarse Mycenaean pottery.

DR. ROBERT ARNOTT
Dept. of Ancient History and Archaeology
University of Birmingham, U.K.

132 JUG WITH GRAPES

M.M. 623

LC I (c. 16th century B.C.)
Akrotiri, Thera, Complex D, room 4
H: 50 cm.; D: (max) 34 cm., rim 14 cm.,
base 14 cm.

Mended from fragments and restored in places on the body. Brown-red fabric with inclusions, off-white slip, brown paint, flaked on one side of the vase. Piriform body with cylindrical everted neck and flattened cylindrical handle. Painted bands on the body, base, rim, and at the base of the handle. One relief and two painted bands at the base of the neck, where it is joined to the shoulder. From the band at the neck hang four large bunches of grapes set symmetrically one on each face of the vase. From their stems spring two stylised leaves. The grapes are rendered naturalistically, projected strongly against the light surface of the vase, with no supplementary motifs. This is an excellent, original product of the Thera workshops, depicting grapes - a characteristic subject of local pottery. The representation is a combination of Minoan naturalism and the symmetry of the Cycladic tradition. Grapes are depicted on other vases from the settlement at Akrotiri, Thera, and the inhabitants evidently cultivated vines, ate their fruit, and presumably also made wine. Viticulture in Greece and Crete is attested already in the Early Bronze Age, and installations for making wine have been discovered on Crete.

L.P.-M.

132

WINE IN THE CULT CENTRE AT MYCENAE
(c. 1340-1250 B.C.)

The amphora and the stirrup jars M.M. 24347/EUM-153; M.M. 24345/EUM-157; M.M. 21785/EUM-161 produced the same result: wine. The three vessels came from the Cult Centre (the fill and the shrine/sanctuary store behind the Room with the Fresco). Taking into consideration the organic residue results from the Room with the Fresco as well, the importance of wine to cult practice at Mycenae becomes clear. Wine was also found in the kylix M.M. 24329/EUM-159 which came from the shrine/sanctuary store behind the Room with the Fresco.

The importation of resinated wine in Canaanite jars (EUM-67), to the palace site of Mycenae, details of which follow, provide additional evidence for the drinking habits of the Mycenaeans in the middle of the 13th century B.C.

DR. HOLLEY MARTLEW

MYCENAEAN STIRRUP JARS

Stirrup jars are the type artefact of Mycenaean Greece. The shape originates in Crete and a few early three-handled examples of Cretan type are known from the Mainland. Around the middle of the 14th century B.C. (at the beginning of LH III A2) the shape becomes extremely popular and remains in use until the early Iron Age.

There are three sizes:

1) Large transport jars in "heavy" ware of which some are inscribed with signs in the Linear B script and others are capped and sealed with impressions from signet rings. These are usually ovoid in shape.

2) A much rarer medium size in fine ware. The two examples in a fine but grit-tempered ware from the Cult Centre at Mycenae are unusual.

3) Various small sizes, generally globular or piriform, but other variants are attested. The piriform and globular types are often found as a pair.

The nature of the spout, which lies beside the "stirrup" handles from which the vase takes its English name, make it easy to control pouring. This feature together with textual evidence from the Linear B tablets indicates that the stirrup jar was used for oil, either in bulk for transport or in small quantities of perfumed oil. Indeed one of the transport jars at Mycenae was so "oily" on discovery that the building where it was found (adjacent to a means of heating the oil) was named the House of the Oil Merchant. The connection with oil does not of course preclude other usage.

Both transport jars and small examples are found widely over the entire area of the Eastern Mediterranean to which Mycenaean trade penetrated from Nubia in the south to the upper Euphrates in the east. They are less common in the Western Mediterranean.

DR. ELIZABETH B. FRENCH
Former Director, British School at Athens

133 AMPHORA

M.M. 24347 EUM-153: Wall sherd Exc. No 69-1524

WINE. OLIVE OIL. THE OLIVE OIL WAS PROBABLY USED TO SEAL THE WINE

Evans: See method of analysis.

Mid LH III B (c. 1340-1250 B.C.)
Mycenae, Cult Centre, Room 31, the Room with the Fresco
H: 39.5 cm.; D: rim 16.5 cm.,
body (max) 30.5 cm.

Pinkish buff clay. Partially preserved vessel with linear decoration on the upper body only and a slightly wavy band down the handle. The surface is pitted and encrusted with white calcined material. A sherd was taken for analysis prior to restoration.

E.B.F.

134 STIRRUP JAR

M.M. 24345 EUM-157: Wall sherd Exc. No 69-428

WINE

Evans: See method of analysis.

Mid LH III B (c. 1340-1250 B.C.)
Mycenae, Cult Centre, fill placed in Room 31, the Room with the Fresco.
H: Unknown; D: disk 7.5 cm.
Sherds submitted for analysis averaged between 4 and 6 centimeters in diameter.

Reddish buff clay. Domestic stirrup jar. Decorated with dark paint on lighter ground; two circles, the inner filled, on disk; handles broadly barred; tassel pattern on shoulder; bands on body. This type, not so widely found, seems to have been used alongside the more usual ovoid transport stirrup jar from at least the beginning of the 12th century B.C. This vessel could not be restored.

E.B.F.

135 STIRRUP JAR

M.M. 21785 EUM-161: Wall sherd Exc. No 68-490

WINE

Evans: See method of analysis.

Mid LH III B (c. 1340-1250 B.C.)
Mycenae, Cult Centre, Room 32,
"The Shrine"/sanctuary store behind the Room with the Fresco.
H: 32 cm.; D: (max) 30 cm.

Coarse orange clay with greenish yellow slip. Domestic stirrup jar. Decorated with dark paint on lighter ground; two circles on disk; handles barred; tassel pattern on shoulder; bands on body as M.M. 24345. A sherd was taken for analysis prior to restoration.

E.B.F.

133

134

135

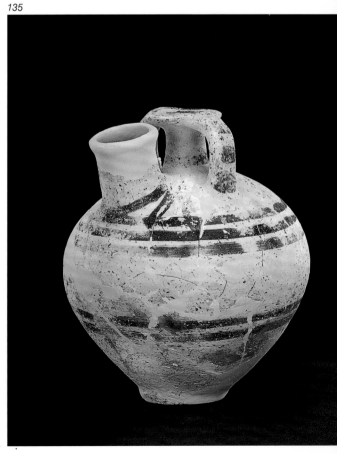

A COLLECTION OF MYCENAEAN KYLIKES

The case of kylikes illustrates the three most common shapes of unpainted kylikes in use at Mycenae in the two centuries between 1350 and 1150 B.C. and the three fabrics in which they are made. The kylix was one of the most popular drinking vessels along with the cup and the mug, but was occasionally used for other everyday purposes, as a lamp or a scoop.

DR. ELIZABETH B. FRENCH
Former Director, British School at Athens

136

137

136   KYLIX

M.M. 24329 EUM-159: Wall sherd   Exc. No 68-493

WINE

Evans: See method of analysis.

Mid LH III B (c. 1340-1250 B.C.)
Mycenae, Cult Centre, Room 32
"The Shrine"/sanctuary store
behind the Room with the Fresco
H: 16.4 cm.; D: rim 16.4 cm.

Pinkish buff clay. Conical kylix (FS 274)
with deep body and lipless rim. This
relatively large type of kylix becomes
extremely prevalent at this period and
remains in use for at least a century. This
type is usually, as this example, made in
the "polished" fabric. A sherd was taken
for analysis prior to restoration.

E.B.F.

137   KYLIX

M.M. 24337 Exc. No 69-1425

Mid LH III B (c. 1340-1250 B.C.)
Mycenae, Cult Centre, Room 32
"The Shrine"/sanctuary store behind
the Room with the Fresco
H: 16.5 cm.; D: rim 17.6 cm.

Fine pale buff clay. Conical kylix (FS 274)
as M.M. 24329 (Exc. No 68-493).

E.B.F.

138   KYLIX

M.M. 24328 Exc. No 66-1406

Mid LH III B (c. 1340-1250 B.C.)
Mycenae, Cult Centre, storeroom of the
Temple, Room 19
H: 10.3 cm.; D: rim 11.5 cm.

Buff slightly gritty clay. Complete rounded
kylix (close to FS 264/5) in the "rough"
fabric which was used for all the unpainted
pottery found in the Temple store.

E.B.F.

139   KYLIX

M.M. 24334 Exc. No 66-419

Probably LH III C early (c. 1185-1130 B.C.)
Mycenae, Citadel House Area, Room xxxiv
H: 11.2 cm.; D: rim 12.1 cm.

Pinkish buff clay. Complete carinated
kylix in "standard" fabric with smoothed
surface. This type is ubiquitous, being
found in all contexts from the middle of
the 13th through the 11th century B.C.
Occasional examples show traces of having been used as lamps.

E.B.F.

138

139

RESINATED WINE IMPORTED TO MYCENAE IN CANAANITE JARS

Canaanite or Syro-Palestinian jars or amphorae are large coarse-ware clay vessels with conical bodies, standing at an average height of around 50 cm. They have an ovoid body, a highly pointed or stumpy base for stability, two large vertical loop handles, situated opposite each other at the shoulder for pouring and a neck and mouth that is narrow enough both to take stopper and to pour with ease. They bear an uncanny resemblance to Classical amphorae.

The finding of jars such as these are irrefutable evidence of the intense trade between the Aegean and Syro-Palestine in the 14th and 13th centuries B.C., being found exclusively in Late Minoan and Helladic III levels. Ships loaded with these locally made jars, filled with wine, oil or resin, left the ports of the Syro-Palestinian coast, such as Ugarit (Ras Shamra), and, as is clear from the archaeological evidence, travelled to all parts of the Aegean, Crete, Attica, the Argolid and Messenia, as well as Cyprus and southwards to Egypt. It is now generally accepted that one of the most important functions of these jars was for the importation of wine into the Aegean, perhaps at a time when a taste for exotic wines from the east was in fashion. Such wines certainly had an honoured place at the table and in the tombs of the Egyptian pharaoh.

Canaanite jars also contained other commodities such as oil and there is ample evidence from the wreck of the 14th century B.C. ship found off the coast of Ulu Burun, that a number contained terebinth resin (*ki-ta-no* in the Linear B script), which has many uses, including medicines. Good sturdy jars such as these may also have been eagerly sought after as water carriers, once all the wine had been drunk.

DR. ROBERT ARNOTT
Dept. of Ancient History and Archaeology
University of Birmingham, U.K.

140 CANAANITE JAR

. . . .

EUM-67: Wall sherd   Exc. No 64-207; 66-518

RESINATED WINE

Mc Govern: See method of analysis.

Mid LH III B (c. 1340-1250 B.C.)
Mycenae, Cult Centre, Area 36
H: (pres.) 16.5 cm.; D: shoulder 12.5 cm.

Red clay with grey core and fine grit. Matching sherd from Exc. No 66-518. Canaanite amphora, probably from the Phoenician coast of the Eastern Mediterranean (information from Professor E. Oren) not unlike those from the well-known group found at Ras Shamra. This shape is one of the very few pottery imports found at Mycenaean sites.

E.B.F.

N.M. 2014; 2015; 2016 are substitutes for EUM-67 above, which only survived in sherd condition and could not be restored.

CANAANITE JAR

. . . .

N.M. 2014

Mid LH III B (c. 1340-1250 B.C.)
Tholos tomb, Menidi, Attica
H: 50.5 cm; D: shoulder (with handles) 31 cm., rim 10 cm., base 4.5 cm.

Mended at the neck, shoulder and one handle, with slight restoration. Reddish fabric with ochre slip. Conical body with angular shoulder and cylindrical neck. Narrow, slightly curved base. Two flattened cylindrical handles, one with an engraved sign in the shape of a rectangle. The term "Canaanite" is applied to these characteristic amphoras, which were the main containers used for transportation and trade between the coast of Syria and Palestine and Crete in the 14th-13th c. B.C. Four Canaanite amphoras were deposited as offerings in the rich tholos

tomb at Menidi, and others like them have been found in houses and tombs at Mycenae, at Pylos, and at Kommos on Crete. Another type of Canaanite amphora, with rounded shoulders, is known from Argos, Asine, the Athenian Agora, and Koukaki in Athens. A picture of the variety of liquid and solid products transported by ship in Canaanite amphoras may be compiled from the finds from the Ulu Burun (Kas) shipwreck off the

coast of Asia Minor. Analysis of the contents of a large number of amphoras has demonstrated that one contained beads made of glass paste, another pigments, and yet others the remains of fruits, while the majority contained resin, presumably for use in the manufacture of perfumes or in the production of wine.

L.P.-M.

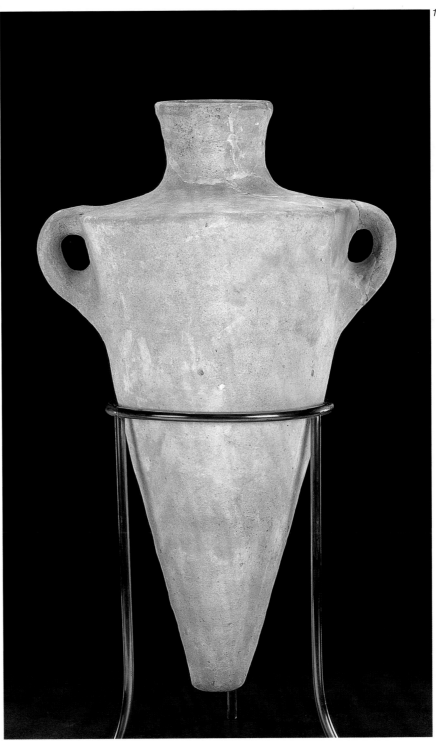

140

141 CANAANITE JAR

N.M. 2015

Mid LH III B (c. 1340-1250 B.C.)
Tholos tomb, Menidi, Attica
H: 53.5 cm.; D: shoulder (with handles) 32 cm., base 4 cm.

Mended at the shoulder and handles, restored at the neck, shoulder and body. Identical in shape and fabric to N.M. 2014 (cat. no 140). See commentary there. Sign incised on the back of one of the handles: three small horizontal parallel lines, intersected by a fourth at about the middle.

L. P.-M.

142 CANAANITE JAR

N.M. 2016

Mid LH III B (c. 1340-1250 B.C.)
Tholos tomb, Menidi, Attica
H: 54 cm.; D: shoulder (with handles) 35 cm., rim 10 cm.

Mended from a large number of pieces. Conical, pointed body with a small, slightly convex base. The upright shoulders rise to cylindrical neck ending in an upright rim with an incised ring at its base. Two vertical handles of cylindrical section. Greenish fabric with off-white slip, characteristic of Syria and Palestine. The Menidi amphora has shoulders with a distinctive angular profile, a feature it shares with the Amiran II B:11 and 12 types, examples of which have also been found in the Aegean. The tholos tomb at Menidi is very rich and has yielded three more Canaanite amphoras; ivories; clay and stone tools; bronze weapons; glass paste and faience jewellery. It evidently belonged to a wealthy family that maintained contacts with the Orient.

E.B.F.

141

142

DID THEY DRINK BEER AT MYRTOS?

This has been one of the riddles of the Minoan/Mycenaean civilisation.

The answer is yes, and they may even have had barley beer in the Early Minoan Period, c. 2200 B.C., at the settlement of Myrtos Phournou Koryphe in southern Crete. The evidence is not conclusive, but at the very least analysis indicates that barley/a barley product had been introduced to two pithoi that contained wine (EUM-104/P. 597; EUM-100/P. 623). The presence of a barley product in pithoi at the Early Minoan, c. 2200 B.C., site of Myrtos Phournou Koryphe, is not strong enough to argue exclusively for barley beer according to McCovern. He interpreted the evidence to include, but not limited to, the following:

1) reuse of some vessels, namely EUM-104, pithos P. 597, and possibly EUM-100, pithos P. 623, for a barley product whether gruel, mead, or beer;

2) the addition of unfermented barley to wine: possibly resinated wine in EUM-104, pithos P. 597;

3) the actual mixture of wine and beer, perhaps foreshadowing the development of a mixed fermented beverage by Late Minoan/Mycenaean times.

DR. HOLLEY MARTLEW

CONTENTS OF THE MYRTOS PITHOI

The pithoi analysed for residues come from five different rooms or areas in the Early Minoan village and all are from the final destruction context of Early Minoan II B, c. 2200-2150 B.C. The combined evidence of six of them is remarkable and it increases knowledge of Early Bronze agriculture in Crete significantly.

All six pithoi are shown to have contained wine, in the case of P. 611 (EUM-98) from South East Magazine 53 and P. 605 (EUM-95) from Room 80 wine on its own; in P. 600 (EUM-97) from Area 26 and P. 604 (EUM-99) again from Room 80 wine possibly resinated; in P. 597 (EUM-104; not exhibited) from the east part of Room 20 wine and a product of barley and in P. 623 (EUM-100; not exhibited), also from Room 80, wine and possibly a barley product. Gruel, mead, beer or an unfermented liquid are possibilities for this barley product and suggest use for different liquids at different times for these two pithoi.

The analytical evidence for P. 605 (EUM-95) nicely confirms the original discovery of pressed grapes, pips, stalks and skins in the pithos itself. P. 600 (EUM-97) had been noted at the time of publication to have been stained red inside; the clay fabric of P. 611 (EUM-98) and P. 623 (EUM-100) was rotted inside, and the acidity present in wine was a suggested cause. The small manufacture hole just above the base of most of the jars would have facilitated cleaning and the imitation of overflowing contents even suggest a dry sense of humour. The function of the piriform jugs found with P. 597 (EUM-104), P. 600 (EUM-97), P. 605 (EUM-95) and P. 623 (EUM-100) may now be seen as an ideal means of drawing out wine from the pithoi, ready for use at table or for transferring it to the elegant long-spouted 'tea-pots' for the same purpose. Finally, the discovery of evidence for wine in no fewer than six out of seven tested pithoi strongly suggests that wine storage was the function of other pithoi among the minimum of 44 in use at Phournou Koryphe at the moment of destruction.

The analytical discoveries also assist interpretation of room function. Room 20, where P. 597 (EUM-104) and its adjacent jug were used for wine and a product of barley, was already known to be a food preparation room with a raised oven and a quernstone *in situ*, as well as other jars. Thus the grinding of wheat or barley took place here, probably for bread-making, when it was not in use for wine. By coincidence a fragment of a potstand from this same room had impressions of wheat and barley from chaff tempering of the clay, indirect evidence to confirm growth of these cereals at the site.

Southeast Magazine 53, already proposed as a storeroom for liquids, may have been specifically a wine magazine. Room 80, with its magnificent array of vessels, may have contained two or even three kinds of wine:
1) Simple: P. 605 (EUM-95), which contained actual remains of grapes, pips, stalks and skins;
2) Possibly resinated: P. 604 (EUM-99);
3) Possibly used before, after or together with a barley product: P. 623 (EUM-100).

Remains of grapes were also found in a bowl with processing vessels in Room 90 and a fragment of the base of a large processing tub elsewhere on the site had a vine leaf impression on its base There were several large, spouted tubs in the settlement, used for treading grapes and/or as olive oil separators. All in all, each of the domestic units on the site is likely to have its own store of wine and equipment for making it, which in turn is an argument for individual families as the basic social unit. The average capacity of the Myrtos pithoi was 89 litres.

Myrtos Phournou Koryphe is one of very few excavated Early Minoan settlements. The available evidence, from Haghia Triadha, Knossos, Myrtos: Pyrgos, Palaikastro, Trypete, Vasilike, for example, indicates that there were similar places. The similarity will certainly have extended to the general agricultural base, namely mixed farming of cereals, pulses, vines and olives, and stock-raising. The dramatic new strengthening of previous evidence for viticulture and wine-making at Myrtos is more than likely to represent the state of affairs at other early Minoan communities too.

PROF. PETER WARREN
University of Bristol, U.K.

143 PITHOS

EUM-104: Wall sherd   P. 597

WINE AND A BARLEY PRODUCT

Mc Govern: See method of analysis.

EM II B (c. 2200 B.C.)

Myrtos Phournou Koryphe, Room 20, east part, fill

H: rim to greatest diameter 35 cm.; D: rim 46.5 cm., body 68.7 cm.

Sherds submitted for analysis averaged between 4 and 6 centimeters.

Coarse fabric with dark, also occasionally white grits, firing from grey to pink or buff. Buff slip and dark painted trickle decoration. Warren's type (1) with band of applied thumb-impressed decoration on the shoulder, producing a deep collar. Everted rim. Base and lower body are missing.

P.W.

144 PITHOS

EUM-100: Wall sherd   P. 623

WINE AND POSSIBLY ALSO A BARLEY PRODUCT

Mc Govern: See method of analysis.

EM II B (c. 2200 B.C.)

Myrtos Phournou Koryphe, Room 80, largest room in settlement, used for living and working

H: 65.8 cm.; D: rim 42.3 cm., body 57.4 cm., base 25 cm.

Sherds submitted for analysis averaged between 4 and 6 centimeters in diameter.

Coarse fabric with dark, also occasionally white grits, firing from grey to pink or buff. Buff slip and dark painted trickle decoration. Warren's type (3): very small collar with applied band or other decoration marking it off distinctly from the body. Barrel-shaped body, everted rim with band of shallow impressed circles just below. Small hole above base. A third of rim and body is missing.

P.W.

Pithos A.N.M. 13100 is a substitute for pithoi EUM-104 (Pub. No 597) and EUM-100 (Pub. No 623), both of which survived only in sherd condition and could not be restored.

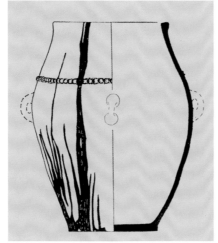

143

PITHOS

A.N.M. 13100   P. 627

EM II B (c. 2200 B.C.)

Myrtos Phournou Koryphe, Room 53

H: 63.5 cm.; D: rim 42.4 cm., body c. 58 cm., base 24.2 cm.

Coarse fabric with dark, also occasionally white grits, firing from grey to pink or buff. Buff slip and dark painted trickle decoration. Warren's type (4): wide mouth, with no distinct collar. Band of impressed circles just below rim. Small hole just above base. Restored.

P.W.

144

DID THEY DRINK BEER AT APODOULOU?

By the Middle Minoan II B period (c. 1700 B.C.), the evidence for beer is stronger at the settlement of Apodoulou, Rethymnon. An acid that was found in beer brewing vats in pre-dynastic Egypt, was found in two tripod cooking pots. One of them (EUM-21) provides evidence.

DR. HOLLEY MARTLEW

145 TRIPOD COOKING POT

EUM-21: Wall sherd

BEER BREWING?
This vessel contained phosphoric acid. This acid has been found in pre-dynastic (earlier than 3000 B.C.) beer brewing vats in Hierako-napolis, Upper Egypt. As this acid is a component of all living cells, a definite conclusion cannot be drawn.
However, the results also produced 2-octanol. This is commonly thought to indicate beer.

Beck: See method of analysis.

MM II B (c. 1700 B.C.)
Apodoulou, Room 9, a storage area under the stairs
Sherds submitted for analysis averaged between 4 and 6 centimeters in diameter.

Elliptical vessel. The type normally had an incurving mouth and no spout. This type is known to have been in use at the palace site of Phaistos betwen MM I B and MM III A (c. 2000-1640 B.C.).

H.M. F. 65 5112 is a substitute for EUM-21, which only survived in sherd condition and could not be restored.

TRIPOD COOKING POT

H.M. F. 65 5112

MM I B (c. 2000-1900 B.C.)
Phaistos, town area, Room C III. One of 3 tripods listed in the Great Landslide deposit. H: 25.5 cm.; D: rim 13 cm.

Restored. Brown-yellow fabric. Elliptical vessel. It has an incurving mouth and no spout. Two horizontal handles, coil in section, set on shoulder. The base is flat and legs are oval in section.

A.K.-E.K.

145

MINOAN AND MYCENAEAN DRINKING HABITS: WINE WITH HERBS

Tripod cooking pots yielded evidence for herbs in wine/resinated wine both in Crete and on the Mainland. EUM-33 from Chania, which dated to the Late Minoan I period, the first half of the 15th century B.C., could have contained one or a group of herbs. Dating to a later time, the first half of the 12th century B.C., a tripod pot (M.M. 24323/EUM-72) had an even more startling result: resinated wine with rue, a narcotic and stimulent. That gives scope to the imagination about what life might have been like in the Greek Bronze Age.

DR. HOLLEY MARTLEW

146 TRIPOD COOKING POT

EUM-33: Base/leg sherd

RESINATED WINE WITH HERBS
Large amounts of camphor which appear to indicate any one (or more) of the following: laurel, lavender, sage.

Beck: See method of analysis.

LM I (c. 1600-1425 B.C.)
Chania, Splanzia, Room ST, found at pillar base
Sherds submitted for analysis averaged between 4 and 6 centimeters in diameter.

Cylindrical vessel. The type normally had a small, pulled-out spout. It is known to have been in use in West Crete between MM III and LM III A (c. 1700-1340 B.C.).

CH.M. 8323 is a substitute for EUM-33, which only survived in sherd condition and could not be restored.

TRIPOD COOKING POT

CH.M. 8323

LM I (c. 1600-1425 B.C.)
Chania, 1989. Splanzia - Papadopoulos plot. Well (Pit 4). Exc. No 18
H: 32 cm.; D: rim 22 cm., body 21.2 cm.

Restored. Light reddish brown, gritty clay; buff wash. Cylindrical body; flat base. Rim slightly incurving with small pulled-out spout. Roll handle, horizontally set just below rim. A large sealing with geometric designs dominates the centre of the base underneath, as a trade mark. Plain. Burnt inside, and badly burnt outside.

M.A.-V.

147 TRIPOD COOKING POT

EUM-65: Base/leg sherd

RESINATED WINE WITH AROMATIC ADDITIVES

Beck: See method of analysis.

LM I (c. 1600-1425 B.C.)
Chania, Splanzia, drain area.
Sherds submitted for analysis averaged between 4 and 6 centimeters in diameter.

Cylindrical vessel. The type normally had a small, pulled-out spout. It is known to have been in use in West Crete between MM III and LM III A (c. 1700-1340 B.C.).

M.A.-V.

147

148 TRIPOD COOKING POT

M.M. 24323   EUM-72   Exc. No 64-505

RESINATED WINE WITH RUE
Rue is a narcotic and stimulant according to Willis' Dictionary of Flowering Plants and Ferns.

Beck: See method of analysis.

LH III C early (c. 1185-1130 B.C.)
Mycenae, Citadel House Area, Room 34.
H: 22.8 cm.; D: rim 21 cm.

Red sandy clay. Open version of FS 320 which copies metal prototypes. The legs, squared with a channel on all four sides, bend to join the body of the pot just below a distinct carination; two flat vertical handles from carination to just below rim. Burnt outside and at the base inside. A sherd was taken for analysis prior to restoration.

E.B.F.

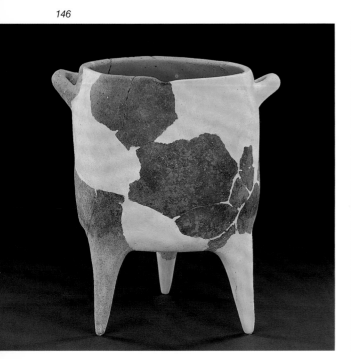

146

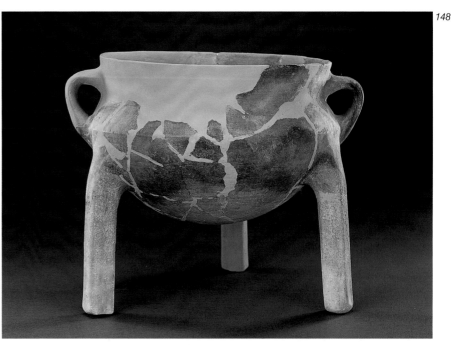

148

149 BAKING BASIN

EUM-180: Wall/base sherd

GRAPE/WINE PRODUCT

Mc Govern: See method of analysis.
LM III C1 (c. 1190-1130 B.C.)
Chamalevri, Palaeoloutra, Hadjidakis Peris
Sherds submitted for analysis averaged
between 4 and 6 centimeters in diameter.

The type is similar to CH.M. 3442

Baking Basin CH.M. 3442 is a subtitute for
EUM-180, which only survived in sherd
condition and could not be restored.

150

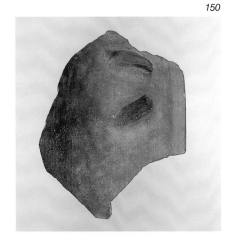

151 COOKING JAR

EUM-93: Base sherd

WINE? OIL

Evans: See method of analysis.

LH III B (c. 1340-1185 B.C.)
Midea, sanctuary area
Sherds submitted for analysis averaged
between 4 and 6 centimeters in diameter.

Sherd material from typical medium-
sized coarse red cooking jar.

G.W.

49

151, 152

BAKING BASIN

CH.M. 3442

LM III (c. 1390-1190 B.C.)
Chania, 1971. Kastelli hill, Greek-Swedish
Excavations. Exc. No P. 848 & 758
H: 15 cm.; D: rim 48 cm.

The whole base is missing; restored.
Reddish gritty clay; traces of buff slip.
Large semi-globular body; vertical rim
with broad spout and opposing wall
inverted. Convex base. Plain. Heavily
burnt outside.

M.A.-V.

150 COOKING JAR

M.M. 28093   EUM-90: Base sherd

WINE. OIL?

Evans: See method of analysis.

LH III B (c. 1340-1185 B.C.)
Midea, sanctuary area
H: 18 cm.; W: 21 cm.; D: rim c. 28 cm.
Sherds submitted for analysis averaged
between 4 and 6 centimeters in diameter.

Coarse red clay. Rim and handle fragment
of a typical cooking jar with a collar
neck and stubs of one handle. Burnt near
base and on outside of handle stubs.

G.W.

152 COOKING JAR

EUM-94: Base sherd

WINE? OIL?

Evans: See page method of analysis.

LH III B (c. 1340-1185 B.C.)
Midea, sanctuary area
Sherds submitted for analysis averaged
between 4 and 6 centimeters in diameter.

Sherd material from typical medium-
sized coarse red cooking jar.

G.W.

MIXED FERMENTED BEVERAGES
DURING THE LATE BRONZE AGE: c. 1600-1100 B.C.

The conclusion drawn by the chemists was that both Minoans and Mycenaeans probably indulged in a "cocktail" comprised of wine, barley beer and honey mead, and that this cocktail was used in cult practice (EUM-111). The other interpretation is for successive uses of the relevant vessels for wine, barley beer and honey mead.

A firm conclusion cannot be drawn from the evidence we have so far, but the argument for the "mixed fermented beverage" is strengthened by the relatively large number of finds (taking into consideration the actual number of drinking vessels from which sherds were sent for analysis) of the three ingredients in the same vessel, both at sites in Crete and on the Mainland, and the timespan of these finds (roughly 400 years). The problem is a mixture which seems so peculiar to modern taste.

Three vessels that Greek prehistorians have always drawn to one's attention are the "mug", the "feeding bottle" and the "rhyton". The organic residue results for these vessels therefore have a special significance.

The "mug" which was analysed (EUM-195) indicated wine and honey, or possibly wine and honey mead. Beer? Maybe. Since we now know they had beer, it is possible that we just sampled the wrong mug.

The oddest occurrence of the proposed "mixture" of wine, barley beer and mead came from a vessel traditionally called a "feeding bottle" (EUM-331), a shape that archaeologists have previously suggested was probably used for feeding babies.

Rhytons have always had ritual connotations. Therefore to find wine in a rhyton (EUM-330) — especially when we have had several organic residue results of wine in cult contexts — is not a surprise. To find wine and barley beer, however, is remarkable.

The same mixture of fermented beverages was also found in four conical cups (EUM-36, EUM-47, EUM-61 and EUM-58), from the Kastelli area at Chania.

DR. HOLLEY MARTLEW

153 CONICAL CUP

EUM-36: Wall/base sherd

THE POSSIBILITY OF A MIXED FER-MENTED BEVERAGE COMPRISED OF WINE, BARLEY BEER AND HONEY MEAD

Mc Govern: See method of analysis.

LM I A (c. 1600-1480 B.C.).
Chania, 1997. Splanzia - Daskaloyiannis St.
Room ST at pillar base
Sherds submitted for analysis averaged between 4 and 6 centimeters in diameter.

The type is similar to CH.M. 9378.

CH.M. 9378 is a substitute for EUM-36, which only survived in sherd condition and could not be restored.

CONICAL CUP

CH.M. 9378

LM I A (c. 1600-1480 B.C.)
Chania, 1997. Splanzia - Daskaloyiannis St.
Room ST with pillar base. Exc. No 593
H: 6 cm.; D: small rim 8.1 cm., base 3.9 cm.

Almost complete; restored. Reddish brown, gritty clay; buff wash. Conical body; rounded rim; narrow flat base. Strong wheel ridges inside. Plain.

M.A.-V.

154 CONICAL CUP

EUM-47: Wall/base sherd

THE POSSIBILITY OF A MIXED FERMENTED BEVERAGE COMPRISED OF WINE, BARLEY BEER AND HONEY MEAD.

Mc Govern: See method of analysis.

LM I A (c. 1600-1480 B.C.)
Chania, 1997. Splanzia - Daskaloyiannis St.
Drain area
Sherds submitted for analysis averaged between 4 and 6 centimeters in diameter.

The type is similar to CH.M. 9361.

CH.M. 9361 is a substitute for EUM-47, which only survived in sherd condition and could not be restored.

CONICAL CUP

CH.M. 9361

LM I A (c 1600-1480 B.C.)
Chania, 1997. Splanzia - Daskaloyiannis St.
Drain area. Exc. No 354
H: 3.8 cm.; D: rim 8.3 cm., base 4.1 cm.

Almost complete; restored. Reddish yellow, gritty clay; wet-smoothed. Conical body; slightly outward flaring rim; narrow flat base. Plain.

M.A.-V.

155 CONICAL CUP

EUM-61: Wall/base sherd

THE POSSIBILITY OF A MIXED FERMENTED BEVERAGE COMPRISED OF RESINATED WINE, BARLEY BEER, AND HONEY MEAD.

Mc Govern: See method of analysis.

LM I A (c. 1600-1480 B.C.).
Chania, 1997. Splanzia - Daskaloyiannis St.
Drain area
Sherds submitted for analysis averaged between 4 and 6 centimeters in diameter.

The type is similar to CH.M. 9372.

CH.M. 9372 is a substitute for EUM-61, which only survived in sherd condition and could not be restored.

CONICAL CUP

CH.M. 9372

LM I A (c. 1600-1480 B.C.).
Chania, 1997. Splanzia - Daskaloyiannis St.
Drain area. Exc. No 356
H: 4.5 cm.; D: small rim 3.6 cm., base 7.7 cm.

Completely preserved. Reddish yellow clay; wet-smoothed. Conical body with a low ridge in the middle. Vertical rounded rim; narrow flat base. Plain.

M.A.-V.

153

154

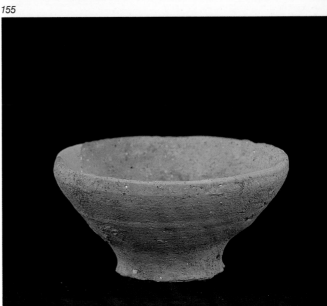

155

156   CONICAL CUP

EUM-58: Wall/base sherd

THE RESULTS FOR THIS CUP WERE LESS CERTAIN, BUT IT IS POSSIBLE THAT IT TOO CONTAINED A MIXED FERMENTED BEVERAGE

Mc Govern: See method of analysis.

LM I A (c. 1600-1480 B.C.).
Chania, 1997. Splanzia - Daskaloyiannis plot.
Drain area
Sherds submitted for analysis averaged between 4 and 6 centimeters in diameter.

The type is similar to CH.M. 9363.

CH.M. 9363 is a substitute for EUM-58, which only survived in sherd condition and could not be restored.

157   MUG

EUM-195: Wall sherd

WINE AND HONEY. THE HONEY CONTENT INDICATES THE POSSIBILITY OF MEAD

Beck: See method of analysis.

LH III A2 (c. 1370-1340 B.C.)
Helleno-British Excavations at Mycenae.
Sherds submitted for analysis averaged between 4 and 6 centimeters in diameter.

EUM-195 came from a typical mug decorated with FS 225 running spiral.

E.B.F.

M.M. 8011 (Exc. No 50-148) is a substitute for EUM-195, which only survived in sherd condition and could not be restored.

MUG

M.M. 8011   Exc. No 50-148

LH III A2 (c. 1370-1340 B.C.)
Mycenae, "Cyclopean Terrace Building: South West Trench", a domestic context on the northwest slope of the settlement outside the walls
H: 14.8 cm.; D: rim 16.6 cm.

Restored. Fine buff clay. Typical example of this shape with ridges and bands at rim and waist and running spiral pattern with fill in both zones; concentric circles under the base.

E.B.F.

156

CONICAL CUP

CH.M. 9363

LM I A (c. 1600-1480 B.C.).
Chania, 1997. Splanzia - Daskaloyiannis plot.
Drain area. Exc. No 332
H: 3.1 cm.; D: rim 7 cm., base 3.6 cm.

Almost complete; restored. Reddish yellow, gritty clay; buff wash. Conical body; rounded rim; narrow flat base. Plain.

M.A.-V.

157

158 FEEDING BOTTLE

N.M. 28092 EUM-331: Base sherd Exc. No 1038

TRACES OF BEESWAX: HONEY? FERMENTED PRODUCT. MEAD? BEER? MIXTURE?

Evans: See method of analysis.

LH III B (c. 1340-1185 B.C.)
Midea, a room against the citadel wall, northeast of Megaron
H: 7.2 cm.; D: 3.5 cm.

Hand-made, fine ware. Decorated with a band around the neck and groups of vertical lines from neck to belly. There are two horizontal bands on the belly and also a band around the spout (FS 161). A sherd was taken for analysis prior to restoration.

G.W.

159 PITHOS

EUM-313: Wall sherd

FERMENTED PRODUCT? OIL. BEESWAX. TARTARIC ACID. HONEYED WINE? MEAD? IT IS PRESUMED THE OIL WAS TO SEAL THE SURFACE.

Evans: See method of analysis.

LH III B/C (c. 1200 B.C.)
Thebes, room with evidence for both ceremonial and working activities, site 13
H: (pres.) 15.5 cm.; W: 18 cm.
Sherds submitted for analysis averaged between 4 and 6 centimeters in diameter.

Undecorated pithos.

E.A.

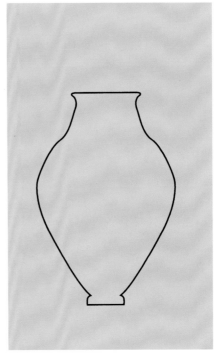

159

158

160 ASKOS

T.M. 27425 EUM-322: Wall sherd

TRACES OF RESIN. RESINATED WINE? BARLEY? BREWING RESIDUES. A MIXED FERMENTED BEVERAGE?

Evans: See method of analysis.

LH III B1 (c. 1340-1250 B.C.)
Thebes, room with evidence for both ceremonial and working activities, site 13
H: (pres.) 22 cm.; D: rim 6.5 cm., body (max) 22.5 cm.

Light brown fabric. The lower part of the askos is missing. It has a squat globular body, cylindrical neck, spreading lip and flattened handle. It is decorated in black paint. Pale yellow slip. Group of bands below the decorative zone of the shoulder. Band around the rim and the base of the neck. Bands drawn freehand on the edges of the handle continue and cover the shoulder. Another band, part of it on the neck and part on the shoulder, encircle the vase. A sherd was taken for analysis prior to the restoration that was possible.

E.A.

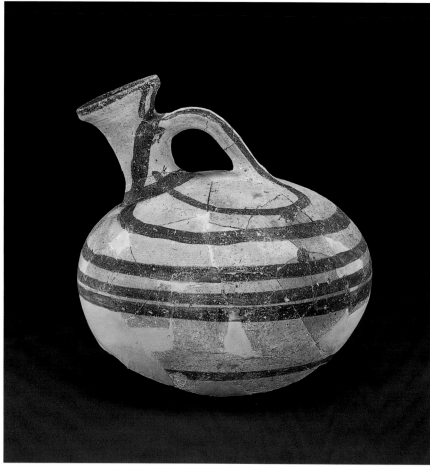

160

162

163

161

161 TRIPOD COOKING POT

EUM-188: Wall/base sherd

RESINATED WINE, A BARLEY PRODUCT AND POSSIBLY HONEY

"I think it is very unlikely that Chamalevri EUM-188 was used for beverages; rather ingredients such as barley, honey and wine were ingredients used to prepare a food in this vessel."

DR. PATRICK E. Mc GOVERN

Mc Govern: See method of analysis.

However, there is evidence for the possibility of heating fermented beverages at other sites (e.g. Thebes: tripod cooking pot EUM-33 and cooking jars EUM-329 and EUM-321; Mycenae: tripod cooking pot EUM-72)

LM III C1 (c. 1190-1130 B.C.)
Chamalevri, 1996. Tzambakas House. Pit Sherds submitted for analysis averaged between 4 and 6 centimeters in diameter.

R.M. 15272 is a substitute for EUM-188, which only survived in sherd condition and could not be restored.

TRIPOD COOKING POT

R.M. 15272

LM III C1 (c. 1190-1130 B.C.)
Chamalevri, 1991. Bolanis field: Pits Δ+E.
Exc. No 11
H: 17 cm.; D: rim 11.7 cm., body 15 cm., base 6 cm.

Half of the body is preserved; restored. Reddish, brown, gritty clay. Globular body; vertical, roll handle; high flaring rim with a small spout opposite to the handle. Narrow, convex base; legs ovoid in section. Plain. Heavily burnt.

M.A.-V.

162 COOKING JUG

EUM-316: Wall sherd

COMPLEX, INCLUDING TARTARIC ACID AND RESIN. RESINATED WINE? BARLEY. OLIVE OIL. BARLEY BEER? BARLEY WINE? A MIXED FERMENTED BEVERAGE?

Evans: See method of analysis.

LH III B/C (c. 1200 B.C.)

Thebes, room with evidence for ceremonial and working activities, site 13
Sherds submitted for analysis averaged between 4 and 6 centimeters in diameter.

Wall fragment of a typical ovoid cooking jug.

E.A.

M.M. 6995, Exc. No 52-586, is a substitute for EUM-316, which only survived in sherd condition and could not be restored.

COOKING JUG

M.M. 6995   Exc. No 52-586

LH III B (c. 1340-1185 B.C.)
Mycenae, 1962. Prehistoric Cemetery South
H: 20.3 cm.; D: rim 11.5 cm., belly 18.4 cm., base 7.2 cm.

Restored from many pieces. Grey to reddish clay. Cooking jug with one vertical handle from the junction of the vertical lip to the belly. Discoid raised base. Typical example of the shape, burnt black on most of the outside and on the inside of the rim. Unusual in that it had been repaired in antiquity and reused as a funerary offering.

E.B.F. - EL.P.

163   COOKING JAR

T.M. 27435   EUM-321: Rim sherd

COMPLEX, INCLUDING BARLEY, RESIN, OIL. RESINATED WINE. BARLEY WINE? A MIXED FERMENTED BEVERAGE?

Evans: See method of analysis.

LH III A2 (c. 1370-1340 B.C.)
Thebes, habitation deposit, site 13
Sherds submitted for analysis averaged between 4 an 6 centimeters in diameter.

Rim fragment of a typical ovoid cooking jar.

E.A.

T.M. 27435/EUM-321 only survived in sherd condition and could not be restored.

164   RHYTON

EUM-330: Base sherd

BARLEY BEER. WINE

Rhytons are considered by most Greek prehistoric archaeologists to have ritual connotations.

Evans: See method of analysis.

LH III A2 - LH III B (c. 1370-1190 B.C.)
Midea, Surface find, west of Megaron, Lower Terraces
H: 3 cm.; D: 2 cm.

Pierced base fragment of conical rhyton with pointed body. Slightly convex above the base. The entire fragment is covered with dark paint. FS 194.

G.W.

M.M. 24362 is a substitute for EUM-330, which only survived in sherd condition and could not be restored.

RHYTON

M.M. 24362

LH III A2 (c. 1370-1340 B.C.)
Mycenae, 1986, Koutsoubela Cemetery, tomb 1, Exc. No 4
H: 27.3 cm.; D: base 1.6 cm., rim 11.6 cm.

Conical, long body, pierced at the lower end. Large fat rounded lip, loop handle on the lip. Yellow slip. Red to brown paint. Linear decoration, the upper part with four thick zones of foliate bands and the lower part with thin bands. Monochrome base, lip and handle.

EL. P.

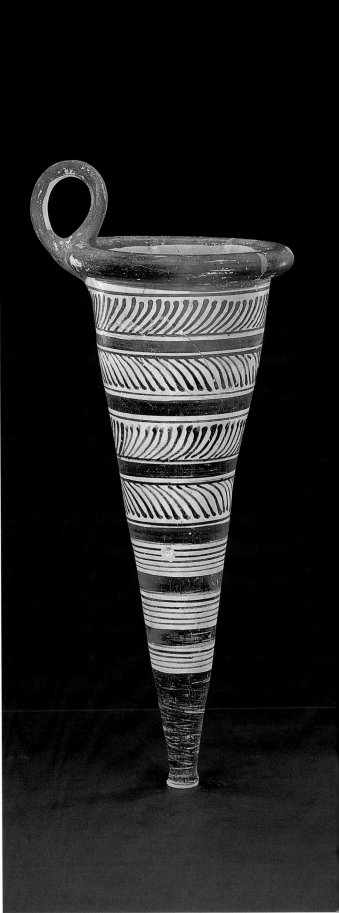

164

MINOAN STIRRUP JARS
WITH MIXED FERMENTED BEVERAGES

Discovering that two Minoan stirrup jars (EUM-269 and EUM-252), found at Kastelli, Chania, held resinated wine is important, and that it was possibly part of the proposed "mixed fermented beverage" makes the discovery of even greater significance.

DR. HOLLEY MARTLEW

165 STIRRUP JAR

EUM-269: Wall sherd

RESINATED WINE, POSSIBLY AS PART OF A MIXED FERMENTED BEVERAGE.

Mc Govern: See method of analysis.

LM III (c. 1390-1190 B.C.)
Chania, Kastelli hill
Sherds submitted for analysis averaged between 4 an 6 centimeters in diameter.

The type is similar to CH.M. 8267.

CH.M. 8267 is a substitute for EUM-252 and EUM-269, which only survived in sherd condition and could not be restored.

STIRRUP JAR

CH.M. 8267

LM III B (c. 1340-1190 B.C.)
Chania, Kastelli hill - Greek -
Swedish Excavations
H: 47 cm.; D: body 38 cm., base 14 cm.

Many pieces are missing; restored. Light brown, gritty clay; pale yellow slip. Red to orange paint. Kydonian workshop. The upper half of the body is decorated by a large octopus with its tentacles embracing the whole surface. Two groups of horizontal bands on the lower body. Many traces of burning outside.

M.A.-V.

165

166

166 STIRRUP JAR

EUM-252: Wall sherd

WEAK EVIDENCE FOR A MIXED FERMENTED BEVERAGE

Mc Govern: See method of analysis.

LM III (c. 1390-1190 B.C.)
Chania, Kastelli, Trench B
Sherds submitted for analysis averaged between 4 and 6 centimeters in diameter.

EUM-252 only survived in sherd condition and could not be restored.

MINOAN FUNERARY RITUAL

The vessels in this case illustrate the types of vessels found in contexts used for funerary ritual at the Late Minoan Cemetery of Armenoi, c. 1390-1190 B.C., in West Crete.

The presumed occurrence of the "mixed fermented beverage" of wine, barley beer and honey mead (the other possibility is that of successive use) taken into account with the foodstuffs reported in Section II, indicates that eating and drinking played an important role in Minoan funerary ritual (kylix EUM-111; jug EUM-121; cup EUM-122).

The main thrust of our results is that resinated wine was already a preferred beverage in Early Minoan times. Barley beer appears to have been produced then too, and may have been mixed with wine. Later, mead was added for good measure.

DR. HOLLEY MARTLEW   DR. PATRICK E. McGOVERN

THE CEMETERY OF ARMENOI, RETHYMNON

In certain areas of the Late Minoan Cemetery of Armenoi, pits (apothetes) were found, full of kylikes, cups, and cooking pots, all in fragments. This occurrence in connection with similar finds in corridors (dromoi) led us to the conclusion that special ceremonies took place which included the consumption of food and drink as part of funerary ritual. This theoretical approach was confirmed by the organic residue results.

DR. YANNIS TZEDAKIS

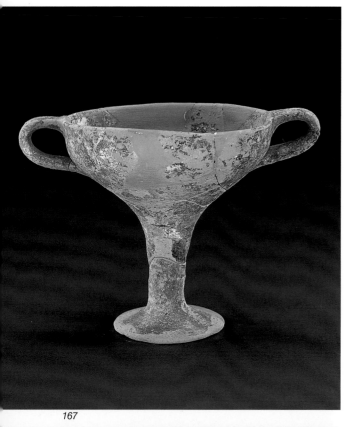

167

168

167 KYLIX

R.M. 17284 EUM-111: Wall sherd

RESINATED WINE, BARLEY BEER AS PART OF A MIXED FERMENTED BEVERAGE ALSO CONTAINING HONEY MEAD

Mc Govern: See method of analysis.

LM III A2 (c. 1370-1340 B.C.).
Ceremonial pit of Tomb 178
Sherds submitted for analysis averaged between 4 and 6 centimeters. From this context they averaged between 2 and 3 centimeters.

Fragments of the discoid base, the low stem and the globular body survives. Traces of black paint survive on the outside. White slip inside.

R.M. 3459 is a substitute for R.M. 17284 /EUM-111, which only survived in sherd condition and could not be restored.

KYLIX

R.M. 3459

LM III A2/B1 (c. 1370-1250 B.C.)
LM Cemetery of Armenoi, Tomb 159
H: 11.8 cm; D: rim 12 cm.

Mended from a large number of sherds. Red fabric, slip of same colour. Shallow conical body (FS 274), strap handles at the level of the rim, cylindrical stem of average height (5.2 cm.). Discoid base with hole at centre. Tin-plated surface. Imitation of Mycenaean tin-plated kylikes.

E.P.

168 JUG

R.M. 17340 EUM-121: Wall sherd

(POSSIBLY RESINATED) WINE AND ALSO THE POSSIBILITY OF THE PRESENCE FOR BARLEY BEER AND HONEY MEAD AS PART OF A MIXED FERMENTED BEVERAGE. THE ORGANIC EVIDENCE WAS NOT AS STRONG AS FOR THE KYLIX R.M. 17284/EUM-111.

Mc Govern: See method of analysis.

LM III A2 (c. 1370-1340 B.C.)

LM Cemetery of Armenoi, Ceremonial Pit of Tomb 178
Sherds submitted for analysis averaged between 4 and 6 centimeters in diameter. From this context they averaged 2 to 3 centimeters.

Only fragments of the discoid base and body survive.

R.M. 1592 is a substitute for R.M. 17340 /EUM-121, which only survived in sherd condition and could not be restored.

JUG

R.M. 1592

LM III B1 (c. 1340-1250 B.C.)
LM Cemetery of Armenoi. Tomb 10
H: 21.6 cm.; D: body 18.8 cm.

Restored from many fragments. Yellowish brown fabric and slip. Brown to black paint. Globular body with high neck. Rounded rim. Vertical handle, elliptical in section, from rim to shoulder. Flat base. Horizontal bands around the vessel from base to rim. Three wavy lines decorate the shoulder.

E.P.

169 CUP

R.M. 17337 EUM-122: Wall/base sherd

RESINATED WINE AND POSSIBLY BARLEY BEER AND HONEY MEAD AS PART OF A MIXED FERMENTED BEVERAGE. THE ORGANIC EVIDENCE WAS NOT AS STRONG AS FOR THE KYLIX R.M. 17284/EUM-111.

Mc Govern: See method of analysis.

LM III A2 (c. 1370-1340 B.C.)
LM Cemetery of Armenoi. Ceremonial pit of Tomb 178
Sherds submitted for analysis averaged between 4 and 6 centimeters in diameter. From this context they averaged between 2 and 3 cm.

Body fragments only survive.

R.M. 2228 is a substitute for R.M. 17337/ EUM-122, which only survived in sherd condition and could not be restored.

ONE-HANDLED CUP

R.M. 2228

LM III B2 (c. 1250-1190 B.C.)
LM Cemetery of Armenoi. Tomb 98
H: 6.01 cm.; D: rim 10.6 cm.

Complete. Grey fabric. Cream slip. Red to black paint. Semi-globular, shallow body with slightly flaring rim. Flattened vertical handle. Conical stem. Base is concave inside. Hastily decorated in trickle pattern.

E.P.

Shallow conical body. Tall stem ending in a discoid base with a concave bottom and cavity at the centre. Handles of circular section rising above the rim. Tin-plated surface.

E.P.

169

170 KYLIX

R.M. 3460

LM III A2/B1 (c. 1370-1250 B.C.)
LM Cemetery of Armenoi. Tomb 159
H: 20.1 cm.; D: base 8.5 cm., rim 18.5 cm.

Mended and restored. Ochre-brown fabric, slip of same colour, brown-black paint, covering the interior of the vase.

171 CONICAL CUP

R.M. 2214

LM III A (c. 1390-1340 B.C.)
LM Cemetery of Armenoi. Tomb 104
H: 4.5 cm.; D: rim 10.2 cm., base 3.1 cm.

Mended and restored. Raised base. Unpainted.

E.P.

171

70

172

172 MINIATURE HANDLELESS CUP

R.M. 1667

LM III B (c. 1340-1190 B.C.)
LM Cemetery of Armenoi. Tomb 24
H: 2.8 cm.

Intact. Brown-grey fabric, slip of same colour. Shallow conical body (FS 204). Rounded rim. Raised base. Unpainted.

E.P.

TSIKOUDIA AT THE MIDDLE MINOAN PALATIAL CENTRE
AT MONASTIRAKI, PETHYMNON

The Minoans drank resinated wine, barley beer and honey mead, possibly all together. The evidence points to the possibility of distilled wine spirits in Middle Minoan II, c. 1900-1700 B.C. Could the Minoans have invented the extremely popular Cretan fire water, tsikoudia? We think yes.

DR. HOLLEY MARTLEW

THE EXCAVATION

The discovery of a number of pithoi which contained carbonised remains of grapes and grape pits suggests that they were placed here for the fermentation/distillation process required to produce tsikoudia, the strong alcoholic beverage consumed on Crete. The statement by the excavator of the palace of Phaistos, together with the stalks and pits, were placed in a large pithos similar to a Minoan vessel and left for about two weeks, according to a practice with striking similarities to the Minoan, to allow fermentation to take place. They were then sealed in a bronze cooking pot. A second, empty vase was placed inside the first,

Doro Levi, that pithoi of similar content were discovered during his excavations there, is of particular importance. Although the technique of distillation presupposes expert knowledge and special vessels, the inhabitants of the settlement at Monastiraki seem to have discovered other ways of producing this strong alcoholic drink, which were probably similar to the traditional methods still used in Crete today.

An experiment was carried out to produce tsikoudia by the traditional method, without the use of special vessels or tools. The remains of the trodden grapes, and the pot was closed with a lid and sealed with dough/yeast to prevent the vapour from escaping. The pot was then placed on a slow fire, and the lid was cooled continuously with a piece of cloth dipped in cold water. When the vapour from the grapes/pits rose to the lid, it condensed and fell into the smaller vessel. The experiment produced tsikoudia of good quality.

PROF. ATHANASIA KANTA
University of Rethymnon, Crete

Food and Drink

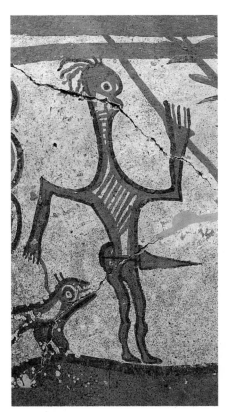

INTRODUCTION

The tests have enabled everyday Minoan/Mycenaean life to come alive in a way that was not possible before.

Pots like the ones shown in this section can give us a real sense of life's carrying on in ways with which we can identify. The years that separate us vanish, as we see these people doing things that we do every day. Preparation of food and drink. Serving of food and drink. Choosing the vessel to put on the table, and making a conscious decision of what to serve in it. We do these things.

Four thousand years may have passed, but we can meet with the Minoans and the Myceaneans "at table" - now - in a way that we could never do before, because we now have a clearer picture of how they cooked, what they brewed, and what they ate and drank.

DR. HOLLEY MARTLEW

VESSELS OF MULTIPLE USES...
I. APODOULOU (c. 1900-1700 B.C.)

Only in the hands of a clumsy cook would a pot have been used just once, and the normal practice of repeated uses would be likely to have involved the preparation of many different foods. A tripod cooking pot (EUM-22) from this site had organic residues which indicated a variety of possible uses. These were ordinary cooking (plant and animal products); production of aromatics (oil of iris and olive oil); beer brewing (an acid that was found in beer brewing vats in pre-dynastic Egypt).

DR. HOLLEY MARTLEW   PROF. DR. CURT W. BECK

173 TRIPOD COOKING POT

EUM-22: Wall/base sherd

RUMINANT ANIMALS (COWS; SHEEP; GOATS). PLANT MATERIAL. OLIVE OIL
These indicate that meat and vegetables must have been prepared in this vessel

THE POSSIBILITY OF OIL OF IRIS. OLIVE OIL
The organic residue results indicate that aromatic oils/unguents might have been produced in this pot

BEER BREWING?
This vessel contained phosphoric acid. This acid has been found in pre-dynastic (earlier than 3000 B.C.) beer brewing vats in Hierakonapolis, Upper Egypt. As this acid is a component of all living cells, a definite conclusion cannot be drawn, but the vessel also contained dimethyl oxalate, which is commonly thought to indicate beer

MM II B (c. 1700 B.C.)
Apodoulou, Room 9, a storage area under the stairs
Sherds submitted for analysis averaged between 4 and 6 centimeters in diameter.

Box-shaped vessel. The type normally had a small, pulled-out spout. It is known to have been in use between MM II and LM III A/B (c. 1900-1190 B.C.).

HM F.55 1822b is a substitute for EUM-22, which only survived in sherd condition and could not be restored.

TRIPOD COOKING POT

H.M. F. 55 1822b

MM II-III (c. 1900-1600 B.C.)
Palace of Phaistos, Room LX, waiting room
H: 22 cm.; D: rim 21 cm.

Restored. Yellowish-brown fabric. Box-shaped vessel. It has a small, pulled-out spout and a boss on the side opposite the spout, below the narrow rim. Two horizontal/coil in section handles are set on the shoulder. The base is flat and the legs are oval in section.

A.K.-E.K.

173

II. THEBES

The second site is at Thebes, in an area near the palace, on the Mainland. The artefacts date to the mid-13th century B.C. According to Evans who analysed the Theban vessels, they gave him the impression of being used for different things at different times. The incongruity of the results is readily apparent. An example is the bowl EUM-315: barley beer and wine; figs; olive oil, pulses, meat. It is perfectly reasonable to say that the evidence suggests that this deep painted bowl was used to serve drink on some occasions and food on others. Uses like this are logical, and it is important to realise that never before has anyone been able actually to point to an artefact from Bronze Age Greece and to say on the basis of its residual contents, that here is a vessel which had a specific use or uses.

Results like this make our knowledge of the Bronze Age in Greece, much more immediate. It is the detail that is important and which gives them a meaning beyond that of the purely scientific.

DR. HOLLEY MARTLEW

174 DEEP BOWL

EUM-315: Wall sherd

TARTARIC ACID. BARLEY. FERMENTATION WINE. BEER? BARLEY WINE? BARLEY BEER AND WINE? A MIXED FERMENTED BEVERAGE?

OLIVE OIL. PULSES? MEAT? FIG?

Evans: See method of analysis.

LH III B/C (c. 1200 B.C.)
Thebes, room with evidence for ceremonial and working activities, site 13
Sherds submitted for analysis averaged between 4 and 6 centimeters in diameter.

Only a wall fragment from the lower part of the body of a painted bowl that appeared to be deep survived. The body was monochrome inside with brown-red paint, unevenly applied.

E.A.

T.M. 1961 is a substitute for EUM-315, which only survived in sherd condition and could not be restored.

DEEP BOWL

T.M. 1961

LH III B2 (c. 1250-1185 B.C.)
Thebes, Linear B Tablet Archive, site 10
H: (pres.) 11.5 cm.; D: base 5.7 cm, rim 14.5 cm.

Restored with one handle completed. Brown fabric. Light brown slip. Deep hemispherical bowl, with slightly spreading lip, and ring base. Horizontal cylindrical handles. Decorated in brown paint. Outside, a band at the lower part of the belly. In the decorative zone of the handles, three continuous stemmed spirals on each side. Three blobs on the handles. Inside, a broad band around the lip and three concentric circles at the bottom.

E.A.

175 COOKING JAR

T.M. 26990   EUM-317: Wall sherd

PULSES? RESIN (WINE?) MEAT. OLIVE OIL

Evans: See method of analysis.

LH III (c. 1390-1165 B.C.)
Thebes, habitation deposit, site 13
H: 22 cm.; D: rim 16.2 cm., base 9.2 cm.

Coarse red-brown fabric. About 3/4 of

175

174

the vessel survive. It has an ovoid body, high spreading lip, vertical cylindrical handle, and a raised discoid base. In the centre of the bottom, is a hole that had been drilled after the vase was fired. This may indicate some special use of the pot for preparing food or beverage, or it may be connected to a secondary use of the vessel. Clear traces of burning on the upper part outside and on the lower part inside. A sherd was taken for analysis prior to restoration.

E.A.

176 COOKING JAR

T.M. 27435 EUM-320: Base sherd

BEER. MEAT. OIL. COMPLEX

Evans: See method of analysis.

LH III B/C (c. 1200 B.C.)
Thebes, room with evidence for ceremonial and working activities, site 13
H: (pres.) 7 cm.; D: (max) 28 cm.
Sherds submitted for analysis averaged between 4 and 6 centimeters in diameter.

Part of the bottom of the jar survived, and has been mended. The base is broken off. Outside, the surface is cracked and flaking. Inside, there are clear wheel marks. Some sherds are burned. A sherd was taken for analysis before the restoration that was possible, was carried out.

E.A.

T.M. 1951 is a substitute for T.M. 27435/ EUM-320, which only survived in sherd condition and could not be restored.

177

COOKING JAR

T.M. 1951

LH III B2 (c. 1250-1185 B.C.)
Thebes, Linear B Tablets Archive, site 10
H: (pres.) 19.8 cm.; D: rim 12.4 cm., base 7.7 cm.

Restored. Light brown coarse fabric. Ovoid body, high spreading lip, and discoid base. Two cylindrical handles from rim to shoulder. Undecorated and rough.

E.A.

177 PITHOS

EUM-308: Base sherd

FERMENTED PRODUCT. BEER? MEAT. OLIVE OIL. PULSES. CEREAL

Evans: See method of analysis.

LH III B1 (c. 1340-1250 B.C.)
Thebes, storeroom, site 13
Sherds submitted for analysis averaged between 4 and 6 centimeters in diameter.

The vessel had a flat base and piriform body. Only a small area of the pithos survived. Clear traces of burning at the bottom.

E.A.

176

THE DISCOVERY OF RETSINA IN BRONZE AGE GREECE

The organic residue result from the cooking jar M.M. 24350/EUM-68 which was found in the destruction level of a cult context, c. 1250 B.C. at the palace of Mycenae, the Room with the Fresco, was wine with pine resin. So the Greek tradition of retsina, wine with pine resin, can now be traced to the Greek Bronze Age.

The organic residue result from the cooking jar EUM-68 shows that retsina was used in a ritual context at Mycenae, during the lifetime of that palace. The organic residue result from the cooking jar EUM-82 found in a domestic context at Thebes indicates that retsina was being produced and drunk by ordinary people after the major destructions of the Mainland palaces.

Organic residue analysis has indicated the possibility of resinated wine at Myrtos Phournou Koryphe at the end of Early Minoan (c. 2200 B.C.). A clear organic residue result for resinated wine was found in a vessel from Monastiraki, dating to the Middle Minoan II Period (c. 1900-1700 B.C.). Clear results were also obtained at the site of Splanzia, Chania, in the Late Minoan I Period (c. 1600-1425 B.C.), and from the Late Minoan Cemetery of Armenoi (c. 1390-1190 B.C.).

Different kinds of resin can be and were used to resinate wine, the most common of which was terebinth. In all the examples cited above, analysis was either not able to specify which resin had been used, or the result indicated terebinth resin (Apodoulou, MM II, c. 1700 B.C.). At Mycenae (c. 1250 B.C.), and later at Thebes (LH III C middle, c. 1130-1090 B.C.), it was possible, and the resin was pine.

DR. HOLLEY MARTLEW

Subsequent to the opening of the Exhibition, Beck and McGovern reported the positive identification of "wine flavoured with Greek pine vesin" in tripod vessel EUM-30 (Palatial Centre at Monastiraki, see p. 144). The report also identified the presence of castor oil and vegetable oils in EUM-30. This research project has therefore traced retsina to Minoan Crete c. 1700 B.C.

178 COOKING JAR

M.M. 24350   EUM-68: Wall/base sherd
Exc. No 69-667

RETSINA: WINE WITH PINE RESIN
A clear indication that retsina was produced in Bronze Age Greece

Beck: See method of analysis.

LH III B (c. 1250 B.C.)
Mycenae, Cult Centre, Room 31, the Room with the Fresco. Sealed area of the fill placed in the Room with the Fresco
H: 34 cm.; D: 38 cm.

Red gritty clay. Cooking jar with a heavily globular body, collar neck and two horizontal handles on the shoulder. Heavy burning outside except in the areas that would have been protected from the flame, i.e. under the rim and above the handle. One handle is very burnt, but the other shows only a tiny bit of burning. A sherd was taken for analysis prior to restoration.

E.B.F.

179 COOKING JAR

EUM-82: Wall sherd

WINE WITH PINE RESIN

Beck: See method of analysis.

LH III C middle (c. 1130-1090 B.C.)
Thebes, habitation deposit, site 11
Sherds submitted for analysis averaged between 4 and 6 centimeters in diameter.

The sherd appears to come from a typical ovoid cooking jar which would have had a collar neck and two handles.

E.A.

178

179

M.M. 985 is a substitute for EUM-82, which only survived in sherd condition and could not be restored.

COOKING JAR

M.M. 985

LH III B (c. 1250 B.C.)
Mycenae, 1984. Room M5
H: 18.3 cm.; D: rim 16.1 cm., belly 19.3 cm., base 7.4 cm.

Restored from many pieces. Gray clay. Cooking vessel, crater, with two vertical coil handles that extend from the junction of the upright collar to the belly. Discoid raised base.

EL.P.

THE ROOM WITH THE FRESCO AT THE CULT CENTRE, MYCENAE.

FOOD AND DRINK IN A RITUAL SETTING

The tableau has been created to show food and drink in an original setting. There is the added interest that it is a ritual setting.

Organic residue results were obtained from three vessels found near the altar (stirrup jar, amphora and tripod cooking pot) as well as from other vessels that came from outside the area which is reproduced in the Exhibition. This includes other vessels found in the room, shattered vases found in the hearth, vessels found in the shrine/sanctuary store behind the Room with the Fresco, and vessels found in the fill.

This group of vessels was the most varied of any group that was tested from a single location. It included decorated vases (amphorae and stirrup jars), plain vessels (bowls and a kylix), and coarse cooking pots (a tripod cooking pot and examples of the most common Mycenaean cooking utensil, the cooking jar).

It is unique to the project that results were obtained from every one of the vessels from the Cult Centre which were submitted for analysis.

It is important to take note of the other artefacts which were found near the altar, and of the fresco itself. It is a rare opportunity to enjoy a whole range of things: the types of food and drink that were present, the vessels that contained them, and a wide assortment of other artefacts. These included an Egyptian faience plaque that must have been an heirloom, and three outstanding ivory pieces including an ivory lion that is certainly one of the more beautiful and appealing *objet d'art* produced in the Greek Bronze Age.

THE SUMMARY

Whether the contents of the vessels were used for cult meals or offerings, the importance of these results, positive indications of what types of food and drink were used and/or consumed in the Cult Centre at the palace of Mycenae in the middle of the 13th century B.C., can hardly be over-estimated.

THEY HAD WINE... AND SOME OF IT WAS RETSINA

Next to the altar in the Room with the Fresco, 2 vessels contained wine: a small stirrup jar (M.M. 24335/EUM-162) and a very large amphora (M.M. 24349/EUM-151).

A much smaller decorated amphora (M.M. 24347/EUM-153) from the Room with the Fresco, contained wine.

A decorated stirrup jar (M.M. 24345/EUM-157) from the fill in the Room with the Fresco, contained wine.

A decorated domestic stirrup jar (M.M. 21785/EUM-161) which came from the shrine/sanctuary store behind the Room with the Fresco, contained wine.

A plain kylix (M.M. 24329/EUM-159) found in the shrine/sanctuary store behind the Room with the Fresco contained wine.

In all the above cases it was not possible to determine whether the wine was resinated.

A cooking jar (M.M. 24350/EUM-68) found in the Room with the Fresco, but outside the area of the tableau, did produce a result of true retsina, wine with pine resin.

THEY PREPARED FOOD...

A large tripod cooking pot (M.M. 24353/EUM-152) contained meat, olive oil and lentils.

Interestingly, a cooking jar (Exc. No 69-673/ EUM-156) from the fill gave the same organic residue results as the tripod cooking pot EUM-152 which was found near the altar: meat, olive oil and lentils.

The sherds from two cooking jars that were found

shattered in the decomposed burnt pottery in the hearth appeared also to have been used for food preparation. EUM-163 contained meat and olive oil. EUM-164 contained olive oil and wine, and possibly fish. This was the only Minoan/Mycenaean organic residue result that indicated marine food. (There was one other marine result, but it dated to the Neolithic period. This sherd was from a bowl, R.M. 1003/EUM-138, found in the Neolithic Cave of Gerani in West Crete: see Section II.)

OLIVE OIL...

A decorated stemmed bowl (M.M. 24318) from the Room with the Fresco gave a result of olive oil.

HONEY...

The shallow angular bowl M.M. 24343/EUM-158 which came from the shrine/sanctuary store behind the Room with the Fresco, gave this result.

DR. HOLLEY MARTLEW

THE EXCAVATION

The northwest section of the Cult Centre comprised a group of four rooms of which the central one was dominated by the Fresco from which it takes its name. In the main period of usage in the mid 13th century B.C., the Fresco would have been visible as one entered the main room from an anteroom, seen through wooden columns that stood at either end of a central hearth of unusual type. Immediately on the left of the entrance to the room was a clay bathtub which may have served for the ritual cleansing of those entering the room.

In front of the Fresco was an altar 60 cm. high with three small hearths near the outer edge. Beside and left of the altar and the painted doorway that formed part of the Fresco itself, was the doorway into a small room which was used both as an inner sanctum and for the storage of dedications.

On the floor of the main room lay a mass of objects: above all, pottery of many different types. Immediately in front of the altar was a group of nine pots, seven for storage and two for cooking. With them was a large lead vessel in which was resting part of an Egyptian plaque that had been carefully split. At the south end of the altar lay tumbled a group of rich items: a Cretan stone bowl; two handsome ivories, the pommel from a sword and a couchant lion originally mounted on a sceptre or on a piece of furniture. More puzzling was the quantity found throughout the room of small stone conuli whose function is still a matter of fierce discussion.

A short distance in front of the altar there lay on the floor the ivory head of a presumably male figure. This had probably fallen off the altar where, mounted on a wooden armature or frame draped in cloth, it would have served as a cult object, representing a deity. In the fallen debris to the left of the altar, over the raised dais in the corner, there was a miniature hydria which had probably rested on the surface of the altar holding some kind of offering.

Not long after the room was completed, the whole Cult Centre was damaged, probably by earthquake, and this complex was "mothballed": the Fresco itself was whitewashed and a filling of fine soil laid over the cult items and dedications. Over this, along the sides of the room where such items were known to lie, a series of large slabs were tidily laid. Thus the whole complex remained out of use, though apparently partially visible, until this section of the Citadel of Mycenae was destroyed by fire at the end of the 13th century B.C.

DR. ELIZABETH B. FRENCH
Former Director,
British School at Athens

FINDS FROM THE ROOM:		
Pottery:		
Drinking vessels:	9 kylikes	2 cups
Pouring vessels:	4 jugs	1 "askos"
	3 ladles	1 spouted cup
	1 funnel	
Mixing:	2 stemmed bowls	
Storage:	1 vat (of unbaked clay)	
	3 large jars (1*)	
	2 medium jars (2*)	
	3 small piriform jars (1*)	
	4 small stirrup jars (2*)	
	3 "alabastra"	
Cooking:	1 tripod cooking pot (1*)	
	1 cooking pot jar	
	1 cooking pot jug (1*)	
Miniatures:	4 hydriae	1 bowl (1*)
	1 kylix	* = from area in front of Fresco
Metal:	1 Lead vessel	
	5 Bronze arrowheads etc.	
Ivory:	Male head	Couchant lion
	Sword pommel	
Bone:	Hilt plate	Pin
Stone:	Cretan bowl	
	Agate lentoid seal	
	27 Conuli	2 pounders
Waste materials		
Beads, small	11	
Faience	Egyptian plaque	

THE FRESCO: AN INTERPRETATION

One of the most complete of Mycenaean wall paintings comes from the area of the joint Helleno-British excavations at Mycenae itself. Found *in situ* on the back wall of Room 31, it and the platform in front of it should be considered as a single conception representing an architectural setting with three female figures on two different levels. The painting, although competent, shows signs of haste and may have been intended to be part of a larger composition never completed. Part of the adjacent south wall was covered with plain plaster.

Area A represents a blank doorway framed with rosettes (similar decoration is also known from the doorway of a chamber tomb at Mycenae).

Area B shows, on the left, a cloaked female figure holding a sword with the point down who is facing another woman who is holding a staff. Between them are two small naked male figures in mid-air, one red and the other black. These figures are framed in a room with a brick or tile floor and a ceiling supported by two spiral columns reminiscent of the columns and their capitals on the facade of the Treasury of Atreus.

Area C represents a room with one column on the left. Within is a standing female with her hands raised, holding sheaves of corn (also to be seen on an ivory pyxis lid in Mycenaean style from Syria). The yellow tail and forepaws are all that remain of a lion accompanying her.

Area D is a platform or altar which was once completely plastered and probably painted all over. The decoration of "horns" and the painted ends of beams on the side suggest that it represents the exterior of a building. On top at the edge were three circular depressions with traces of burning and a square hole which may originally have held a post.

All three figures are dressed in the kind of clothes familiar to us from Minoan and Mycenaean illustrations on gold rings, sealstones, ivory carvings (such as the "ivory trio" from Mycenae), pottery and wall paintings. The detail of clothing is particularly clear in wall paintings at Akrotiri on Thera.

The left-hand woman has an elaborate cloak with braid around its border. It was probably woven in wool, and on the inside flokati is indicated by the threads down the front of the cloak. The red blobs below the hems represent the tied warp ends of the material. Similar cloaks can be seen in the miniature wall paintings at Akrotiri. On her wrists are bracelets with a single sealstone. Her feet are bare. There are traces of her hair at the top and back of her cloak, but her face and upper hairstyle are missing. She wears a white chemise or top with two black bands on the sleeves.

She faces another slightly smaller female figure wearing a typical wrapover skirt of the kind often called "flounced" in grey/blue, white and red material. A red bodice is edged with a blue, white and yellow braid. The bodice leaves her breasts bare. In the worn upper half of this painting traces of her face, hair and "polos" headdress can be made out with difficulty.

The third lower figure is wearing a white chemise or top with two black bands on the sleeve - the same pattern as worn by the woman with the cloak. Over this she has a length of a grey/blue material wrapped around her and tied with a knot over her right shoulder (like a modern beach sarong) as in the wall painting of the "priestess" in the West House at Akrotiri. She too

has sealstone bracelets. On her head she wears a "polos" hat with a central plume or flower, of the kind to be seen in a wall painting at Pylos and often associated with sphinxes or figurines. Her feet are bare.

We cannot tell whether these figures are intended to represent deities or mortals. Parallels have been drawn with Classical goddesses such as Athena Polias for the figure with the sword and with Demeter for the small figure with the corn sheaves. The blank doorway has been interpreted as the entrance to the underworld or to the adjacent room with the female figure. It is not even certain whether the two small male figures, whatever they represent, were part of the original composition or added later.

DIANA WARDLE
Archaeologist

CONULI FROM THE ROOM WITH THE FRESCO

Conuli are the most enigmatic of all Mycenaean finds. In the form of small cones, bicones or elaborations of the cone they were made originally (in the 15th century B.C.) from clay (and still made in clay later in provincial areas) but later from stone, generally steatite. This could be a plain mottled black/grey or an attractive red or pale green. It was once thought that they were used as spindle whorls, but the large number found precludes this. The wear patterns around the central hole indicate that often they were suspended on strings which, through long usage, caused damage. No satisfactory explanation of their function has yet been put forward, though use as buttons, dress weights or curtain weights has been suggested. They can be divided into four types on the basis of the shape.

The small group from the east end of the Room with the Fresco, despite being in a good functional context, gives no indication of purpose. Moreover, the group is in no way homogeneous except in being relatively well-preserved. The only point of interest is the fact that the total number of conuli found in the Room with the Fresco Complex (with its ancillary areas) is surprisingly large, even without including the large group associated with the Figure.

DR. ELIZABETH B.FRENCH
Former Director,
British School at Athens

IVORIES FROM THE CULT CENTRE, MYCENAE

The Citadel House Area, within the Cult Centre of Mycenae, provides us with finished ivories of outstanding quality and valuable new insights into the craft of Mycenaean ivory carving. Mycenaean ivories carved in the round (or substantially so) are very rare. The lion (Cat. No. 204) is by far the largest attested; it is also one of the finest ivories that survive from the Aegean Bronze Age. The original function of the lion is, however, uncertain. The mortise indicates that it was meant to be attached to a support or base made of another material, presumably wood, now lost. This may have been a specially constructed plinth, designed to show off the lion to best effect. One cannot, however, rule out the possibility that the lion originally decorated a piece of wooden furniture. In either case, the use of the lion in the Cult Centre –whether as a furnishing in the room or as an offering– may have been secondary.

The well-known ivory head of a young man (Cat. No. 205) found nearby, is equally hard to interpret. The head evidently once belonged to a statuette, since provision is made for attachment to a wooden support running vertically through the head. There is, however, no proof that this statuette served as a cult image in the room, or indeed that the head remained attached to its support until the time of destruction. Thus, the head (alone) could also represent secondary use, e.g. as commentators' seeing it as a Near Eastern import. Unique pieces are always hard to assess, but detailed comparisons with the lion strongly support the view that the head is indeed a Mycenaean product.

With the ivory pommel (Cat. No. 203), detached from its sword, we are on more certain ground; swords with ivory pommels are most frequently attested in burials of the Early Mycenaean period, especially in the Shaft Graves at Mycenae. Relatively few are known from later Mycenaean contexts, although one should note the recent discovery of three fine pommels (one each of ivory, alabaster, and lapis lacedaemonicus) found in a niche in the Megaron at Midea. It thus seems reasonable to interpret the Citadel House pommel as an offering, a view which is perhaps further supported by the iconography of the Fresco.

From the adjacent storeroom 32, along with a terracotta figurine known as the Lozenge Lady, were recovered further ivories, including hilt-plates detached from a Naue II sword and a small knob or pommel perhaps from a dagger. They were found in association with ivory workshop material, comprising workers' waste, mistakes or rejects, and partially finished pieces. These items, together with comparable material, were recovered from an ivory workshop. This must have been located somewhere at Mycenae, although not necessarily in the Cult Centre itself. Whether the pieces served as dedications or were simply stored for their salvage value remains an open question.

DR. OLGA KRZYSZKOWSKA
Institute of Classical Studies
University of London, U.K.

180

180   STIRRUP JAR

M.M. 24335   EUM-162: Wall sherd   Exc. No 68-582

WINE. OLIVE OIL
It is presumed the oil was used to seal the wine

Evans: See method of analysis.

LH III B (c. 1250 B.C.)
Mycenae, Cult Centre, Room 31, the Room
with the Fresco.
H: 16 cm.; D: base 7 cm.

Pinkish buff clay. Small piriform stirrup
jar. The shape is common in the late
13th and early 12th centuries B.C. both
on the Mainland of Greece and as an
export, particularly to the Eastern
Mediterranean. This version is, as here,
often found paired with the small
globular one. A sherd was taken for
analysis prior to restoration.

E.B.F

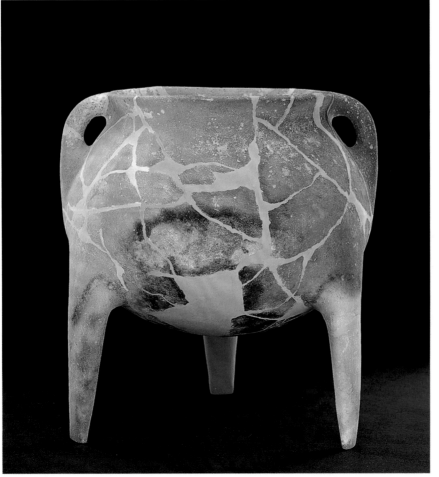

181

181   TRIPOD COOKING POT

M.M. 24353   EUM-152: Base/wall sherd
Exc. No 68-486

MEAT. OLIVE OIL. LENTILS?

Evans: See method of analysis.

LH III B (c. 1250 B.C.)
Mycenae, Cult Centre, Room 31, the Room
with the Fresco
H: 41 cm.; D: rim 27.3 cm.

Large example of FS 320 with distinct
marks of burning on the sides away
from the surviving handle. Coarse
orange-yellow clay, which according to
Dr. Peter Day, was almost certainly
imported from Aegina (report for the
Exhibition). A sherd was taken for
analysis prior to restoration.

E.B.F.

182   COOKING JUG

M.M. 24324   Exc. No 68-487

LH III B (c. 1250 B.C.)
Mycenae, Cult Centre, Room 31, the Room
with the Fresco
H: 25 cm.; D: (max) 21.5 cm., base 7.8 cm.

Almost complete. Pink gritty fabric with
buff core; smoothed. Typical ovoid
cooking jug with high collar and one
handle (FS 105). Burning outside on
base and on the side opposite the handle.

E.B.F.

182

183   AMPHORA

M.M. 24349   EUM-151: Wall sherd   Exc. No 68-488

WINE. OLIVE OIL
It is presumed that the oil was used to seal the
wine

Evans: See method of analysis.

LH III B (c. 1250 B.C.)
Mycenae, Cult Centre, Room 31 the Room
with the Fresco
H: 54 cm.; D: rim 14.4 cm., body: (max) 43 cm.

Pink gritty clay with yellow slip. Large and
unusual storage vessel. FS 69 with twisted
handles. As well as linear decoration
there are two crossed circles, one on each
shoulder. (FM 41:21). It has been
suggested that at Akrotiri on Thera this
type of decoration may have been a code
to the contents of the vessel. A sherd was
taken for analysis prior to restoration.

E.B.F.

183

184 COOKING JAR

EUM-164: Wall/base sherd Exc. Unit 109

OLIVE OIL. WINE. FISH?

Evans: See method of analysis.

LH III B (c. 1250 B.C.)
Mycenae, Cult Centre, Room 31, the Room with the Fresco, in the lower part of the destruction level. It was found in a hearth, in a group of brilliant orange and yellow shattered and decomposed burnt coarse pottery
Sherds submitted for analysis averaged between 4 and 6 centimeters in diameter. This sherd was 3 centimeters maximum.

Coarse gritty red clay. The sherds appeared to have been from an ovoid jar that was a typical cooking shape from at least the late 13th until the middle of the 11th century B.C., at Mycenae.

E.B.F.

185 COOKING JAR

EUM-163: Wall sherd Exc. Unit 111

OLIVE OIL. MEAT. COMPLEX

Evans: See method of analysis.

Mid LH III B (c. 1250 B.C.)
Mycenae, Cult Centre, Room 31, the Room with the Fresco, in the lower part of the destruction level. The remains of this vessel were found in the hearth, in a group of brilliant orange and yellow decomposed burnt coarse pottery
Sherds submitted for analysis averaged between 4 and 6 centimeters in diameter. This sherd was 3 centimeters maximum.

Coarse gritty red clay. The sherds appeared to have been from an ovoid jar that was a typical cooking shape from at least the late 13th until the middle of the 11th century B.C., at Mycenae.

E.B.F.

184-185

Reconstruction of the Room with the Fresco, area near the altar.

186 PIRIFORM JAR

M.M. 24338   Exc. No 68-489

LH III B (c. 1250 B.C.)
Mycenae, Cult Centre, Room 31, the Room
with the Fresco
H: 11.8 cm.; D: rim 8.8 cm.

Fine buff clay. Unbroken small two-
handled jar with piriform body, the first
known example of a type which gradually
takes over from the three-handled version
and continues into the Geometric period.
In addition to the usual linear decoration
there is a zone of cross-hatched lozenges
(FM 73:k) between the handles. The
small piriform jar, with the alabastron,
is thought to have served as a container
for thicker unguents.

E.B.F.

187 STIRRUP JAR

M.M. 24340   Exc. No 68-495

LH III B (c. 1250 B.C.)
Mycenae, Cult Centre, Room 31, the Room
with the Fresco
H: 15 cm.; D: (max) 13.3 cm.

Pinkish clay with cream slip. Small
globular jar (FS 173) with typical linear
decoration (including concentric circles
under the base), flower (FM 18:128) in
the shoulder zone and a spaced zig-zag
(FM 61:3) in the body zone. This type is
often, as here, paired with a small piriform
stirrup jar like M.M. 24338 above.

E.B.F.

188 AMPHORA

M.M. 24330   Exc. No 68-496

LH III B (c. 1250 B.C.)
Mycenae, Cult Centre, Room 31, the Room
with the Fresco
H: 23.8 cm.; D: rim 5.6 cm., max 18 cm.

Yellowish buff slightly gritty clay with
greenish slip. Unusual example of a
simple linear amphora with very narrow
neck.

E.B.F.

189 MINIATURE CONICAL SPOUTED BOWL

M.M. 24339   Exc. No 68-581

LH III B (c. 1250 B.C.)
Mycenae, Cult Centre, Room 31, the Room
with the Fresco
H: 5.4 cm.; D: rim 11 cm.

Fine orange clay. Small vessel, almost complete, with linear decoration only. Room
31 contained four miniature hydriae
and this bowl; other such miniatures
were found in Room 32, in storage in
Area 36 and in the surrounding debris.
Their exact function cannot be determined.

E.B.F.

190 MINIATURE HYDRIA

M.M. 16488   Exc. No 68-494

LH III B (c. 1250 B.C.)
Mycenae, Cult Centre, Room 31, the Room
with the Fresco, over the altar
H: 6.8 cm.; D: (max) 6.8 cm.

Fine buff clay. Typical example of this
version of the small hand-made vessels,
FS 126; baggy globular body, rounded
base and short flaring neck; a vertical
handle rises from shoulder to slightly
above the rim; two horizontal loop lug
handles on the upper body. Linear
decoration only. Four examples of the
hydria type occur in Room 31 and none
of the jug type.

E.B.F.

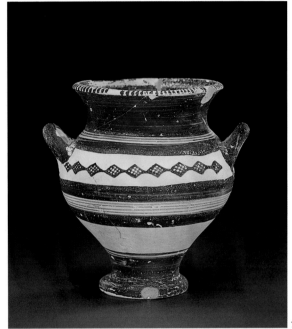

186

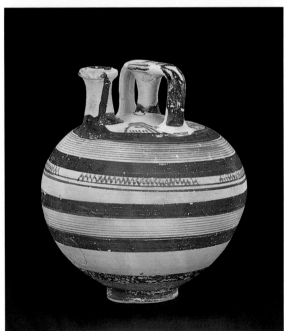

187

188

189

191 JAR

M.M. 24346 Exc. No 68-497

LH III B (c. 1250 B.C.)
Mycenae, Cult Centre, Room 31, the Room
with the Fresco
H: 19.1 cm.; D: rim 11 cm.,
body (ext.) 28.6 cm.

Yellow buff clay with creamy slip. Upper
section of a vessel from the bottom of
the pile; lower body possibly corroded
by contents; sharply offset neck on
globular body, flaring rounded rim;
strap handle from rim to shoulder.
Linear decoration only.

E.B.F.

192 MINIATURE JUG

M.M. 16593 Exc. No 69-523

LH III B (c. 1250 B.C.)
Mycenae, Cult Centre, from the doorway
between the Room with the Fresco (Room
31) and Room 32, "The Shrine"
H: 8.3 cm.; D: (max) 7 cm.

Pinkish buff clay. Miniature hand-made
jug (one type of FS 126) with baggy
globular body, narrow neck and
rounded base; vertical handle from
shoulder to rim. Four sketchy stemmed
spirals pendant from band at base of
neck; accessorial linear decoration. Two
examples of the jug type occur in Room
32 and none of the hydria type.

E.B.F.

193 STIRRUP JAR

M.M. 16596 Exc. No 69-524

LH III B (c. 1250 B.C.)
Mycenae, Cult Centre, from the doorway
between the Room with the Fresco (Room
31) and Room 32, "The Shrine"
H: 10.5 cm.; D: (max) 10.2 cm.

Fine pale buff clay. Typical globular
stirrup jar of FS 171. Multiple stem
decoration in the shoulder zone and
small vertical parallel chevrons continuously in the body zone; concentric
circles under the base.

E.B.F.

191

192

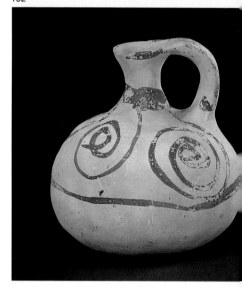

194 CONULUS

M.M. 18263 Exc. No 68-1095

LH III B (c. 1250 B.C.)
Mycenae, Cult Centre, Room 31, the Room
with the Fresco
H: 1.5 cm.; D: 2.7 cm.; W: 10.2 gm.

Dark green steatite. Large conical example
of type 3: convex base with flat facet
around the counter-sink; conical flanges;
short cylindrical shank with flat top. All
surfaces highly polished, but the shape
in general is slightly irregular. Manufacture marks are more visible on the
flange and shank than elsewhere. The
counter-sink and flat facet are irregularly
formed but highly polished. An unusual
combination of sloppy shape and fine
surface treatment.

E.B.F. - S.D.

190

193

4-198

for chips on base edge and "chewed" top. Tall conical shape, a bit tall for its size; flat base, flush hole, rounded top; lower part well preserved but the top is rather battered.

E.B.F. - S.D.

196 CONULUS

M.M. 18242   Exc. No 68-1092

Mid LH III B (c. 1250 B.C.)
Mycenae Cult Centre, Room 31, the Room with the Fresco
H: 1.2 cm.; D: 1.9 cm.; W: 6 gm.

Dark red veined steatite. Small and well-preserved conical example of type 1; flat base, bevelled edge (some slight chipping), flat/round top. Unusual base edge bevel, well-made top, some vertical striations on the side.

E.B.F. - S.D.

197 CONULUS

M.M. 18292   Exc. No 68-1093

Mid LH III B (c. 1250 B.C.)
Mycenae, Cult Centre, Room 31, the Room with the Fresco
H: 2.1 cm.; D: 3.1 cm.; W: 23 gm.

Mottled olive grey steatite. Big fat conical example of Warren type 1; flat base, flush hole, rounded top. Unusually high surface polish even though rather battered and scratched.

E.B.F. - S.D.

198 CONULUS

M.M. 18170   Exc. No 68-890

Mid LH III B (c. 1250 B.C.)
Mycenae, Cult Centre, Room 31, the Room with the Fresco
H: (est.) 1 cm.; D: 1.8 cm.; W: 3.5 gm.

Olive green steatite. Partially preserved hybrid version of Warren types 2 and 3 with the shank broken and possibly reworked. The base is slightly convex with a big deep counter-sinking, sharp edge and conical flange.

E.B.F. - S.D.

195 CONULUS

M.M. 18302   Exc. No 68-1096

LH III B (c. 1250 B.C.)
Mycenae, Cult Centre, Room 31, the Room with the Fresco
H: 1.8 cm.; D: 2.1 cm.; W: 9 gm.

Dark red steatite. Small but typical example of Warren type 1, whole except

199 ARROWHEADS

. . . .

M.M. 18295 Exc. No 68-1090

LH III B (c. 1250 B.C.)

Mycenae, Cult Centre, Room 31, the Room with the Fresco

L: 4 cm.; W: (max) 1.2 cm.; Thickness: 0.1 cm.

Group of six dart-shaped arrowheads of thin flat sheet metal, probably bronze, of a type known from elsewhere on the site of Mycenae. All six are corroded together into a bundle, but no trace of the original binding survives.

E.B.F.

201 EGYPTIAN FAIENCE PLAQUE

. . . .

M.M. 18340 Exc. No 68-1000

Early 14th century B.C. manufacture found in a context of LH III B (c. 1250 B.C.) Mycenae, Cult Centre, Room 31, the Room with the Fresco

L: (ex.) 9.8 cm.; W: 11.2 cm.;

Thinkness: 1.25>1.55 cm.

White faience originally green-glazed. The larger of two fragmentary plaques of Amenhotep III found in the Room with the Fresco. The extant inscription read "the good god Meb-Ma'at-Re, son of Re" on both the obverse and reverse sides.

E.B.F.

199

201

200 STONE BOWL

M.M. 18339 Exc. No 68-1193

LH III B (c. 1250 B.C.)

Mycenae, Cult Centre, Room 31, the Room with the Fresco

H: 8.9 cm.; D: (max) 14.8 cm., mouth: 7.2 cm.

Blue-green serpentine. Warren Type 3. Broad flat base, curving into regular body, the line continues smoothly to high shoulder and thence to rim, with its sunken interior lip. The inside profile undercuts the rim a little, before curving down to a flat bottom. Exterior polished; interior smoothed, but with rotary abrasion marks in undercut rim area.

E.B.F.

200

202

203

203 IVORY POMMEL

M.M. 18336 Exc. No 68-1193

LH III B (c. 1250 B.C.)
Mycenae, Cult Centre, Room 31, the Room
with the Fresco
H: 3.4 cm.; D: 6.9 cm., W: mortise c. 1.6 cm.

Large pommel carved from elephant
ivory. Splitting along laminations, it is
otherwise intact. In shape the pommel is
a low dome on a slightly flaring neck,
into which is cut a deep square mortise
to take the tang of a sword. This would
have been secured by rivets, for which
circular holes survive in the flaring neck.

O.H.K.

204 IVORY LION

M.N. 14521 Exc. No 68-1191

LH III B (c. 1250 B.C.)
Mycenae, Cult Centre, Room 31, the Room
with the Fresco
H: (max / head) 7.8 cm.; L: 17.7 cm.; W:
(hindquarters) 7.5 cm.; Mortise: L 13.5 cm.,
W 1.0-1.7 cm., Depth c. 0.5 cm.

Couchant lion, carved almost wholly in
the round, from a large section of
elephant tusk. A long rectangular mortise
for attachment is provided on the flat
underside. The carving skilfully captures
the latent power of a lion, with strongly
modelled hindquarters, legs and paws.
In the front view, the lion is depicted
with flattened nose and deeply drilled
nostrils. One eye is preserved: a raised
disc for the eyeball within an almond-
shaped relief ridge. The mane is poorly
preserved, but is apparently indicated
by conventional incised 'feather' pattern. The tail, with tufts, curls round to
the right side of the body.

O.H.K.

202 LEAD VESSEL

M.M. 24363 Exc. No 68-999

LH III B (c. 1250 B.C.)
Mycenae, Cult Centre, Room 31, the Room
with the Fresco
H: (max. ex.) 0.1 m.; D: body (max): 0.34 m;
Thickness: sheet 0.001 cm., rim 0.003 cm.;
L: reconstructed rim cirumference (c.) 0.6
cm.; W: 1457.4 gms.

Squashed alabastron; broken and most
of lower part of body is missing. Plain
rim, slightly flaring? Collar neck? Some
encrustation; crumpled and distorted.

S.M.

204

205

206 KYLIX

M.M. 16528 Exc. No 69-1421

LH III B (c. 1250 B.C.)
Mycenae, Cult Centre, sealed area of the fill placed in Room 31, the Room with the Fresco
H: 15 cm.; D: rim 16.5 cm.

Pinkish buff clay, lightly polished inside and out. Typical unpainted conical kylix (FS 274) which is the most common drinking vessel at this period.

E.B.F.

207 STEMMED BOWL

M.M. 24320 Exc. No 69-424

LH III B (c. 1250 B.C.)
Mycenae, Cult Centre, Room 31, the Room with the Fresco
H: 22.5 cm.; D: rim 23 cm., base 6 cm.

Almost complete. Pinkish buff well-levigated fabric, with some impurities; well-smoothed, but some wheelmarks inside. Lustrous brownish red, streaky paint. Monochrome (FS 303).

E.B.F.

208 STEMMED BOWL

M.M. 24318 EUM-155 Exc. No 69-439

OLIVE OIL

Evans: See method of analysis.

LH III B (c. 1250 B.C.)
Mycenae, Cult Centre, fill placed in Room 31, the Room with the Fresco
H: 20.4 cm.; D: rim 22.3 cm.

Pinkish buff clay well-levigated and smoothed. Paler slip polished lightly. Lustrous paint shading from dark to light tawny brown. Typical example of the version of this shape common at this period and well paralleled from Mycenae and elsewhere. Narrow pattern zone (4.8 cm. high) completely filled. Central tri-

205 IVORY HEAD

M.N. 15022 Exc. No 69-42

LH III B (c. 1250 B.C.)
Mycenae, Cult Centre, Room 31, the Room with the Fresco
H: 6.8 cm.; Top of head: 6.3 cm.x5.9 cm.

Male head carved in the round from a large section of elephant tusk, splitting concentrically along laminations; nose damaged and carved surface lost in places; wedge-shaped portion of neck is missing on right side; consolidated. The natural pulp cavity of the tusk has been exploited and slightly modified to provide a central tapering hollow which runs vertically from the neck to the top of the head. This feature and the irregularly spaced holes around the neck to the top of the head indicate that the head was to be mounted on a wooden support. The proportions of the head —broad at the temples and cheeks, tapering to a small rounded chin— emphasise the individual features. These are finely executed and seem designed to produce both a calm and a compelling apppearance. Especially striking are the large eyes, which are rendered as raised discs within almond-shaped relief ridges. These are further accentuated by the long arching eyebrows, also rendered in relief. In turn, the eyebrows are echoed by the hairline, with its central parting on the forehead and which loops on the cheeks in front of the ears. The ears themselves are fairly small but prominent, with well-modelled lobes and deep drill holes, possibly for the provision of earrings. The mouth is broad, but the actual lips are rather thin and compressed. Especial care has been taken in rendering the hair —a series of fine incised wavy lines— hugging the contours of the head. The hair is bound by a plain band or fillet which sits high on the head.

O.H.K.

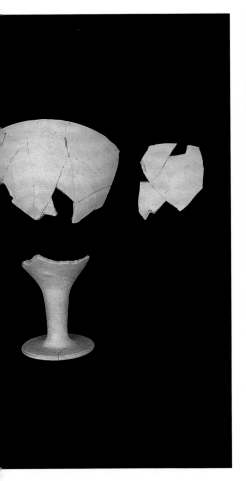

207

glyph of semi-circle-fringed verticals, 6 or 7 flanking a scalenet. On either side a pair of opposed concentric semi-circles with a second pair or one only at centre. No centre in one. On far side of these semi-circles, by handles, 6 or 7 vertical lines. Standard rim painting outside of 2 belly bands, 2 fine lines well down bowl, a narrow and a broad band on the stem; a band on outer edge of foot. Inside, a band well down the bowl. The vessel was shattered and shows marks of burning on some sherds from the final destruction of the room. A sherd was taken for analysis prior to restoration.

E.B.F.

208

RETSINA, MIXED FERMENTED BEVERAGES, AND THE CUISINE OF PRE-CLASSICAL GREECE

The origins of winemaking and viticulture in Greece are shrouded in the mists of human prehistory. If winemaking is best understood as an intentional human activity rather than a seasonal happenstance, then the Neolithic period, from about 8500 to 4000 B.C., is the first time in prehistory when the necessary preconditions for this momentous innovation came together. Once humans were settled into permanent villages in the Neolithic period, based on the first domesticated plants and animals, the conditions were ripe not only for experiencing and elaborating upon wine's psychotropic effects, but also for developing more predictable means of assuring a better quality wine and a more productive grapevine. Pottery, which was invented at this time, was ideal for forming shapes such as narrow-mouthed vats and storage jars, for producing and keeping wine.

The Archaeological Chemistry Laboratory of the Museum Applied Science Center for Archaeology (MASCA), under the direction of Dr. Patrick E. McGovern, has provided the earliest chemical confirmation of wine inside pottery jars from the Neolithic site of Haji Firuz in the northern Zagros Mountains of Iran, dated c. 5400-5000 B.C. This finding implies that wine had already been incorporated into the economic, social and religious fabric of human life, a phenomenon which is now expressed in many cultures around the world. Wine was evidently part of everyday "Neolithic cuisine," which includes many other foods and beverages—including bread, beer, and many meat and cereal entrees—that we enjoy today. Moreover, Neolithic peoples already had an appreciation for the preservative and medicinal properties of tree resins, which were added to their

wines. The use of wine and tree resins continued to expand in later times, until it dominated the pharmacopoeias of literate civilizations of the ancient world, in particular Greece.

Greek villages, like those in upland regions of the Near East, were possibly already producing wine in the Neolithic period. Pips or seeds of what have been identified as the wild Eurasian grape (Vitis vinifera sylvestris) have been recovered from Franchthi Cave in the Argolid of the Peloponnese, dating to the late Palaeolithic/Mesolithic periods (c. 11,000 B.C.), and sites throughout Greece have yielded such evidence for the Neolithic period proper. As yet, however, no Neolithic remains have been found of the domesticated grapevine (Vitis vinifera vinifera), which was the sine qua non for large-scale production and today accounts for almost all the wine that is produced around the world.

From an archaeological and historical standpoint, a good case can be made for a single origin of the domesticated grapevine in a northern upland region of the Near East, such as the Caucasus, the northern Zagros, or eastern Taurus Mountains. From here, viticulture probably spread out to other parts of the Near East, Egypt, and Greece during the Chalcolithic and Early Bronze periods (c. 4000-2160 B.C.). Prestige exchange of wine and special wine-drinking ceremonies among elite individuals, as can be documented for Mycenaean palace life and as best exemplified by the Classical Greek symposion, encouraged the adoption of winemaking and the successive transplantation or cloning of the domesticated grapevine in areas where even the wild grape had never grown. For example, a thriving royal winemaking industry had been established in the Nile Delta of Egypt by c. 3000 B.C. The limited production of wine, coupled with its range and subtlety of tastes and bouquets which improve with age, contributed to the value of this unique beverage wherever and whenever it has been drunk.

The chemical research that has been carried out by the University of Pennsylvania laboratory and Prof. Dr. Curt Beck's laboratory at Vassar College, in preparation for this exhibit, have shown that the large pithoi in some 80 storerooms of an extensive Early Bronze II (c. 2200 B.C.) at Myrtos Phournou Koryphe on Crete contained wine. This wine was probably resinated. It should be emphasized that modern Greece is the only region of the ancient world that still carries on the ancient tradition of adding a tree resin to wine, which dates back at least 7000 years. Grape remains, which might have provided added flavor or coloration, were found in some of the "noble jars" at Myrtos. Dark reddish residues, probably representing the pigmentation from a red wine, were noted on the vessels' interiors. Several features of these jars — holes drilled through their lower sides to decant off the wine and clay appliques forming rope designs — are common for wine jars of earlier and later date elsewhere in the ancient Near East.

By the Middle Minoan II period (c. 1900-1700 B.C.), resinated wine was probably used in cooking, because it is attested inside a tripod cooking pot (EUM-30) from Room 3 of the Monastiraki palatial centre on Crete. As was common in later Greek and Roman cookery, wine was a popular ingredient in many different foods, including meat marinades, fish sauces, flavored cheeses, and desserts. Vinegar, another grape product in which the alcohol in wine has fermented to acetic acid, might also have been used in food preparation. The presence of a resin in EUM-30, which was a common additive to wine in antiquity, implies that wine, rather than vinegar, was used in the Monastiraki (and Apodoulou?) cooking pots. Most ancient wines were probably somewhat vinegary, and the tree resin helped to cover up off-flavors and odors, besides acting as a preservative.

The wine in the Monastiraki tripod cooking pot

EUM-30 was highly interesting for another reason: a specific compound that results from the toasting of oak wood, called cognac or whiskey lactone, was present. Either the wood was toasted to bend the staves for making barrels in which the wine was stored, or toasted wood chips were added to the wine to give it a distinctive taste, similar to what is done to produce fine Scotch today. Another possibility is that oak resin, derived from processing the bark as was done for tanning leather, was directly added to the wine. No wood barrels have been found in excavations prior to the Roman period, when it has often been argued that barrels were first invented under Celtic influence. Ancient ship-building, however, must have employed a similar technology, so that barrels might well have been introduced at a much earlier period. The ageing of wine in oak barrels, a long-standing European tradition, might even have been an earlier pedigree. California winemaking in the last few decades has "rediscovered" how French oak adds "more complexity" and "mellows" out the tannins, compounds found in grape skins and pips that give wine much of its taste, better than ageing in American oak barrels. Other more "primitive," ancient methods have since been adopted and gained wide acclaim for New World winemaking.

By at least 1480-1425 B.C. (Late Minoan I B) at Daskaloyianni, Chania on Crete, a different kind of beverage –combined resinated wine, barley beer and honey mead– was being drunk from or presented ceremonially in conical cups. The popularity of this mixed fermented beverage is most evident by Late Minoan/Mycenaean III, when it was being served in kylikes, e.g. EUM-111, at Armenoi (LM III A2, c. 1370-1340 B.C.) and a "beer mug", EUM-195, (LH III A2, c. 1370-1340 B.C.). The kylikes are of special interest, because they were depicted being "held high" on fresco scenes at Knossos and Pylos that have a clear ceremonial and/or religious significance. Wine was an important commodity in palace life, since the wine ideogram, showing a trellised grapevine that is related to an older Egyptian hieroglyph, appears often in Linear B texts at Pylos and Mycenae. Moreover, a "honeyed wine" is referred to in one of Pylos texts. Nestor's "toddy" (kykeon) in which grated cheese, barley and honey were mixed together with Pramnian wine might well hark back to the "Minoan ritual cocktail" of heroic times.

Intriguingly, later Greek writers and gourmands dismissed beer as a barbarian drink, and resinated wine came to be mixed only with water. Most scholars have thus assumed that beer was never drunk by the Greeks. Yet, barley grows well on thin soils, and was already cultivated as early as the Neolithic period in Greece. Bread-making, which employs many of the same techniques as beer-making, was well-established in ancient Greece, and, given the close contacts between Greece and Egypt where barley beer reigned supreme, the Greeks could have produced beer if they wanted. The available evidence, at present, suggests that they did not drink barley beer pure and simple, but mixed it with other fermented beverages. One may propose that this custom was introduced by peoples migrating into Greece from the north c. 1500 B.C. A mixed fermented beverage is documented in northern Europe in the 3rd millennium B.C.

The Classical Greek wine-set of krater, jug, ladle, and kylix/cup/mug/bowl had its origins in Middle-Late Minoan Crete, and served equally well for any combination of fermented beverages and/or water for more than 1500 years.

A mixture of resinated wine, honey, and barley was attested inside a tripod cooking pot (EUM-188) found at Chamalevri on Crete, a Late Minoan III C1 (c. 1190-1130 B.C.) site. Like the Middle Minoan cooking pot from Monastiraki (above), the assumption is that these were standard ingredients for foods, which could also be fermented into beverages.

Archaeological chemistry promises to open whole new perspectives on the exciting history of foods and beverages in ancient Greece. It has revealed that retsina dates back to the 2nd millennium B.C. and that it was probably aged in toasted oak barrels in c. 1700 B.C. By the end of the millennium, a mixed fermented beverage of resinated wine, barley beer and honey mead, which was possibly introduced from outside Greece, was the preferred drink. Greeks of the 1st millennium B.C. returned to their roots, as it were, and mixed their retsina only with water. Honey, wine and barley were also popular ingredients in an emerging Greek cuisine, which laid the foundation for later Greek cookery as described by Archestratus, Athenaeus, and others.

DR. PATRICK E. McGOVERN
MASCA
University of Pennsylvania Museum, U.S.A.

The Tests

Your bones are formed using components taken from all the foods you have eaten during your lifetime. By analysing the chemical composition of your bones, we can determine the significant features of your diet. This is called: **Stable Isotope Analysis**

The Sample

A small piece of bone, half a gram preferably, taken from a femur (leg bone).

The Time

Two weeks

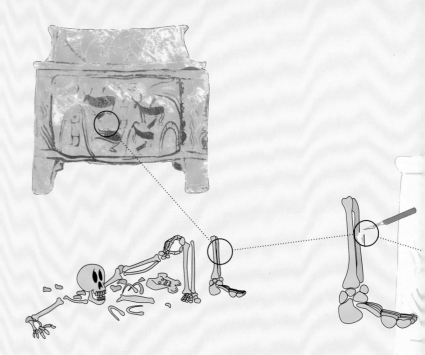

The main use of this equipment is Radiocarbon Dating

This research started as scientists noted interesting patterns of ST Isotope values in samples they were preparing for radiocarbon dating.

The Results: An Explanation

The tests revealed types of protein in the diet over a period of about 10 years. It can tell us whether people had protein from seafood, or from land plants and animals. It can also tell us whether people had more meat or plants in their diets. By way of example, if the diet is around 20% fish, it means the person ate fish roughly once every five days, or for two months per year.

You are what you eat

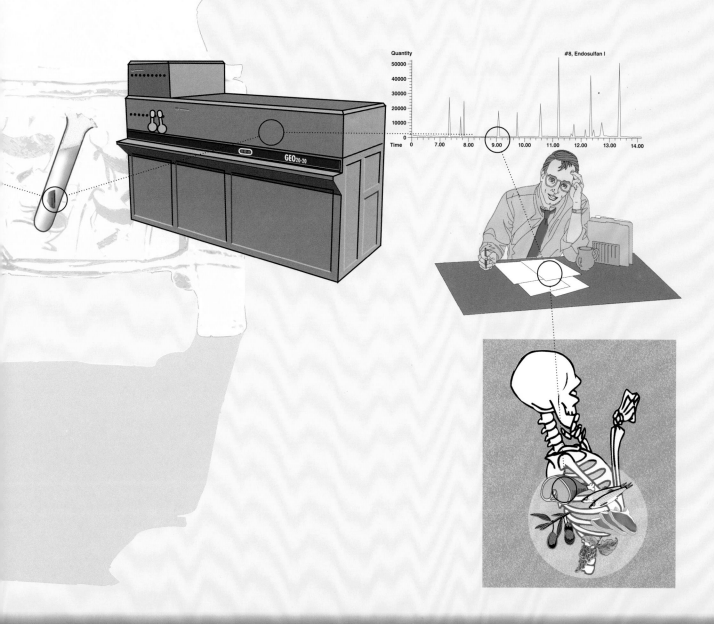

YOU ARE WHAT YOU EAT

The difference between Section V and Sections I-IV of the Exhibition, is between pots and bones.

The value of the scientific analyses of pottery is that they indicated what food and drink residues were contained in individual vessels.

The value of stable isotope analysis on Neolithic, Minoan, and Mycenaean bones is that it indicated what types of protein residues were contained in individual people.

The Exhibition comes full circle in Section V: from naming individual foodstuffs, Section V proceeds to give an overall picture of diet, as much as can be deduced by the extraction and analysis of the protein content found in the collagen that survived in the bones of adults. The survival of collagen depends on the condition of the skeletal material, and this depends on the type and method of burial, and on climatic conditions. Burial customs varied, but the real problem was the Greek climate, as moisture is the enemy of the survival of collagen. There was no way to predict whether collagen had survived without carrying out analysis. The plan was to start with the Cemetery of Armenoi, and then to add sites if these results were positive. Samples from the first 80 skeletons (half male and half female) from Armenoi gave positive and interesting results. Additional sites were therefore added. Altogether five groups of skeletal material were tested.

The five groups of skeletal material that were analysed, and whose results are summarised in the Exhibition are:

CRETE:
Neolithic Cave of Gerani (estimated date of skeletons: c. 3800 B.C.)
Late Minoan Cemetery of Armenoi (c. 1390-1190 B.C.)

GREEK MAINLAND:
Grave Circle B at Mycenae (c. 17th-16th century B.C.)
Grave Circle A (c. 16th century B.C.)
A group of Late Helladic Chamber Tombs in the Argolid (c. 1600-1200 B.C.).

The most important point to remember when studying the results in Section V, is that there is a progression from c. 3800 B.C. to 1200 B.C. on Crete; from c. 1700 to 1200 B.C. on the Mainland. No one group can be compared directly with any other.

Nevertheless, certain points can be made. The most significant feature is that from 3800 B.C. to 1200 B.C., there is a dependence on animal protein far greater than anyone has suspected and many have argued against. The only real evidence for consumption of fish on a level that showed up in the diet was in Grave Circles A and B, and according to Dr. Michael Richards, even then consumption of marine foods would have been no more than once a week. Grave Circles A and B were elite burials. The group of Late Helladic Chamber tombs were from a later date, but they were the tombs of ordinary people. In this group there was no evidence of the consumption of marine foods in measurable amounts.

In all cases where it could be quantified, there appeared to be a difference between the diets of males and females. The difference was that men consumed more animal protein.

The wall panels summarise the status of the health of each group. The outstanding feature is that the inhabitants of Grave Circle B (c. 17th-16th century B.C.) were by far the most robust. Men and women were taller and more muscular. The condition of their teeth was excellent.

The Minoan couple that shared the larnax found in tomb 132 at Armenoi (c. 1340-1190 B.C.) had, as was typical of the inhabitants of Armenoi, very bad teeth. This was perhaps exacerbated in the case of the man, as he was thought to have used his teeth to ply his trade, which is suggested was that of a weaver.

Skeletal material revealed information about diet and health in Bronze Age Greece. It also showed how the Minoans and Mycenaeans practiced medicine. Lesions on bones survive after thousands of years and from these lesions it is possible to see how surgery was performed: cranial trepanation, bones skillfully set, and basic but precise surgery carried out.

The reconstruction of an imaginary chamber tomb at Armenoi illustrates Minoan burial practice in the 14th-13th century B.C., and displays the types of interesting and beautiful artefacts that were buried with the dead and the types of vessels used in funerary ritual.

DR. HOLLEY MARTLEW

HOW CHEMICAL ANALYSIS OF HUMAN BONES CAN TELL US THE DIETS OF PEOPLE WHO LIVED IN THE PAST

As "You Are What You Eat" the basic building blocks that have been used to make all of your body tissues, including your bones, have been taken from foods you have eaten. At archaeological sites, bones are the part of the human body that remains after a long period of burial, and from chemical analysis of a small piece of bone we can determine important information about an individual diet.

Bones buried in the ground over a long period of time undergo all sorts of chemical changes and alterations, but often a part of the bone, the protein (called "collagen") survives well. This is the part of the bone that is extracted for radiocarbon dating, as well as for dietary analysis.

Your bone protein has been constructed from protein you have eaten over your lifetime, and that protein retains a chemical signature, called a stable isotope value. We know the stable isotope values of a wide range of foods, so we can compare these with the stable isotope values of the human bone, in order to determine what foods were eaten by that person and then were subsequently used to make bone protein.

We look at two elements in the bone collagen, which tell us about different aspects of the past human diets. The carbon isotope value tells us how much marine protein (e.g. fish, shellfish) there was in the diet, compared with terrestial proteins (e.g. grains, breads, cattle and goat milk). The nitrogen isotope tells us how much plant food there was in the diets, compared with animal foods (like meat and milk).

In addition, we can use isotope analysis to look at differences in diets within sites, perhaps between men and women, or between rich and poor people, or to see if there are changes in diet with time.

The advantage of stable isotope analysis is that it give us a direct measure of past diet. More traditional methods of diet reconstruction at archaeological sites, such as analysis of the remaining animal bones and plant foods, only give us information about specific foods eaten, and may only reflect a single meal or a special, perhaps ritual meal. Stable isotope analysis tells us about long-term diets, perhaps revealing as much as ten years worth of dietary information in a long bone such as a femur. However, the best approach is to combine stable isotope analysis with more traditional methods, and together they can be powerful tools for telling us about past human diet.

PROFESSOR ROBERT E. M. HEDGES
DR. MICHAEL P. RICHARDS
Research Laboratory for Archaeology and History of Art
University of Oxford, U.K.

OSTEOARCHAEOLOGY, THE STUDY OF BONES

Archaeologists learn about the past by studying the objects that ancient people left behind. Osteo-archaeologists learn about the past by studying skeletal remains of these ancient peoples. What better way to find out about the lives of past peoples than to examine the people themselves? An ancient human skeleton is like a closed book just waiting to be opened and read. It can provide a wealth of information relating to the life of the person to whom it once belonged. Gender, height, age at death, ethnic affiliation, general state of health and nutrition, previous injuries, type of activities performed, and cause of death, is just some of the information a human skeleton can provide.

In order to interpret all this information, an osteoarchaeologist, in addition to his or her archaeological skills, must have knowledge of human anatomy and skeletal biology and pathology. The first two things an osteoarchaeologist tries to ascertain from an individual skeleton is its gender and age at death. The first step in determining the age at death involves establishing whether the individual was an adult. A certain sign of adulthood is the complete fusion of the ends of the bone, called the epiphyses, to the shafts of the bones. In children the epiphyses will be completely separate, while in adolescents, they will be in various stages of fusion to the shafts. If it has been determined that the skeleton belonged to a child, a precise age at death can be assigned. Children's bones grow at a well-recognised rate, and by measuring the length of a bone, an age can be determined. Teeth are good indicators of a child's age, as certain teeth erupt in the upper and lower jaws at specific ages. It is not as easy to assign a precise age to an adult skeleton. In an adult skeleton, age can be determined by examining the amount of attrition or "wear" on the teeth, by the appearance of the pelvic bones, by the appearance of the ends of the rib bones, and by the degree of fusion amongst the bones of the skull. It is best to try as many

of the aging methods as possible to get an average estimate for the age at death. Once an age has been assigned to a skeleton, it is time to determine the gender. It is very difficult to assign gender to children's skeletons because until puberty is reached, boys' and girls' skeletons are virtually identical. The hormones that are released during puberty cause the female and male skeleton to differentiate primarily in the pelvis and skull. A female's pelvis will be broader than a male's and will be orientated to facilitate childbirth. A male's skull will be likely to have pronounced brow ridges, a prominent chin, and conspicuous muscle attachments. A female's skull will be more gracile, with the features' having a finer appearance. A male skeleton will generally be larger than that of a female. The long bone of the arms and legs will be longer and thicker and the muscle attachments will be bigger.

After the age and sex of the skeleton have been determined, it is necessary to examine the skeleton for signs of pathology. In order to determine if something pathological has affected the skeleton, it is important to know what a "normal" skeleton looks like in all its many variations. A deviation from the normal might have pathological implications. It is also necessary to determine if the deviation in the skeleton occurred when the individual was living or occurred because of the burial process. It is not always possible to diagnose specific pathological conditions in every skeleton, but the types of pathologies that can be identified in skeletons fall into the following categories: trauma, arthritic conditions, infectious diseases, diseases of the metabolism (e.g. scurvy or rickets), circulatory disorders (problems involving the heart and blood vessels), birth defects, and cancers. The dental health of the individual can also be assessed by noting cavities, abscesses, plaque, and missing teeth.

DARLENE WESTON
Institute of Archaeology
University College, London, U.K.

This is a graph of the stable isotope values of Neolithic humans from the cave site of Gerani, West Crete.

The δ13 C value tells us about the amount of marine protein (e.g. fish) in diets, where a δ13 C -20‰= no fish and a δ13 C -12‰=all fish.

The δ15 N value tells us about the amount of animal protein (e.g. meat or milk) vs. plant protein in diets, where a δ15 N 9-11‰ = almost 100% meat, and a δ15 N 3-5‰ = almost no meat.

The two individuals here did not have marine foods (e.g. fish) in their diets, as indicated by the δ13 C values. The δ15N values are fairly high, indicating that they did eat a fair amount of animal protein (meat or milk).

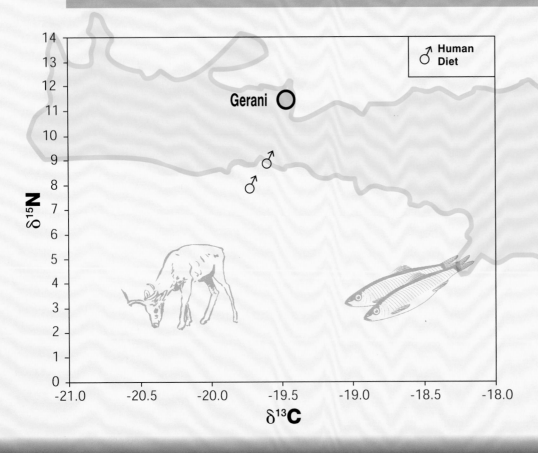

What did they eat?

We don't have much evidence for Neolithic diets, beyond discoveries of domesticated animals like cattle and sheep, and plants like grains.

How much meat or milk did they eat?

Did men and women have different diets?

Neolithic Cave of Gerani

Late Neolithic I
c. 3800 B.C.

Chemical analysis of bones tells us

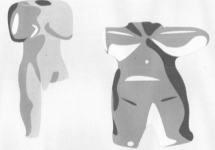

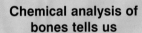

• No marine foods

• They ate a mixture of meat and plants

• We did not know the sex of the two samples, but one had more animal protein in the diet than the other.

THE TECHNIQUE OF FACIAL RECONSTRUCTION

The basic principle behind the technique of facial reconstruction is extremely simple: the bony skull provides the frame for the fleshy face that lies over it. Every skull is different in its shape and proportions, and so every face must be different too.

The first step is to make an accurate cast of the skull: the original skull is never used, for (as in the case of the Minoans from Armenoi) it may be extremely fragile. The thickness of the flesh of the face is known from measurements taken for more than a century, and so marker pegs can be inserted into the cast, and the face built up around them in clay, muscle by muscle, taking into account the age, sex and race of the dead person. These muscles give the basic structure of the face: a further layer of clay represents fat, other tissue and finally the skin.

The skeleton can provide other evidence about the individual's health and lifestyle, and this too is incorporated into the reconstruction: it becomes a three-dimensional report on research by many different specialists, much easier to understand than a printed report, and much more exciting.

Because the evidence comes from the bones, the reconstruction cannot be a true portrait, which would show all the surface details such as laughter lines or a furrowed brow which betray a person's character, but it will give a recognisable image of how that person will have looked in life. Superficial details such as hair are only added afterwards: for Mycenaeans and Minoans one relies on the evidence of near-contemporary frescoes, gems and figurines, whereas in later periods, where the person can sometimes be positively identified from other evidence, literary descriptions or actual portraits may provide more accurate information.

Computers have a place too. Where one cannot make a cast of the skull –from Egyptian mummies, covered in tissue and bandages, or from living people– computerised tomography enables one to take a series of X-rays at close intervals across the skull (CT-scans), and then through a computer program to use these to carve or mould an exact replica of the skull in plastic, on which the face is then built up. Methods for using the computer to model the face over the skull are being developed: though quicker and cheaper than the "manual" method, their results are still less lifelike and much less effective.

DR. JOHN PRAG
The Manchester Museum,
University of Manchester, U.K.

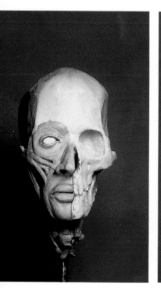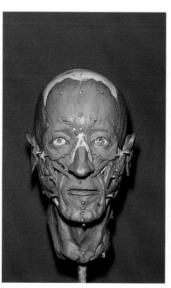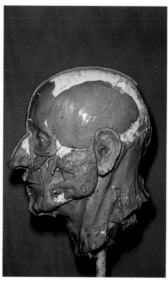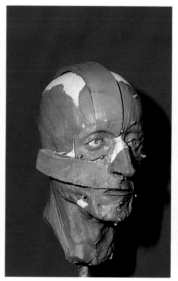

209

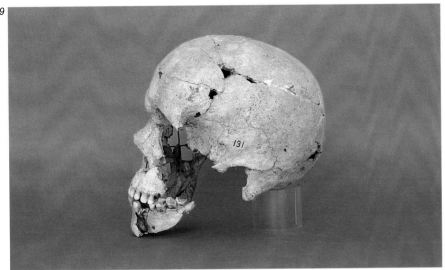

209

209 CRANIUM OF A MIDDLE-AGED MALE

N.M. 10.085 (Sigma-131)

MH (c. 1660 B.C.)
Grave Circle B, Mycenae,
Grave Sigma, the earliest grave in circle

The cranium of an approximately 55 years old male. Fragmentary and restored. Only cranium from Grave Circle B to have its mandible intact, which indicates reasonably good dentition, although he had a large abscess upon his upper right permanent lateral incisor. Traces of cribra orbitalia and possibly of porotic hyperostosis. Rest of skeletal remains indicate extensive arthritis and that he suffered from gallstones.

R.G.A.

210 CRANIUM OF A MIDDLE-AGED FEMALE

N.M. 10.085 (Gamma-58)

LH I A (c. 1550 B.C.)
Grave gamma (south body), Grave Circle B, Mycenae

The cranium of a tall, probably slender and strongly built young woman aged approximately 36 years. Fragmentary and restored, but mandible missing. No apparent pathology, but presentation of the cranium makes it difficult to determine if there was any. Rest of skeletal remains indicate arthritics in her lower lumber vertebrae and hands. At some stage in her life she broke her right humerus, which had healed well, obviously with medical attention (see cat. No 292).

R.G.A.

210

210

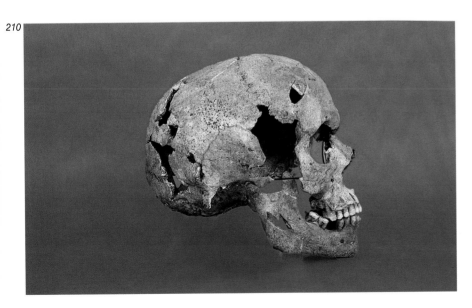

GRAVE CIRCLE B

Grave Circle B lies to the west end of the Middle Helladic Cemetery of Mycenae. It was excavated by the Archaeological Society at Athens (J. Papademetriou and G.E. Mylonas, 1952-1954). It contained 14 royal shaft graves of the 17th and 16th centuries B.C., some earlier and some contemporary to the first graves of Grave Circle A, similarly marked by upright stelae, five of which were found in their original position. This group of tombs was also enclosed by a strong circular stone wall, which surrounded, apart from the royal tombs, another 12 small and shallow graves intended for ordinary citizens. The excavators numbered them by letters of the Greek alphabet. The larger tombs are similar to those in Grave Circle A. The largest one - Grave Gamma- was found to contain the bones of three men (one of whom had a trepanned skull) and a

woman. The other graves contained one, two, or three burials. The grave goods were less opulent than those discovered in Grave Circle A, but they included a mask (Grave Gamma) and some masterpieces of early Mycenaean art, which are exhibited in the Mycenaean Room of the National Museum at Athens. These include the small amethyst seal engraved with a male portrait from Grave Gamma; the gold sword hilt from Grave Delta; finely ornamented sword blades from Graves Iota and Lambda; the gold cup from Grave Nu; and the magnificent rock crystal vase with a duck's head handle, from Grave Omicron. After the last burials the graves were left undisturbed except when Grave Rho was excavated, emptied and enlarged during the 15th century B.C., in order to accommodate a vaulted chamber tomb of stone slabs with a roofed entranceway (dromos), of the type known only in Mycenaean settlements outside mainland Greece, such as those at Ras Shamra Ugarit on the Syrian coast, and Trachona in Cyprus.

S. E. IAKOVIDIS, HON. FSA
Prof. Em. of Archaeology
Member of the Academy of Athens

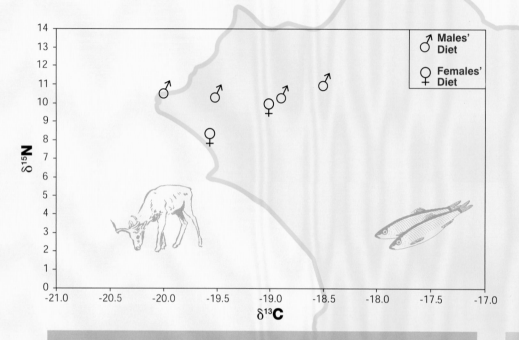

This is a graph of the stable isotope values of humans from Grave Circle B at Mycenae.

The δ13 C value tells us about the amount of marine protein (e.g. fish) in diets, where a δ13 C -20‰ = no fish, and a δ13 C -12‰ = all fish.

The δ15 N value tells us about the amount of animal protein (e.g. meat or milk) vs. plant protein in diets, where a δ15 N 9-11‰ = almost 100% meat, and a δ15 N 3-5‰ = almost no meat.

The human δ13 C values indicate that two of the males plotted here (on the right side of the graph) got some of their protein, 10-20%, from the sea (e.g. fish), but the rest of these people did not. The δ15 N values for all individuals plotted at the upper end of the graph indicate that they had a lot of animal protein in their diets, while the one woman who is lower down on the graph, did not have as much.

Grave Circle B consisted of 26 graves of varying shapes and styles. There were simple pit graves that contained a single skeleton and more elaborate shaft graves that contained multiple burials of family groups. The remains of 35 individuals were found, but only 22 were complete enough to be studied. Of the 22 studied, sixteen were male, four were female and two were children, aged two and five years. The males ranged from 23 to 55 years of age, with an average age of adult death at 36 years.

Grave Circle B
Mycenae

c. 17th-16th century B.C.

...e bones of the males and females were generally more robust ...an these of other ancient Greek populations. The males had ...ge hands and feet and the bones of both sexes had prominent ...arkings for muscle attachments. The females averaged a height ... 159.1 cm. (5'2"), while the males averaged a height of 171.5 ...n. (5'7"), 4-5 cm. taller than the average ancient Greek male at ...s time.

...ere is a remarkable lack of dental disease and lines of enamel ...owth arrest, and little sign of infectious or diet-related disease, ...dicating these people enjoyed better health than their ...ntemporaries, though one male did suffer from gallstones. ...ounds on the heads of several males, healed spinal column ...ctures and extensive arthritis, together with the signs of extra-...uscular strength indicate that the men were probably involved ...fighting. Both the men and the women led an active and ...gorous lifestyle.

What did they eat?	Chemical analysis of bones tells us...
Pottery depicts marine life. How much did they eat?	• Almost no marine foods.
How much meat or milk did they eat?	• They ate a mixture of meat and plants.
Did men and women have different diets?	• Maybe. The two oldest men had more marine foods in their diet than the others.

GRAVE CIRCLE A

Grave Circle A consisted of a group of large shaft graves used for royal burials, dug in the 16th century B.C. on the slope within the Helladic Cemetery of Mycenae. They were enclosed by a circular stone wall of which a very small section remains. The construction of the Lion Gate and of the west fortification wall to a much higher level relegated the graves to the bottom of a deep hollow. In order to bring the burial ground to the level of the citadel entrance a stout supporting wall with a distinct batter was built over the graves. This wall was topped by upright sandstone slabs forming a circular parapet. On the north side there is an entrance between two square cross-walls which terminate the circle on either side. The enclosure contained a number of small and shallow ordinary graves and six large shaft graves numbered I to VI (I to V excavated by H. Schliemann; VI by P. Stamatakes). All six are family tombs, large rectangular pits measuring 3 x 3.50 m. (II) to 4.50 x 6.40 m. (IV) containing several individuals. They had low rubble walls along the sides upon which lay horizontal beams that supported the roof of each grave, about 0.75 m. from the floor, made of slate slabs or wattle covered with an insulating layer of clay. The dead were laid on the bottom of the pit and the dug-out soil was piled on over the roof. Finally the grave was marked by an upright plain or sculpted sandstone slab (stele). The burial ceremony was followed by a funeral banquet; the remains of this banquet were covered with a few handfuls of soil. Whenever a new

burial was about to take place, the stele, the covering soil and the roof were removed and then put back into place, after the burial. Abundant grave gifts were buried along with the corpses, such as gold funerary masks, gold and silver vessels and jewellery, swords and daggers with gold and ivory hilts and blades inlaid with gold and silver decoration. These are now exhibited in the Mycenaean Room of the National Museum at Athens. When the later supporting wall, contemporary with the Lion Gate, was built in the 13th century B.C. the stelae were removed from their original positions and placed at random over the graves. The evidence supplied by these and other Mycenaean tombs seem to indicate that in spite of the opulence of the grave goods and the obvious reverence for the tombs themselves, Mycenaeans did not practice a cult of the dead.

S. E. IAKOVIDIS, HON. FSA
Prof. Em. of Archaeologgy
Member of the Academy of Athens

211 COPY OF GOLD MASK

c. 16th century B.C.

Mycenae, Grave Circle A, Tomb V

Copy of the gold mask thought by Schliemann to belong to Agamemnon. It renders the face of the Achaean king very realistically.

211

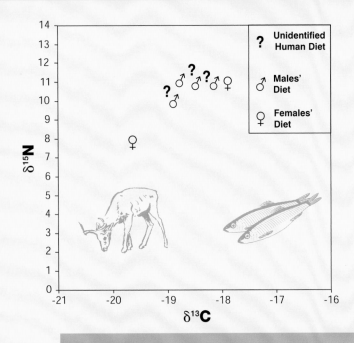

This is a graph of the stable isotope values of humans from Grave Circle A at Mycenae.

The δ13 C value tells us about the amount of marine protein (e.g. fish) in diets, where a δ13 C -20‰ = no fish, and a δ13 C -12‰ = all fish.

The δ15 N value tells us about the amount of animal protein (e.g. meat or milk) vs. plant protein in diets, where a δ15 N of 9-11‰ = almost 100% meat, and a δ15 N of 3-5‰ = almost no meat.

Most of the humans plotted here (with the exception of a single woman) got a portion (about 20%) of their protein from the sea, probably from fish, as indicated by the δ13 C values. The one woman who is on the left side of the plot above did not.

Grave Circle A consisted of six shaft graves, all but one multiple burials. The remains of 19 individuals were found: eight males, nine females, and two children. Five of the individuals had gold masks, and the children were covered with plain gold sheets. Unfortunately, the remains of the nineteen individuals were in a poor state when they were excavated and the details of only six of the skeletons could be recorded. The six were all males, ranging in age from approximately 25 to 45 years of age. Height could only be estimated for two of the individuals, with them standing 166 cm. (5'5") and 182.5 cm. (6'0") tall. These individuals were as solidly built as those from Grave Circle B were, exhibiting pronounced musculature. Among the pathologies evident in this group of six was osteoporosis, arthritis of the spine, and a well-healed fractured vertebra.

Grave Circle A
Mycenae

c. 16th century B.C.

Mycenae

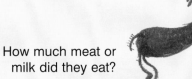
What did they eat?

Pottery depicts marine life. How much did they eat?

Chemical analysis of bones tells us...

- Some marine foods.

How much meat or milk did they eat?

- They ate a mixture of meat and plants.

Did men and women have different diets?

- Yes! Men had a diet with more marine foods than women.

MYCENAEAN CHAMBER TOMBS

On the slopes of the hills around the acropolis at "rich in gold" Mycenae, a number of cemeteries have been identified, each consisting of a group of chamber tombs. These cemeteries served as the burial sites of the inhabitants of the small villages scattered in the outlying areas around the palace of Mycenae.

The people who were buried in the chamber tombs from which the skeletal material was submitted for stable isotope analysis, appear to have come from the middle class of Mycenaean society. The chamber tombs did not belong to the upper social class of acropolis officials, because such people would have had more elaborate burials situated closer to the centre of power.

The chamber tombs are of middle size, and they

are cut into natural rock. They contain relics of many generations. It is clear that the tombs were opened many times, either for a new burial, or in order to clean a burial level.

Only in a few cases, is the last burial preserved undisturbed and *in situ*. In most cases, bones mixed with offerings had been put aside in order to prepare for new burials. In rare cases, there is a burial in a cist at the entrance to the dromos of a chamber tomb.

The greater part of the offerings consisted of known shapes of Mycenaean vases of excellent quality. The shapes are mostly closed vessels, piriform three-handled amphorae of small and medium size; jugs; and a great number of small and large alabastra. Also

found were drinking vessels such as kylikes and cups, and feeding bottles.

Clay figurines, females of standardised types, were offered in the tombs. Of particular note was an exceptional respresentation of a chariot drawn by two horses guided by two charioteers, who sit under a parasol fixed onto the chariot. Two small ivory pyxides were found without their context. They were either used for cosmetics or for the embellishment of the dead.

A few beads of glass paste used for some type of decoration or adornment were among the finds. A sealstone of steatite was found, and another of green jasper. These seals suggest a more luxurious taste. On the seal made of green jasper, two "Minoan" dragons are engraved in a style typical of Crete, proving relations in early Mycenaean times, between Minoan Crete and areas around the eastern Mediterranean.

The cosmopolitan character of the Mycenaean culture is also clear, as evidenced by two souvenirs of a traveller which found their way into one of the chamber tombs. These are: a Mittanean cylinder seal and an Egyptian (scaraboid) seal. It is supposed that these two artefacts travelled in some way to Syria, were acquired by a Mycenaean, and arrived in Mycenae, to serve as amulets considered to have apotropaic value, and finally they were deposited in a chamber tomb. They might have been used as amulets equally by the inhabitants on the coast of Anatolia as well as by the Mycenaeans who finally acquired them.

DR. ELENI PALAEOLOGOU
Archaeologist, 4th Ephorate P.C.A.

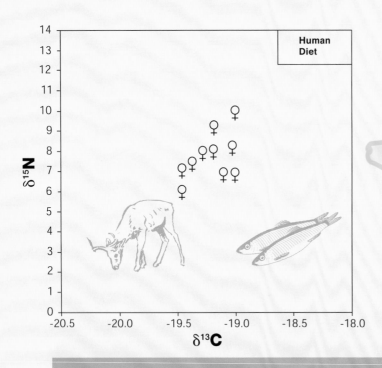

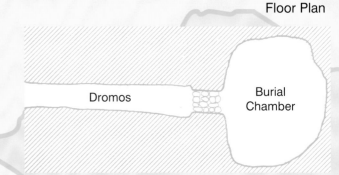

Floor Plan

Dromos

Burial Chamber

These are the tombs of ordinary people

This is a graph of the stable isotope values of humans from chamber tombs at Mycenae.

The δ13 C value tells us about the amount of marine protein (e.g. fish) in diets, where a δ13 C -20‰ = no fish, and a δ13 C -12‰ = all fish.

The δ15 N value tells us about the amount of animal protein (e.g. meat or milk) vs. plant protein in diets, where a δ 15 N 9-11‰ = almost 100% meat, and a δ15 N of 3-5‰ = almost no meat.

The δ13 C values indicate that marine protein (e.g. fish) was not eaten by these people. There is a range of δ15 N values, indicating that the same people had a lot of meat in their diets (at the top end of the plot) while others had more plant protein (at the lower end).

Longitudinal
Section

Burial
Chamber

Mycenae

Chamber Tombs
Mycenae

Late Helladic I-III
c. 1600-1200 B.C.

What did they eat?

Chemical analysis of bones tells us...

Pottery depicts marine life.
How much did they eat?

- Almost no marine foods.

How much meat or milk did they eat?

- They ate a mixture of meat and plants. Some people had more plants in their diets than others.

Did men and women have different diets?

- We did not know the sex of these adults, but there is a range of diets, and this may be linked to gender.

REPORT ON TWO SKELETONS FROM TOMB 132 AT ARMENOI, RETHYMNON

SKELETON 1

Summary: Female, 40's, 141cm., remarkably little pathology, suffered childhood illnesses.

INVENTORY

This skeleton is relatively complete, with most of the bones represented, including the hyoid bone. The presence of the hyoid bone indicates that this was most likely a primary burial, as this bone is not usually recovered in secondary burials. Missing elements include the left clavicle and scapula, patellae, carpals, finger phalanges, and toe phalanges. Incomplete elements include the frontal bone, parietals, right radius, left and right ulnae, left femur, left and right fibulae, left innominate, and the 12th thoracic vertebrae. All the rib were present but in a fragmentary and incomplete state.

CONDITION

Overall, the skeleton is in fair condition. Some elements, specifically the left femur, left proximal tibia, and ribs were in poor condition. Bits of bone flaked off the various skeletal elements when they were handled. The skull has suffered post-mortem erosion on the frontal bone and some bones have large concretions of calcium carbonate deposited on them.

SEX

The assignation of biological sex was based on methods described by Bass (1987), Buikstra and Ubelaker (1994), and Krogman and Iscan (1986). The left innominate of the pelvis was too poorly preserved to sex. The overall shape of the right innominate was very female, with a pronounced ventral arc, a prominent subpubic concavity, and a large preauricular sulcus. The greater sciatic notch was neither male nor female in appearance.

The skull had a small nuchal crest, small mastoids, no supraorbital ridges, no glabella, a small mental eminence, and a small jaw - all very female traits. The long bones appeared very gracile and small, also female traits. Based on the appearances of the right innominate bone of the pelvis, the skull and the long bones, the skeleton can confidently be sexed as female.

AGE

All of the epiphyses of the bones, including those of the clavicle, the iliac crests of the pelvis, and the basioccipital synchondrosis, had completely fused, indicating that bone growth had been completed and the skeleton was fully adult. The right pubic symphysis of the innominate bone was available for ageing. Morphological changes in the pubic symphyseal face are regarded as among the most dependable criteria for estimating age at death in human remains (Buikstra and Ubelaker, 1994). Using Todd's method (Todd, 1921), the age was estimated as being between 45 and 49 years. Using the Suchey-Brooks method (Brooks and Suchey, 1990), the age was estimated as 48.1 ± 14.6 years.

The auricular surfaces of the innominate bones show regular age-related changes that are more intricate and harder to score than those of the pubic symphyses. However, because the auricular surface is more frequently preserved in archaeological contexts than the pubis, it provides a way to attempt ageing when the pubic symphysis is not available (Buikstra and Ubelaker, 1994). The right auricular surface of the innominate bone was available for ageing. This method (Lovejoy et al., 1985) gave an age estimate of between 40 and 44 years.

As the skull was in fairly good condition, cranial suture closure was also used as an ageing method. Cranial sutures generally fuse together with increasing age, but there is a great deal of variability in fusion rates. Therefore, this method should only be used in conjunction with other ageing methods, or when no other ageing methods can be attempted (Buikstra and Ubelaker, 1994). Using Meindl and Lovejoy's (1985) method, the sutures of the lateral-anterior region gave an age of 32 ± 8.3 years and those of the external cranial vault gave an age of 34.7 ± 7.8.

Based on the ageing methods employed on this skeleton, an age estimate of between 35 to 50 years (middle adult) can be confidently given. A more precise, but less confident, age estimate would place this individual in her early forties at the time of death.

STATURE

As an osteometric board was not available for measuring the long bones, the measurements may not be accurate. Using Trotter and Gleser's (1958) formulae, stature was estimated as 140.77 ± 3.55 cm. or 4'71/2", making this woman very short.

HEALTH

DENTAL PATHOLOGY

Two teeth were lost post-mortem, the maxillary right third molar and the mandibular right second molar. Teeth present but not in occlusion included the maxillary right canine, right second incisor, right first incisor, left first incisor, left third molar, and the mandibular right and left second premolars. Teeth congenitally absent included the mandibular third molars. Several teeth were damaged post-mortem due to splitting, the maxillary right second premolar, right canine, and left first and second incisors. Finally, teeth lost pre-mortem, with the alveolus fully resorbed, included the mandibular right first molar and left first premolar.

Tooth wear for incisors, canines and premolars was scored according to Smith's (1984) method and molar wear was scored according to Scott's (1979) method. The maxillary incisors, canines, and premolars exhibited little wear. The canines and incisors had point or hairline dentin exposure and the premolars had moderate cusp removal or blunting. The maxillary first and second molars were moderately worn with the first molars slightly more worn than the second, as would be expected. The first molars were worn flat with some dentin exposure, while the second molars were worn flat without dentin exposure. The third molar exhibited little wear. The mandibular incisors and left canine were worn such that dentin with a line of distinct thickness was showing. The premolars exhibited moderate cusp removal or blunting. The mandibular first molar was slightly more worn than the maxillary first molars, but the second molars were less worn. The first molar was flat with dentin exposure, and the second molars had cusps that were not completely worn flat. In generally, the wear pattern can be described as moderate, indicating a diet that was not particularly coarse.

Dental caries were found on the maxillary left second and third molars, and the mandibular left second molar. Caries on second molars were on the occlusal surface, while caries on the third molar was on the interproximal surface. The presence of these caries indicates a diet rich in carbohydrates. There were no dental abscesses present, but as was previously mentioned, two teeth were lost pre-mortem, the mandibular right first molar and left first premolar. These two teeth could have been lost due to abscesses, as this frequently leads to tooth loss followed by alveolar repair involving bone resorption and a partial refill of the alveolus (tooth socket). There was no dental calculus present on the teeth. A lack of calculus (calcified plaque) could mean that some form of dental hygiene was practised.

Enamel hypoplasia in the form of linear horizontal grooves were present on the maxillary left first and second molars, the left and right first and second premolars, and the left canine. Linear horizontal grooves were also present on the mandibular second premolars, the right first premolar and the second incisors. The presence of enamel hypoplasia in this female indicates that during her childhood, when her teeth were forming, enamel formation was disrupted via a systemic stressor, such as malnutrition or infectious disease.

SKELETAL PATHOLOGY

There is very little evidence of skeletal pathology in this individual, and that which does exist is extremely mild in nature. On the left and right fibulae, there are mild healed periosteal reactions in the form of striations on the lateral proximal thirds of the shafts. This could be caused by an inflammation of the soft tissue in this area, possibly because of muscle strain.

There are small holes on the proximal articular surfaces of the right second and third metatarsals and one distal hand phalanx has lipping of the articular surface on the anterior side. These could be the beginnings of osteoarthritis in these toe joints and finger joint, respectively.

Unusually, for an individual in her 40's, there is no sign of degenerative joint disease in the spine. Based on the lack of joint disease and small muscle insertions, it is conceivable that this woman enjoyed a life free from any demanding physical labour. She was free from chronic pathological conditions, and most likely died from an acute illness.

SKELETON 2

Summary: Male, 35-50 years, 167 cm., poor dental health, osteoarthritis in spine, particularly severe in neck.

INVENTORY

The skeleton is almost complete with most of the bones represented. Missing elements include carpal bones, finger phalanges, and toe phalanges. Incomplete elements include the occipital bone, mandible, and innominate bones. All the ribs are present, but in a fragmentary condition.

CONDITION

Overall, the skeleton is in fair condition. Bits of bone flake off when the bones are handled. Some of the bones have large concretions of calcium carbonate deposited on them and insect burrow holes are present on the ulnae.

SEX

Sex determination was based on the criteria described by Bass (1987), Buikstra and Ubelaker (1994), and Krogman and Iscan (1986). As the pubic symphyses were not present on either innominate bone, it was difficult to assign a sex to the pelvis. The pelvis, in general, presented ambiguous features and could not be confidently assigned to either sex. The sacrum definitely exhibited male traits, being much curved, and having a wide sacral body in relation to the alae.

The skull had a moderate sized nuchal crest, moderate sized mastoids, prominent supraorbital ridges, a moderate sized glabella, a moderate sized mental eminence, and a slightly flaring gonial angle in the mandible. These traits indicate that the skull is probably male.

The long bones had a gracile appearance, though the humeri had very large deltoid insertions, which is more of a male trait. It was difficult to assign a sex based on appearance of pelvis and skull. With these bones alone, a conclusion of indeterminate sex would have had to be made, but the appearance of the sacrum was such that this individual can be classified as male.

AGE

The epiphyses of the bones, including those of the clavicle, the iliac crests of the pelvis, and the basioccipital synchondrosis, had completely fused, indicating that bone growth had been completed and the skeleton was fully adult.

No pubic symphyses were available for ageing, nor were the auricular surfaces viable for study, thus cranial suture closure was used. Using Meindl and Lovejoy's (1985) method, the external cranial vault gave an age of 39.4 ± 9.1 years and the lateral-anterior region gave an age of 41.1 ± 10 years. Based on the unreliability of cranial suture closure as the sole indicator of age, this individual can be cautiously classified as between 35 and 50 years of age (middle adult).

STATURE

As an osteometric board was not available for measuring the long bones, the measurements may not be accurate. Using Trotter and Gleser's (1958) formulae, stature can be estimated as 167.29 ± 2.99 cm. or approximately 5'6".

HEALTH

DENTAL PATHOLOGY

Three teeth were lost post-mortem, the maxillary right canine (with part of the root still present), and the maxillary first incisors. Teeth lost pre-mortem with the alveolus fully resorbed include the maxillary third molars, second molars, right first molar, premolars, left canine, and second incisors, and the mandibular molars, premolars, and right canine.

Tooth wear for incisors, canines and premolars was scored according to Smith's (1984) method and the molars were scored based on Scott's (1979) method. The maxillary right second molar exhibited little wear. The wear facets were large, but the cusps were still present. The maxillary left first molar was considerably worn with the cusp worn flat and dentin exposed. The mandibular incisors were moderately worn with large areas of dentin exposed. The mandibular left canine was considerably less worn, exhibiting a hairline of dentin exposure, while the right canine was extremely worn with only a small remnant of its enamel remaining. The extreme variation in wear between the teeth indicates that factors other than diet were most likely involved in the wear pattern. This man could have been using his teeth as tools.

Dental caries were present on the maxillary right second molar, left first molar, mandibular left and right canines, and left first and second incisors. The caries on the maxillary molars are on the inter-proximal surfaces, while the caries on the mandibular incisors and right canine are cervical caries. The mandibular left canine has three caries, two interproximal ones and one cervical one. The presence of so many caries indicates a diet high in carbohydrates.

There were no abscesses present, but many teeth, the maxillary third molars, second molars, right first molar, premolars, left canine, and second incisors, and the mandibular molars, premolars, and right canine, had all been lost pre-mortem. The loss of these teeth could have been due to previous healed abscesses, as the alveoli of all the teeth had been resorbed and healed. There was no dental calculus and no enamel hypoplasia present on the teeth.

Several teeth suffered from post-mortem damage and were split vertically; namely the mandibular left first and second incisors.

SKELETAL PATHOLOGY

This man exhibited a moderate amount of skeletal pathology, representative of his age. There was new lamellar bone deposited on lateral distal metaphyses, proximal to the fibular notch on the left and right tibiae. This is the site of attachment of the interosseous ligament that binds the tibia and fibula together at the ankle joint. An ankle injury, such as a sprain, could have caused inflammation at the site of muscle attachment, resulting in the production of the new lamellar bone.

There were sclerotic (healed) periostitic striations on the lateral proximal third of shafts of the right and left fibulae. The right fibula also had sclerotic new bone on the medial distal metaphysis. These new bone deposits were probably a result of soft tissue inflammation, possibly muscle strain. The right and left humeri had very large deltoid muscle insertions, indicating that this man may have been involved in some strenuous physical work.

Several bones indicated that this man suffered from degenerative joint disease. The right clavicle had lipping on the medial postero-lateral articular surface, the sternum had lipping on the sternal rib articulations, and one hand phalanx had lipping of the distal articular surface.

The most profoundly affected area of the skeleton was the spine. Osteoarthritis was present in the lumbar, thoracic, and cervical vertebrae. The lumbar vertebrae exhibited lipping on superior borders of their vertebral bodies. The seventh thoracic vertebra had schmorl's nodes on the superior and inferior surfaces of body. Schmorl's nodes are created by the pressure of intervertebral disks on the superior or inferior surfaces of vertebral bodies. The first, second, third and fourth thoracic vertebrae had lipping on inferior edges of their vertebral bodies.

The cervical vertebrae were deeply affected by osteoarthritis. The third cervical vertebra had an elongation of the inferior border of the vertebral body and exhibited severe pitting of the inferior vertebral body. The fourth cervical vertebra had severe lipping of the inferior and superior borders of the vertebral body. The fifth cervical vertebra had severe lipping of inferior and superior borders of vertebral body, with pitting on superior side of vertebral body. The bodies of the cervical vertebrae had cup-shaped articulations.

This man was severely stressing his back, with particular strain being placed on his neck. If he were using his teeth as a tool, as indicated by the dental pathology, considerable strain would have been placed on his neck, as indicated by the extreme osteoarthritis in this area.

This combination of dental and spinal pathologies could be suggestive of a working life spent weaving.

There is no indication for what ultimately was the cause of death.

DARLENE WESTON
Institute of Archaeology
University College, London, U.K.

CONDITION AND CONSERVATION REPORT

FEMALE SKULL

The skull is very fragmented at the forehead, the powder-like bones are disintegrating, the surface is damaged and some small pieces are missing. The right side of the orbit is broken off; teeth are missing in the upper jaw. The bone of the mandible was quite stable; a few teeth were loose, and most had fallen out.

MALE SKULL

The skull shows two small cracks at the back of the head; otherwise it is complete; the mandible is broken into three pieces on the left. The loose teeth are all covered with a thick deposit of salt; one upper tooth was broken in two, one molar was broken into three pieces.

The condition of the bones did not make it easy to choose the appropriate treatment, because the bones had been stored for a while and were very dry. They were fragile, powder-like and salty. To eliminate the salt content within the bones it would normally be necessary to soak them in deionised water. In this case this was not possible with risking damage through collapse or cracking of the bones because of their dryness.

A common and safe consolidant used for treating bones shortly after excavation is Acrysol WS-24, an acrylic dispersion resin supplied in a water solution; the water gives it a high viscosity, allowing it to penetrate deep into the bone structure. Again in this case this was not possible without running a high risk of further deformation.

On the Internet (http://nautarch.tamu.edu/class/anth605/file2.htm) I found a similar consolidant (Acryloid B72) with the same range of advantages to the one chosen:

1. Protection against light, humidity and physical strain.
2. Reversibility through solvents (acetone).
3. Desalination is still possible, and would simply take longer.

TREATMENT

The bones were checked for damage, and fragments kept in a sample bag.

Where the salt was visible on the surface it was removed with a soft dry brush. To lift more stubborn particles of salt, a wooden stick was used. Where the surface appeared stable, cotton wool compresses soaked in deionised water and acetone 50:50 were applied until the salt content was reduced.

Research in libraries and on the Internet showed that the most suitable consolidant solution was Paraloid B72 in ethyl-methyl-ketone.

The solution was first diluted to 3% to allow deep penetration. Complete immersion in a vacuum would penetrate even deeper, but the risk of the skulls collapsing was too great. The process of soaking the bones in this solution was repeated seven times: the skulls were left in the solution until no further air bubbles appeared. The solution was then thickened to 5% and the process repeated five times. The last three times the solution was increased to 10%. In order to protect the particularly fragile parts of the skulls such as the nose and eye sockets these were given extra strengthening by applying a 20% solution with a pipette.

After the bones were completely dry, the broken portions were reattached with HMG (cellulose nitrate adhesive) and the broken jaw was repaired. Loose teeth which were still in place were also secured with HMG, an adhesive which can be reversed with acetone.

The teeth could not be desalinated with water; they were already broken or cracked. Using a scalpel, the thick layer of salt was removed under a microscope. The last traces of salt crystals were cleaned off with acetone and a soft brush. The same consolidation treatment with the same solution was then applied to the teeth.

After drying, the broken tooth was fixed with HMG; because the damaged molar is not complete, it could not be reattached.

STORAGE

The best way to prevent further damage due to the salt of which traces still remain in the bones is to store them at a low humidity, not over 45% and not too far below this figure to prevent further drying and cracking. A cool dark place with controlled humidity would be the best environment to preserve these objects from further damage.

MICHAELA AUGUSTIN-JEUTTER
The Manchester Museum
University of Manchester, U.K.

AGE DETERMINATION OF THE MALE

The state of the art scientific technique for determining age in an individual after death, is the Gustafson Technique. The technique is based on the extent of root translucency in the dentin. The upper left canine of the male skeleton in the larnax from Tomb 132 at Armenoi was submitted for analysis. I am fairly confident that the person was 45 years of age ± 6 years.

DAVID K. WHITTAKER
University of Cardiff, U.K.

212

213

212 MALE SKELETON

. . . .

R.M. 132 a

LM III B (c. 1340-1190 B.C.)
Late Minoan Cemetery of Armenoi, Tomb 132

The male was delicately built, and stood 167 cm. (5'6") tall. He had particularly bad teeth, with 23 out of 32 teeth lost ante-mortem. Dental caries were present on six teeth, but again there was no dental calculus. There was an extreme variation in amount of tooth wear among the remaining teeth, indicating that factors other than diet were involved in the wear pattern. This man could have been using his teeth as a kind of tool. He exhibited a moderate amount of skeletal pathology, representative of his age. He had large upper arm musculature, indicating that he must have been involved in some type of strenuous physical work. There was an indication that he had sustained an ankle injury, probably a sprain. He suffered from mild osteoarthritis in one collarbone, the breastbone and hand, and he suffered from severe osteoarthritis in his back and neck. If he were using his teeth as a tool, as indicated by the dental pathology, considerable strain would have been placed on his neck, as indicated by the extreme osteoarthritis in this area. The dental pathology, coupled with the severe osteoarthritis in the back and neck and the well-developed arm muscles, suggests that this man may have been a weaver by trade. There is no indication of what was ultimately the cause of death.

D.W.

213 FEMALE SKELETON

. . . .

R.M. 132 b

LM III B (c. 1340-1190 B.C.)
Late Minoan Cemetery of Armenoi, Tomb 132

The female, in her mid-forties, was very short and delicately built, standing only 141cm. (4' 71/2") tall. Her dental health was not remarkable. She had lost two teeth ante-mortem, had three dental caries, but surprisingly had no dental calculus. Lines of enamel hypoplasia were present on the majority of her teeth, indicating that the enamel formation was disrupted in early childhood through

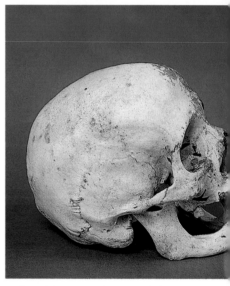

malnutrition or infectious disease. Unusually for an individual in her mid-forties, there was no sign of osteoarthritis in her spine or other joints. Based on this lack of joint disease and her small muscularate, it is conceivable that she enjoyed a life free from any demanding physical labour. She was free from chronic pathological conditions, and most likely died from an acute illness.

D.W.

214 CYLINDRICAL ALABASTRON

R.M. 2671

LM III B (c. 1340-1190 B.C.)
LM Cemetery of Armenoi, Tomb 132
H: 18.1 cm.; D: 16 cm.

Mended and restored. Yellowish fabric, off-white slip, black, fugitive paint, flaked away over the entire surface of the vase. Globular-conical body (FS 59), rather tall neck with concave profile, slightly everted rim. Horizontal handles of oval section, set on the shoulder of the vase. Flat base. The body of the vase is decorated with bands. The main decorative motif is placed on the shoulder, between the handles. It consists of a zone of metopes and triglyphs filled with cross-hatching (FM 75:23) and wavy lines (FM 53:12).

E.P.

215 CYLINDRICAL ALABASTRON

R.M. 2672

LM III B (c. 1340-1190 B.C.)
LM Cemetery of Armenoi, Tomb 132
H: 16 cm.; D: 14 cm.

Intact. Brown-grey fabric, shiny slip of same colour, brown paint. Almost hemispherical body (FS 95?), sloping shoulder with smooth transition to body. Tall cylindrical neck. Everted rim of triangular section. Two horizontal handles of circular section set on shoulder. The main decorative motif is placed on the shoulder of the vase between the two handles and consists of two double hatched semi-circles on each face (FM 43:5). Body of vase encircled by bands down to base.

E.P.

216 STIRRUP JAR

R.M. 2673

LM III B (c. 1340-1190 B.C.)
LM Cemetery of Armenoi, Tomb 132
H: 13.3 cm.; D: 16.3 cm.

Slightly restored at rim. Off-white fabric, slip of same colour, red paint. Cylindrical body, conical at top, with flat shoulder. Narrow closed neck. High narrow spout

215

214

216

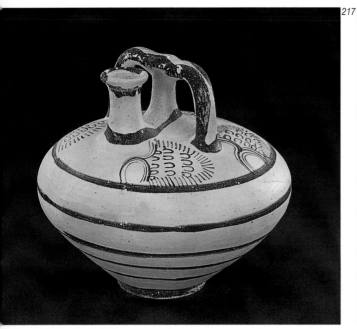

217

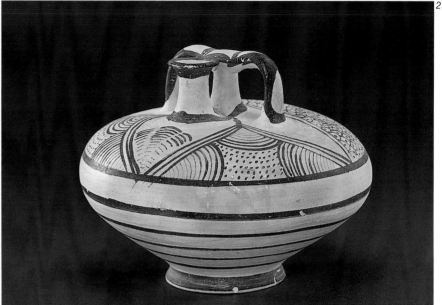

218

219

with angular rim. Handle of elliptical section, and discoid base. The main decorative motif is placed on the shoulder of the vase and consists of oblique hatched lozenges (FM 73) and supplementary semi-circles (FM 43). The rest of the decoration consists of bands.

E.P.

217 STIRRUP JAR

R.M. 2674

LM III B (c. 1340-1190 B.C.)
LM Cemetery of Armenoi, Tomb 132
H: 12.2 cm.; D: 13.75 cm.

Intact. Brown-grey fabric, shiny slip of same colour, brown-black paint. Squat conical body (FS 179). Closed narrow cylindrical neck and spout. Angular spout rim. Flat spherical handle discs, and handles of oval section. Ring base. The main decorative motif is placed on the shoulder of the vase and consists of scale pattern with dots on one side, and on the other triangles with a triple outline, the angles of which are filled by concentric arches of diminishing size. The rest of the decoration consists of bands. Product of a Kydonia workshop.

E.P.

218 STIRRUP JAR

R.M. 2675

LM III B (c. 1340-1190 B.C.)
LM Cemetery ofArmenoi, Tomb 132
H: 10.6 cm.; D: 13.8 cm.

Intact. Brown-grey fabric, shiny slip of same colour, brown-black paint. Squat conical body (FS 179). Closed narrow cylindrical neck and spout. Angular spout rim. Cylindrical handle discs, and handles of oval section. Ring base. The main decorative motif is placed on the shoulder of the vase and consists of scale pattern with dots on one side, and on the other triangles with a triple outline, the angles of which are filled by concentric arches of diminishing size. The rest of the decoration consists of bands. Product of a Kydonia workshop.

E.P.

219 CYLINDRICAL ALABASTRON

R.M. 2676

LM III B (c. 1340-1190 B.C.)
LM Cemetery of Armenoi, Tomb 132
H: 14.2 cm.; D: 13.2 cm.

Intact. Brown-grey fabric, slip of same colour, brown-black to red paint. Cylindrical body (FS 95?), sloping shoulder with angle at transition to body. Tall cylindrical neck with wide horizontal everted rim. Two horizontal handles of circular section set on shoulder. Flat base. The decoration on the body consists of two bands defining zones of triglyphs and metopes. This system is supplemented by cross-hatched motifs (FM 75:23), and parallelograms filled with cross-hatching and a double reserved arch above and below them. The shoulder is decorated with a zone of chevrons (FM 58:33) between the handles. Body encircled by bands.

E.P.

221 SMALL JUG

R.M. 2678

LM III B (c. 1340-1190 B.C.)
LM Cemetery of Armenoi, Tomb 132
H: 8.35 cm.; D: 7.85 cm.

Intact. Brown-grey fabric, shiny slip of same colour, brown-black paint. Squat biconical body (FS 114). Slightly raised ring base, with a concave interior. Hollow neck with concave profile. Rounded everted rim. Vertical strap handle starting from the rim and ending at the shoulder of the vase. The decoration consists of bands.

E.P.

221

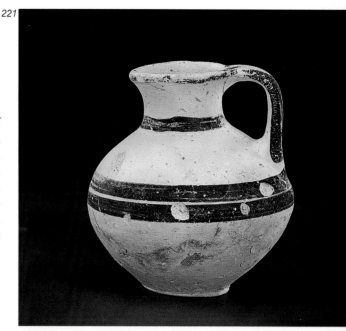

220

220 STIRRUP JAR

R.M. 2677

LM III B (c. 1340-1190 B.C.)
LM Cemetery of Armenoi, Tomb 132
H: 14.8 cm.; D: 18.2 cm.

Intact. Off-white fabric, yellowish slip, orange paint. Squat conical body (FS 179). Narrow closed cylindrical neck. Spout set higher than the handle disc with slightly concave profile, ending in angular rim. Cylindrical handle disc, and handles of oval section. Ring base. The main decorative motif consists of a stylized octopus on each face. The lower part of the body is decorated with bands. Product of a Kydonia workshop.

E.P.

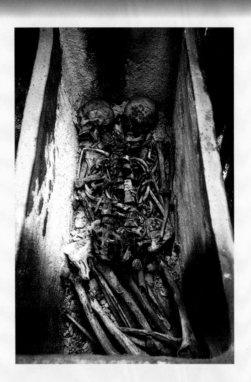

This was the only clay coffin found at the Cemetery of Armenoi that held more than one individual.

Age	Mid-forties
Height	141 cm. (4'7")
General Health	Good
Built	Delicate
Teeth	Poor Condition 2 teeth lost ante-mortem
Cause of death	Acute Illness

The Minoan Couple from Armenoi

Late Minoan III B1
Crete
c. 1340-1250 B.C.

Age	Forty Five - Fifty
Height	167 cm. (5'6")
General Health	Fair
Built	Delicate
Teeth	Bad Condition
	23 out of 32 teeth lost ante-mortem
Cause of death	Unknown
Other interesting features	We think he was a weaver.

CHAMBER TOMB OF ARMENOI

This reconstruction illustrates a wealthy chamber tomb from the Late Minoan Cemetery of Armenoi, Rethymnon.

All chamber tombs are subterranean. They are cut into bedrock, and they consist of a ramp or stairway (corridor) with a chamber at the end. The opening to the chamber was usually closed with a stone slab, but there are instances in which stones of varying sizes were used.

All tombs represent family groups, and the deceased were placed either on the floor of the tomb or in clay larnakes (sarcophagi). In one instance the deceased was placed in a wooden larnax.

Tombs were re-opened as necessary. When there was no room for subsequent burials, the bones already *in situ* were pushed aside including the accumulated grave goods, in order to make room for new burials. The way in which this was done indicates that respect was shown for ancestors.

One should take note of the range and type of goods and where these were found. In the chamber of the tomb you will see beautiful offerings such as decorated vessels, bronze objects, and jewellery. In the chamber there were vessels which appear to have been new and kept for this specific purpose. Vessels used for ceremonial purposes were thrown in the dromos.

DR. YANNIS TZEDAKIS

This is a graph of the stable isotope values of men and women from Armenoi.

The δ13 C value tells us about the amount of marine protein (e.g. fish) in diets, where a δ13 C -20‰ = no fish, and a δ13 C -12‰ = all fish.

The δ15 N value tells us about the amount of animal protein (e.g. meat or milk) vs. plant protein in diets, where a δ15 N of 9-11‰ = almost 100% meat, and a δ15 N 3-5‰ = almost no meat.

The Armenoi humans had no marine food in their diets, as indicated by the δ13 C values, but in general they ate a fair amount of animal protein. Although you cannot tell it from this graph, men at this site had, on average, more animal protein in their diets than women (the men had higher δ15 N values).

The burial population in chamber tombs 1-118 at Armenoi consi approximately 143 adult males, 107 adult females and 114 children, al in tombs of various sizes and shapes. 57 % of the children died before re the age of five, and 34% died before reaching the age of two. The avera at death for the adult males and females was approximately 31 years years respectively, most of the female deaths occurred between the age and 25, probably a result of the dangers associated with childbirth.

Males ranged in height from 158.2 to 180.4 cm. (5'2"-5'11"), with an a height of 167.6 cm. (5'6"); females ranged in height from 144 to 16 (4'8"-5'5"), with an average height of 154.6 cm. (5'1"). This ancient pop was slightly shorter than the modern male and female Cretan who averages 168.1 cm. (5'6") and 156.5 cm. (5'1"), respectively.

Dental disease was a problem for this population. The occurrence of caries (cavities) in the population at 18% and of ante-mortem tooth 29% is very high when compared with skeletal populations at contem Minoan sites. 66% of the population exhibited enamel hypopla disruption in the formation of the enamel due to nutritional deficien infectious disease), 47% suffered from gum disease, and 48% had calculus (plaque).

The people buried at Armenoi suffered from a range of infectio nutritional/metabolic diseases. Among the infectious diseases osteomyelitis (infection of the bone marrow), brucellosis (transm humans through bacteria in goat's milk), and tuberculosis (contracted infected cow's milk). Interestingly, the individuals suffering from tuber were buried together. Nutritional diseases that this population suffere include osteoporosis, scurvy, rickets, and iron-deficiency anaemia.

The people buried at Armenoi led an active lifestyle as evidenced by a of fractured bones. Sixteen individuals had broken bones, with the lo most frequently affected. Most of the fractures were well healed, inc that the Minoans had good knowledge of orthopaedic techniques. Ar lifestyle was also indicated by the fifteen individuals who suffere traumatic arthritis, usually an occupationally related condition.

The Armenoi population was not free from modern societies' most diseases, as two individuals suffered from cancer. An osteoplastic s was discovered on the lower arm of one 45-year-old adult male, metallistic carcinoma was discovered in the spinal column of one mal approximately 29 years.

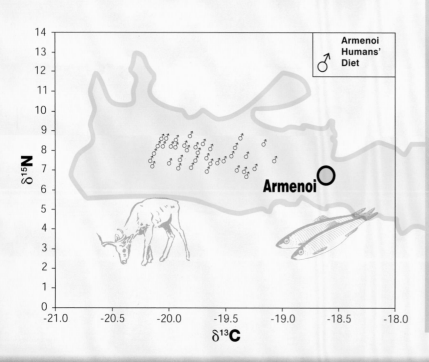

Chamber Tombs
Armenoi

Late Minoan III A-B
c. 1390-1190 B.C.

What did they eat?

Pottery depicts marine life. How much did they eat?

How much meat or milk did they eat?

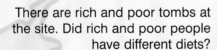

There are rich and poor tombs at the site. Did rich and poor people have different diets?

Did men and women have different diets?

Chemical analysis of bones tells us

• No marine foods.

• They ate a mixture of meat and plants.

• There are no differences in diets between rich and poor people.

• Yes! It seems men had more meat (or milk) in their diets than women.

222   ONE-HANDLED FOOTED CUP

R.M. 6501

LM III B1 (c. 1340-1250 B.C.)
LM Cemetery of Armenoi, Tomb 177
H: 6.8 cm.; D: rim 11.6 cm., base 5.7 cm.

Intact, with some chipping to rim and edge. Reddish fabric, entire surface of vase covered with black, shiny paint, flaked away in places. Conical body. Everted rim. One vertical strap handle. Hollow conical foot.

E.P.

222

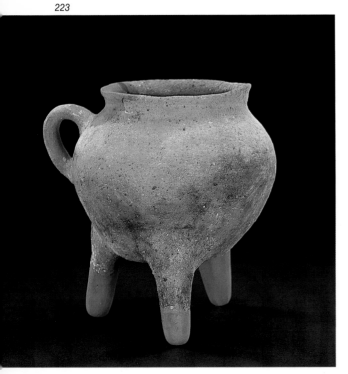

223

223   SMALL ONE-HANDLED TRIPOD COOKING POT

R.M. 47

LM III B (c. 1340-1190 B.C.)
Stavromenos, Rethymnon
H: 15 cm.; D: (max) 17 cm.

Legs restored. Brown-red fabric with inclusions. Squat globular body. Rounded everted rim, with a slight spout. Flat base, sitting on three legs of oval section. Unpainted. Exterior surface has traces of burning, and is flaked away in places.

E.P.

224   JAR

R.M. 7503

LM III B (1340-1190 B.C.)
LM Cemetery of Armenoi, Tomb 201
H: 14.3 cm.; D: mouth 8.5 cm., body 12.5 cm.

Intact, slightly chipped. Brown-red fabric. Biconical body. Flat base. Wide, tall neck. Everted lip. Two vertical strap handles. The surface of the vase is badly worn, and no trace of decoration survives.

E.P.

225   KYLIX

R.M. 3455

LM III B (c. 1340-1190 B.C.)
LM Cemetery of Armenoi, Tomb 159
H: 18 cm.; D: rim 15.5 cm., base 7.9 cm.

Mended and restored. Brown fabric. Deep conical body (FS 273) ending in a rounded rim. The tall stem rests on a wide discoid base with a cavity at the centre. The two handles, of circular section, rise above the rim. The vase is painted solid with black paint, which has largely flaked away. Plated with a layer of tin. Imitation of Mycenaean tin-plated kylikes.

E.P.

226   KYLIX

R.M. 17243

LM III A2-B (c. 1370-1190 B.C.)
LM Cemetery of Armenoi, Tomb 146
(Blocked entrance)

Fragment of a high-stemmed kylix, mended from a large number of sherds. Yellowish fabric with inclusions. Part of shallow conical body preserved, ending

22

22

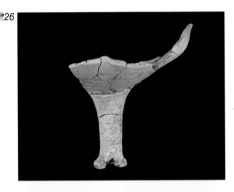

indrical stem preserved intact, and about half the shallow conical body. The vase is undecorated.

E.P.

228 KYLIX

R.M. 20949

LM III A2-B (c. 1370-1190 B.C.)
LM Cemetery of Armenoi, Trench 3, level 3

Fragment of a high-stemmed kylix mended from a large number of sherds. Brown-grey fabric. Larger part of shallow conical body preserved, together with cylindrical stem and a small part of base. No decoration or slip. Surface covered with sediment.

E.P.

229 CONICAL CUP

R.M. 6571

LM III B (c. 1340-1190 B.C.)
LM Cemetery of Armenoi, Tomb 289
H: 5.5 cm.; D: mouth 10.6 cm.

Almost intact, part of rim restored. Brown fabric with inclusions, brown-grey slip. Conical handleless body. Flat base.

E.P.

230 CONICAL CUP

R.M. 1760

LM III B (c. 1340-1190 B.C.)
LM Cemetery of Armenoi, Tomb 39
H: 4.8 cm.; D: rim 10.4 cm.

Mended. Brown-red fabric. Conical handleless body. Flat base.

E.P.

231 RHYTON

R.M. 2324

LM III A2-B (c. 1370-1190 B.C.)
LM Cemetery of Armenoi, Tomb 112, Dromos
H: 30.9 cm.; D: rim 6.1 cm.

Intact, with badly chipped rim. Brown-red impure fabric, off-white slip, black paint. Conical pointed body. Small triangular lug near the rim. Surface badly worn. Very few traces of decoration with narrow bands are preserved.

E.P.

in a thin everted rim, of which little is preserved. Part of vertical handle –of oval section– preserved, and cylindrical stem is intact. The inside of the vase is painted solid with shiny red paint, and on the outside the zone beneath the rim is encircled by a red band. The stem was covered with black paint, of which only a few traces can be detected.

E.P.

227 KYLIX

R.M. 17162

LM III A2-B (c. 1370-1190 B.C.)
LM Cemetery of Armenoi, Tomb 146, Dromos
H: (pres.) 14 cm.

Fragment of a high-stemmed kylix, mended from a large number of sherds. Orange fabric, light brown slip. Cyl-

232 LARNAX

R.M. 1703

LM III A2-B (c. 1370-1190 B.C.)
LM Cemetery of Armenoi, Tomb 55
H: (with lid) 75 cm.; W: long sides 95 cm.,
short sides 40 cm.

Terracotta cist-shaped larnax, with a lid
with a projecting, convex ridge. The
body is supported on four legs, and
there is a projecting border around the
sides. There are 8 holes in the sides and
10 in the lid.
The decoration, in black paint, is as
follows: on one of the long sides are
stylised octopuses (FM 21), and on the
other a row of horns of consecration
with a double axe between them, set in a
zone defined by an isolated spiral above
and below. On one narrow side is a
linear rendering of a flower with thorn-
like projections and a band with a stem.
Above this are supplementary lozenges
filled with chevrons and cross-hatching.
On the other side is a Minoan flower
(FM 18A), with supplementary tongue-
patterns around it (FM 19). The corner-
posts are decorated with wavy bands
(FM 53) and way borders (FM 65).

E.P.

233 BASKET

R.M. 1664

LM III B (c. 1340-1190 B.C.)
LM Cemetery of Armenoi, Tomb 24
H: (with handle) 13 cm.; D: rim 16 cm.,
base 9 cm.

Intact. Light brown fabric, slip of same
colour, red to brown-black paint. Conical
body, wide horizontal rim, flat base.
Vertical handle with a relief applique on
the rim and a small, integral cup.

E.P.

232

233

235 TRIPOD VASE WITH LID

R.M. 1782

LM III B2 (c. 1250-1190 B.C.)
LM Cemetery of Armenoi, Tomb 46
H: (with lid) 33 cm.; D: body 29.4 cm.

Intact, neck chipped. Brown-red fabric, yellow-grey slip, orange to black paint, worn in places. Globular body with narrow cylindrical neck. Four handles of oval section set on the shoulder. Body supported on 3 low legs of oval section. The shoulder zone is decorated with concentric semi-circles (FM 43), filled with small parallel lines. Between them is a system of chevrons (FM 58) at the centre of which are solid semi-circles with dots round them. At each of the four corners of the panel is a system of concentric arches. The main motif is surrounded by supplementary sea anemone motifs.

The lid has a cylindrical body with a basket handle. Its decoration consists of a series of horizontal lines.

E.P.

236 HYDRIA

R.M. 2192

LM III A (c. 1390-1340 B.C.)
LM Cemetery of Armenoi, Tomb 95
H: 27.2 cm.; D: 18.4 cm.

Intact. Pinkish brown fabric, light brown slip, brown-red to red very fugitive

234

234 ALABASTRON

R.M. 1714

LM III A (c. 1390-1340 B.C.)
LM Cemetery of Armenoi, Tomb 27
H: 10 cm.; D: body 12.5 cm.

Intact. Brown-grey fabric, shiny black paint worn in places. Globular body, tall neck with horizontal rim. Flat base. The vase is painted solid.

E.P.

235

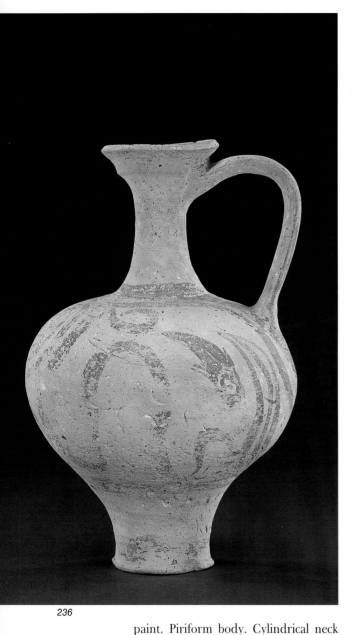

236

paint. Piriform body. Cylindrical neck with a concave profile, ending in a funnel mouth with an exterior relief ring. Vertical strap handle beginning at the relief ring at the mouth and ending at the shoulder of the vase. The main decorative motif is placed on the shoulder of the vase and consists of a stylised octopus (FM 21). The tentacles extend freely around the body, and there is an isolated fish, rendered naturalistically, amongst them. The main motif and the base are encircled by hands. The vase is a copy of a metal model.

E.P.

237 TALL ALABASTRON

R.M. 2193

LM III A (c. 1390-1340 B.C.)
LM Cemetery of Armenoi, Tomb 93
H: 20 cm.; D: body 17 cm, base 13 cm.

Mended and restored. Light brown fabric, slip of same colour, black fugitive paint. Oval body with wide flat base. Tall cylindrical neck with a concave profile, ending in a horizontal everted rim. Horizontal handle of oval section, set vertically on the shoulder of the vase. The shoulder between the handles is adorned with a zone of stylised fish arranged in a zig-zag (recalling FM24:F). The motif is bordered by bands of different thicknesses, and the handles, upper part of the neck, and rim are painted solid.

E.P.

238 CYLINDRICAL ALABASTRON

R.M. 2199

LM III A2 (c. 1370-1340 B.C.)
LM Cemetery of Armenoi, Tomb 100
H: 11 cm.; D: (max) 12.5 cm., base 5 cm.

Intact. Light brown fabric, shiny cream slip, red to black paint. Squat globular body. Flat base. Cylindrical neck with concave outline, ending in horizontal, everted rim. Horizontal handles of elliptical section set at right angles to shoulder. Zone of stylised fish arranged in zig-zag pattern (recalling FM 24:F) on shoulder between handles. Motif bordered by bands of unequal thickness. Upper part of neck and rim painted solid.

E.P.

239 INCENSE BURNER

R.M. 2316

LM III B (c. 1340-1190 B.C.)
LM Cemetery of Armenoi, Tomb 118
H: 14.2 cm.; D: base 10.6 cm.

Lid slightly restored. Light brown fabric, brown-white slip, brown-red to black, rather fugitive paint. The inner part has a cylindrical body with a flat base and a ring around the edge to fit the lid. The handle is vertical, of circular section and extends from the rim to the base. The lid has cylindrical walls and the upper part is conical, has triangular openings, and ends in a funnel-shaped chimney to release the fumes. The inner part is encircled by hands and the lid is decorated with panels, filled alternately with cross-hatching and a naturalistically rendered forked Minoan flower (FM 81C:55). The upper part is encircled by bands, and the chimney is painted completely.

E.P.

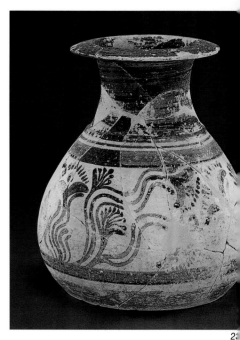

240 ASKOS

R.M. 2657

LM III A (c. 1390-1340 B.C.)
LM Cemetery of Armenoi, Tomb 127
H: 6.7 cm.; D: body 8.6 cm.

Intact. Red fabric, brown-grey slip, brown paint, worn in places. Lower part of body conical with a cylindrical belly and a sloping, almost horizontal, shoulder. Short narrow spout with a concave profile ending in a rim of triangular section. Horizontal handle of oval section on the shoulder. Upright torus base. The entire shoulder is decorated with four stylised Minoan flowers. The motif is bordered by a band, and there are other bands encircling the body and base.

E.P.

238

240

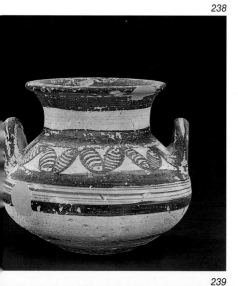

both sides by a stylised octopus (FM 21:5). The motif is bordered by bands. The zone of the handles is adorned by hatched lozenges (FM 73) and a supplementary V-shape on one side, while the other side has elaborate triangles filled with concentric circles and stylised bivalve shells. The rest of the body down to the base is encircled by bands. Product of a Kydonia workshop.

E.P.

239

241

242

241 STIRRUP JAR

R.M. 2658

LM III B1 (c. 1340-1250 B.C.)
LM Cemetery of Armenoi, Tomb 139
H: 12 cm.; D: body 16.5 cm.

Spout slightly restored. Yellowish fabric, shiny yellow-white slip, brown-black semi-fugitive paint. Squat globular-conical body (FS 180). Narrow closed cylindrical neck and spout ending at a rim of triangular section. Handles of circular section. Ring base. The zone of the shoulder is decorated on one side by seven birds with their beaks open upwards, while the other side has an elaborate triangle either side of the spout (FM 71/variation). The rest of the body is encircled by bands, and the handle disc is decorated by a spiral. Product of a Kydonia workshop.

E.P.

242 STIRRUP JAR

R.M. 2709

LM III B (c. 1340-1190 B.C.)
LM Cemetery of Armenoi, Tomb 140
H: 12.7 cm.; D: 17.5 cm.

Spout mended. Off-white fabric, yellowish slip, brown-black paint. Biconical body (FS 179). Closed cylindrical neck and spout ending at a rim of triangular section. The body zone is decorated on

244 SQUAT ALABASTRON

R.M. 6518

LM III A2 (c. 1370-1340 B.C.)
LM Cemetery of Armenoi, Tomb 184
H: 9.1 cm.; D: body 15.2 cm.

Mended from several sherds and restored in places. Ochre-brown fabric, black paint over an off-white slip. Piriform body. Low wide neck with horizontal lip. Three handles of oval section. Flat base. The belly is encircled by rock pattern (FM 32). Lower part of body, base and surface of lip encircled by bands. Neck and back of handles painted solid.

E.P.

246 JAR

R.M. 6544

LM III A2 (c. 1370-1340 B.C.)
LM Cemetery of Armenoi, Tomb 188
H: 18 cm.; D: body (max) 14.3 cm.

Mended and restored in places. Off-white fabric, slip of same colour, black semi-fugitive paint. Piriform body. Low wide neck ending at a flat, sloping rim. Three vertical strap handles on the shoulder. The zone of the shoulders is decorated with a total of five lilies between the handles. The rest of the decoration consists of encircling bands. Neck and foot painted solid.

E.P.

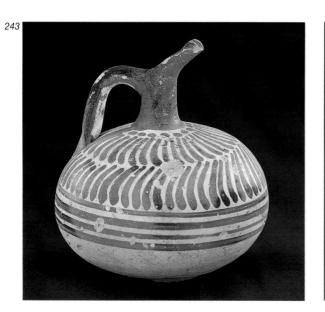

243

24

243 SMALL JUG

R.M. 6515

LM III A2 (c. 1370-1340 B.C.)
LM Cemetery of Armenoi, Tomb 184
H: 9.9 cm.; D: body 9.2 cm.

Intact, considerably chipped. Pinkish brown fabric, black to brown paint over an off-white slip. Squat globular body. Low cylindrical neck ending in a beak spout. Handle of circular section. Flat base. Base of vase decorated by a foliate band (FM 64:13) arranged in two successive rows. Neck and back of handle painted solid. Product of a Kydonia workshop.

E.P.

245 MINIATURE ALABASTRON

R.M. 6527

LM III A (c. 1390-1340 B.C.)
LM Cemetery of Armenoi, Tomb 198
H: 6.1 cm.; D: body (max) 4.7 cm.

Rim restored. Ochre-brown fabric, slip of same colour, brown-red, semi-fugitive paint. Piriform body with a relief ring at the base of the neck. Cylindrical neck with concave profile, ending in a wide flat rim. Flat base. Upper part of body decorated with chevrons (FM 75:8), lower part down to base decorated with irregular horizontal bands. Neck and rim painted solid.

E.P.

247 SMALL DOUBLE JUG

R.M. 21056

LM III A2-B (c. 1370-1190 B.C.)
LM Cemetery of Armenoi, Tomb 208
H: 6.5 cm.; W: (max) 13 cm.

Intact. Brown fabric, yellow slip, red paint. The vase consists of two small jugs connected by a hollow tube at a point of max. diameter. Piriform bodies. Short neck with rim wider on one than on the other. On the first the neck is closed at the top, while the other has four holes, forming a kind of strainer. Basket handle of oval section linking the two parts. The first is decorated with papyri with voluted stems, occupying the body of the vase, and there is a row of dots around the solid-painted spout (FM 11 papyrus). The second is decorated with stylised Minoan flowers (FM 18). On the zone of the shoulder two rows of dots enclose a zone of X-shaped motifs, Here, too, the spout is painted solid. The handle is decorated with small lateral lines. Ritual vase of Cretan type.

E.P.

246

245

247

248 SEALSTONE

R.M. 62

LM III A-B (c. 1390-1190 B.C.)
Rock crystal
LM Cemetery of Armenoi, Tomb 184
1.30×1.50 cm.

Two crossed bands divide the surface into four parts. One pair of opposite parts is cross-hatched and the other pair is decorated with chevrons.

E.P.

turned up. Horns turned behind and down at a right angle. Branches of trees in front of and behind the animal and beneath its belly.

E.P.

250 SEALSTONE

R.M. 102

LM III A-B (c. 1390-1190 B.C.)
LM Cemetery of Armenoi, Tomb 115
D: 1.7 cm.

251 NECKLACE

R.M. 502

LM III A-B (c. 1390-1190 B.C.)
Glass paste
LM Cemetery of Armenoi, Tomb 116

The necklace consists of fifteen rectangular plaques of glass paste, curved at the bottom. Each is decorated with three relief spirals arranged vertically. There is a dentilated protrusion at the centre of each spiral. The decoration is divided into three parts by two hori-

249 SEALSTONE

R.M. 16

LM III A-B (c. 1390-1190 B.C.)
Steatite
LM Cemetery of Armenoi, Tomb 18
D: 1.65 cm.

Lentoid shape. Scene of a wild goat in profile, with its mouth open and tail

Lentoid shape with linear decoration: the sealing surface is divided into two equal halves by a long line, from the centre of which hang radiate oblique lines forming triangles. Each triangle is incised either laterally or longitudinally with a large number of lines.

E.P.

zontal rows of relief dots. A horizontal suspension hole is pierced in both the upper edge, which consists of a series of flutes, and at the bottom, in the middle of the last spiral.

E.P.

252 ARMLET

R.M. 486

LM III A2-B (c. 1370-1190 B.C.)
Bronze
LM Cemetery of Armenoi, Tomb 140
D: 7.1 cm.; Thickness: 0.33 cm.

The armlet is made of thick wire that
gradually tapers, to end in a spiral around
the two parts of the thick wire.

E.P.

253 FINGER-RING

R.M. 560

LM III A-B (c. 1390-1190 B.C.)
Bronze
LM Cemetery of Armenoi, Tomb 86
D: 1.45 cm.; W: 0.65-0.75 cm.;
Thickness: 0.2 cm.

The finger-ring is made of thick wire in
the shape of a triple spiral. One end is
attached, while the thinner end is free.

E.P.

handle with rounded shoulders. The
organic sheathing was held in place by
two nails placed side by side on the
shaft and two more on the shoulder.
The handle is encircled by a lip that
ends at the beginning of the blade. The
pommel is crescent-shaped. The blade
is slightly biconical in section, and
triangular in shape, with sides that run
almost parallel before turning suddenly
to form the angle. A relief line runs
along the lip.

E.P.

251

252

253

254 SAW

R.M. 452

LM III A-B (c. 1390-1190 B.C.)
Bronze
LM Cemetery of Armenoi, Tomb 115
L: 42 cm.; W: 5.5 cm.

Intact. Long, thin blade with a toothed
edge and a straight back in which there
are three holes to attach the sheathing.
Typical Minoan type.

E.P.

255 SMALL SWORD

R.M. 1202

LM III A-B (c. 1390-1190 B.C.)
Bronze
LM Cemetery of Armenoi, Tomb 200
L: 35.5 cm.; W: shoulder 6 cm.,
pommel 4.9 cm.

The small sword belongs to Sandars'
type EII, and has an integral T-shaped

254

255

256 KNIFE-AXE

R.M. 598

LM III A-B (c. 1390-1190 B.C.)
Bronze
LM Cemetery of Armenoi, Tomb 150
L: 21.6 cm.; W: (max) 7.88 cm.

Narrow handle curving outwards distinctly towards the bottom. Two nails are preserved, and a hole for a third, for attaching the wooden sheathing (?), traces of which are preserved along the entire length of the handle shaft. The blade is wide, heavy, and trapezoidal in shape with a straight back. Engraved decorative lines along the blade surface and emphasise the back, which is the thickest part.

E.P.

257 SMALL SWORD

R.M. 613

LM III A-B (c. 1390-1190 B.C.)
Bronze
LM Cemetery of Armenoi, Tomb 186
L: 26.2 cm.; W: 5.31 cm.

256

257

258

259

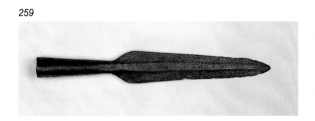

The integral T-shaped handle had a crescent-shaped pommel and a long narrow shaft ending at the blade, where it forms square shoulders. The entire handle down to the beginning of the blade is encircled by a lip. The organic sheathing of the handle was held in place by four nails, two set lengthways.

E.P.

258 DAGGER

R.M. 618

LM III A-B (c. 1390-1190 B.C.)
Bronze
LM Cemetery of Armenoi, Tomb 202
L: 19.7 cm.; W: shoulder 5.21 cm.,
beginning of blade 4.4 cm.;
Thickness: 0.32 cm.

Intact, cutting edges slightly chipped. Long double-edged blade with a fairly square shoulder, in which are set three rivets to attach the wooden sheathing. The cutting edges are straight and end in a point like that of a spear.

E.P.

259 SPEARHEAD

R.M. 35

LM III A-B (c. 1390-1190 B.C.)
Bronze
LM Cemetery at Armenoi, Tomb Gamma
L: 27.5 cm.; W: 3.6 cm.

Conical tube, wider at the beginning, which has two holes opposite each other for attaching the wooden shaft. Leaf-shaped point with rounded heel. Central rib reinforces the back of the spearhead.

E.P.

260 HANDLELESS CUP

R.M. 386

LM III A (c. 1390-1340 B.C.)
Bronze
LM Cemetery of Armenoi, Tomb 35
H: 5 cm.; D: rim 12.4 cm., base 4.24 cm.;
Thickness 0.2-0.3 cm.

Hemispherical body, flat base. Mended from a large number of fragments and chipped around the edge of the rim.

E.P.

260

261 SKELETON

LM III B (c. 1340-1190 B.C.)
LM Cemetery of Armenoi, Tomb 218,
Skeleton 1

Skeleton 1 (burial 218) belongs to a larger collection from the LM Cemetery of Armenoi in Crete. Due to the severe erosion and salt accumulation, the skeleton was cleaned with a soft brush and distilled water was sprayed to the anatomical elements when appropriate. Most skeletal parts were preserved with post-mortem loss primarily limited to bones of the hand and foot. Many ribs, the sternum and both scapulae are fragmentary. Post-mortem erosion has also affected the vertebrae; finally, all 36 teeth are preserved. The individual was a young male (average age at death was estimated at 18.5 years). No pathologies were observed, except cribra orbitalia at the anterolateral sector of both eye orbits.

Chr. B.

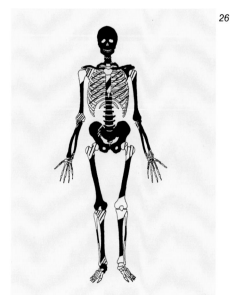

261

MITOCHONDRIAL DNA

We have begun a project on mtDNA in modern day Crete. 85% of those tested are members of a single group of mitochondrial lineages. By counting the number of mutations by which they differ from each other, we can estimate that these lineages are roughly 10,000 years old. This is now in the process of being checked in two ways: by additional sampling; and by extracting mtDNA from bone samples of people buried before the arrival of Greeks on the island. If these samples look similar to the modern-day islanders, they could be related to the Minoans, at least through the female line. This would be a finding of considerable archaeological importance.

Molecular signatures from the past are providing fascinating insights into early human society, the migrations of ancient people, the origins and practice of early agriculture and prevalence of diseases that leave no lesions on bones. There are considerable technical difficulties involved in the analysis of ancient human DNA sequences, but the technology has a unique role to play in our understanding of these questions. One of the ways of looking at ancestry and tracing the movements of people is by the study of mitochondrial DNA (mtDNA), which provides information on actual maternal lineages (mtDNA is maternally inherited), and genealogies which can be traced by the mutation rate.

DR. MARTIN RICHARDS
Institute of Molecular Medicine
University of Oxford, U.K.

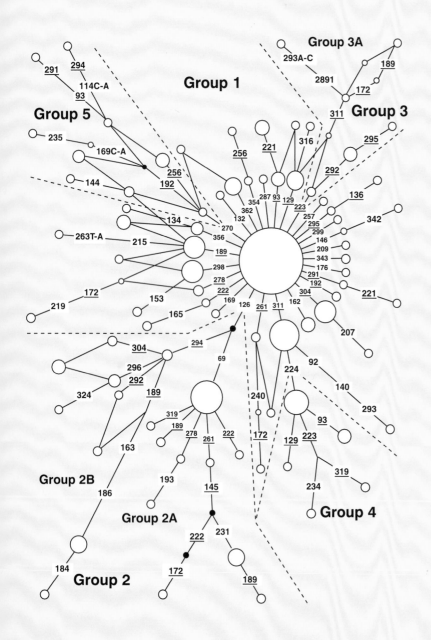

1 Your body is built up from instructions that are encoded in the genes, in the language of DNA. Nearly all of your genes are in the chromosomes, in the nucleus of the cell, but a few occur on a tiny circle of DNA that lives outside the nucleus, in the mitochondria.

2 Mitochondria are the power-packs of the cell. They live in the cytoplasm, where they carry out the energy-producing functions of respiration. They are very unusual, because they have their own DNA molecule. Everyone's DNA is slightly different from everyone else's because when it is passed down the generations, slight changes in the sequence, called mutations, gradually appear.

3 Mitochondrial DNA is unusual because it is inherited only through the female line. This means that when we reconstruct the mutations that have appeared down the generations, we can trace a family tree of lineages back to a common ancestor.

4 The common ancestor of all European mitochondrial DNA was a woman who lived in Africa. Her descendants came out of Africa with a small group of hunters-gatherers who spread out across Europe and Asia about 60-70,000 years ago. We can trace a number of different lineages descended from her in modern-day populations. In Europe, we can see about six main lineages.

5 We have begun a project in mtDNA in modern-day Crete. 85% of those tested are members of a single group of mitochondrial lineages. By counting the number of mutations by which they differ from each other, we can estimate that these lineages are roughly 10,000 years old. This is now in the process of being checked in 2 ways: by additional sampling; and by extracting mtDNA from bone samples of people buried before the arrival of Greeks on the island. If these samples look similar to the modern-day islanders, they could be related to the Minoans, at least through the female line. This would be a finding of considerable archaeological importance.

Mitochondrial DNA
DNA mt

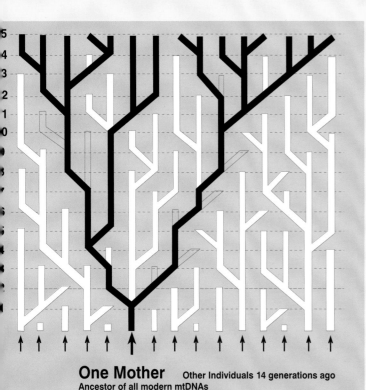

One Mother Other Individuals 14 generations ago
Ancestor of all modern mtDNAs

One Mother

The diagram illustrates the concept that all of the maternal lineages in a population trace back to one of the lineages present in an ancestral population. This hypothetical example follows the history of a population of 15 individuals for 15 generations. Some females from each generation will leave either no surviving offspring or only male offspring. In either case their maternal lineages will go extinct (indicated by the yellow lines), until eventually all of the maternal lineages in some descendant population will trace back to just one of the females in the ancestral population (indicated by solid lines). For a population that is neither increasing nor decreasing in size this process is expected to take about 15 generations, as the diagram indicates.

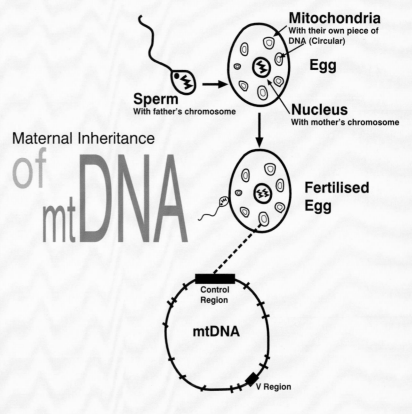

Maternal Inheritance
of mtDNA

Sperm With father's chromosome

Mitochondria With their own piece of DNA (Circular)

Egg

Nucleus With mother's chromosome

Fertilised Egg

Control Region

mtDNA

V Region

HEALING AND MEDICINE

INTRODUCTION

In the prehistoric Aegean it is possible to determine forms of healing and medical practice, from an understanding of the pathology of many skeletal remains found, from both objects found in graves and from what we know of plants that the Minoans and Mycenaeans either grew or gathered.

RELIGIOUS MEDICINE

On Minoan Crete, religious healing was a significant part of popular cult, with its focus centred upon sanctuaries situated on the more accessible peaks of hills and mountains. Offerings of detached human limbs, genitalia, bisected figurines, detached heads and figurines, indicating suffering from particular diseases or afflictions, were dedicated to a deity as a thank offering or as a petition for a cure for a disease. In the peak sanctuary of Mount Vrysinas, south of Rethymnon, were found a number of similar votive offerings, including male and female figurines indicating different pathologies.

DR. ROBERT ARNOTT
Dept. of Ancient History and Archaeology
University of Birmingham, U.K.

262 LOWER SECTION OF MALE FIGURINE

R.M. 949

MM II (c. 1900-1700 B.C.)
Peak Sanctuary of Vrysinas
H: 5.95 cm.

Bronze. A figurine made from the waist down, possibly indicating either a diseased limb or seeking strength in the legs.

R.G.A. - C.D. - E.M.

263 FEMALE FIGURINE

R.M. 16696

MM II (c. 1900-1700 B.C.)
Peak Sanctuary of Vrysinas
H: 10.29 cm.

Clay. This figurine with a pointed base for depositing at the sanctuary is of a woman with possible multiple pathologies.

R.G.A. - C.D. - E.M.

264 LOWER SECTION OF MALE FIGURINE

R.M. 2003

MM II (c. 1900-1700 B.C.)
Peak Sanctuary of Vrysinas
H: 9.8 cm.

Clay. Roughly made pair of male legs with a hole for hanging at the sanctuary.

R.G.A. - C.D. - E.M.

265 LOWER SECTION OF MALE FIGURINE

R.M. 2058

MM II (c. 1900-1700 B.C.)
Peak Sanctuary of Vrysinas
H: 10.7 cm.

Clay. Well-modelled pair of male legs and torso and, like the bronze example, made only from the waist down, perhaps indicating the illness was located on the torso.

R.G.A. - C.D. - E.M.

262

263

264

265

PLANT REMEDIES

The *materia medica* of the Aegean Bronze Age is believed to have been largely derived from the great number of native plants that were at their disposal, as well as others imported from around the Eastern Mediterranean, such as those displayed: Cretan dittany, coriander, saffron, cumin, figs and myrtle. Also used for medicines would have been terebinth and hybiskos or tree-mallow. Unfortunately, the Middle and Late Bronze Age Aegean possesses nothing remotely comparable to the Egyptian medical papyri or Near Eastern medical texts, and because of the lack of documented remedies and their prescriptions, it is only possible to speculate which known plants would have been prized for their medicinal uses, based tentatively on what we know of their medicinal application in both Ancient Egypt and the Near East. In fact, the only possible clue to a remedy we have is on the isolated Linear B tablet from Pylos, which refers to the known medicinal herb ebiskos, but which also contains the word *pa-ma-ko*, or φάρμακα, suggesting a record of medicinal supplies. From the study of further specialized tablets from the palace archives of Knossos, Pylos and Mycenae, which record herbs and spices, it is possible to detect the

existence of a number of plants which have known medicinal properties, although their contexts do not directly concern medicine, and it is only possible to conjecture as to their use, and what precise ailments they may have treated. By the late 13th century B.C., the Mycenaeans had developed a highly organised palace-controlled perfumed oil industry and it is possible that some plants were especially cultivated in gardens as components of a small-scale industry that manufactured remedies. Some popular therapeutics would, of course, have been made up from local ingredients and used domestically.

The Aegean's overseas contacts must have brought awareness of many medical practices and the importation of remedies or their ingredients to the Aegean, and in light of the evidence of the trade in plants with potential medicinal uses in both directions, then a two-way communication in medical knowledge is the most likely scenario. However, there is, in fact, greater evidence for the communication of Minoan medical knowledge and practice to Egypt; for example, the Papyrus Ebers, dated to around 1550 B.C., details a remedy for constipation:

"...another (remedy) to cause purgation..." (then comes a section about an unknown herb) "... which are like beans from the Keftiu land..."

It is quite possible, of course, that the trade in this field from Egypt to Crete was dominated not by plants but by medical preparations, which have not survived.

DR. ROBERT ARNOTT
Dept. of Ancient History and Archaeology
University of Birmingham, U.K.

266 LINEAR B TABLET

N.M. 1314 (PY Un 1314)

LH III B (c. 1200 B.C.)

Pylos

Clay. Leaf-shaped tablet. The flat surface has a text written in a syllabic script, ideograms and Linear B numbers, consisting of three rows. This tablet belongs to group Un, which describes stocks of spices at the Palace at Pylos. Richard Janko has suggested, from a study of this tablet, that the reference to *e-pi-ka* is tree-mallow or hybiscos (ιβί-σκος) (possibly **Althea officinalis L.**), also known from the archaeological record, which was brought to the palace for the sake of its medicinal properties. The dried peeled root of the mallow or althaea is a commonly known remedy for gastro-intestinal disturbances and inflammations, particularly to the mouth: This tablet also includes the word *pa-ma-ko* (φάρμακα), which Ventris and Chadwick suggest may be a record of drugs or medical supplies, presumably for the palace healer.

R.G.A.

267 LINEAR B TABLET

H.M. 705 (KN Gg 705)

LM III A1 (c. 1390-1370 B.C.)

Knossos

Clay. Leaf-shaped tablet. The flat surface has a text written in a syllabic script, ideograms and Linear B numbers, consisting of three rows. This tablet belongs to group Gg, which generally concerns ritual offerings, but in this case, to honey:

One jar of honey to Eleuthia

One jar of honey to all gods

One jar of honey [...]

Honey was also used by the Ancient Egyptians for a number of medical purposes; as an unguent for dressing wounds, in salves for treating eye-disease, and as a sweetener in purgatives. It can be used as a sedative in obstetrics, and is also a known natural antibiotic. A salve made with one part honey and two parts grease (olive oil or animal fat) has the properties of being non-toxic, aseptic, fungicidal, antiseptic and antibiotic. As a salve, honey does not damage tissues and attracts moisture to prevent bandages from sticking to wounds. Recent clinical tests have proved that honey speeds up the healing process in a wound.

R.G.A.

268 LINEAR B TABLET

N.M. 7705 (MY Ge 605+605a+607(+) fr)

LH III B (c. 1200 B.C.)

House of the Oil Merchant, Mycenae

Clay. Page-shaped tablet, used horizontally. Fragmentary. The flat surface has a text written in a syllabic script, ideograms and Linear B numbers, consisting of three rows. This tablet belongs to group Ge, part of a series which concerns spices at Mycenae. Amongst the spices listed, many have medicinal uses, such as *ko-ri-ja-da-na** (coriander), *ku-mi-no* (cumin), *ka-ra-ko* (pennyroyal), and *sa-sa-ma* (sesame).

R.G.A.

266

267

268

269 CONICAL CUP

R.M. 8733

MM II B (c. 1700 B.C.)

Palatial centre at Monastiraki, Amari,
West extension, Room 53 - 88

H: 4.1 cm.; D: rim 7-7.1 cm.

Complete but a small part of the rim is
chipped. Fine buff clay with a little dark
grit. The body has a bell form with a
pinched base. The exterior of the vase
has been smoothed.

ATH. K.

270 CONICAL CUP

R.M. 7512

LM III B (c. 1340-1190 B.C.)

LM Cemetery of Armenoi, Tomb 201

H: 5.8; D: rim 11.2 cm., base 3.9 cm.

Restored. Brown-red fabric, brown slip,
black semi-fugitive paint. Conical body.
Rounded rim. Raised torus base. Solid-
painted.

E.P.

271 CONICAL CUP

R.M. 15573

MM II B (c. 1700 B.C.)

Palatial centre at Monastiraki, Amari,
Room 71-93

H: 4.9 cm.; D: rim 8.6 cm.

Almost complete, but mended in three
places and restored in a small part of
the body. Fine brownish grey clay with
few inclusions. The body has a bell form
with a pinched base. The exterior of the
vase has not been smoothed, thus wheel
marks and impressions of fine vegetable
matter are visible. The vase has turned
grey from the fire which destroyed the
centre.

Ath. K.

272 CONICAL CUP

R.M. 7573

MM III B (c. 1640-1600 B.C.)

Apodoulou, Room 9

H: 5 cm.; D: rim 9.2-9.5 cm., base 4.9 cm.

Intact. Brown fabric with inclusions. Conical body. Rounded, slightly everted rim.

E.P.

273 CONICAL CUP

R.M. 6510

LM III B (c. 1340-1190 B.C.)

LM Cemetery of Armenoi, Tomb 179

H: 4.9; D: rim 10-10.3 cm., base 3 cm.

Small part of body restored. Brown
fabric, slip of same colour. Conical
body. Rounded oval rim. Torus base.

E.P.

274 HANDLELESS CUP

R.M. 2145

LM III A (c. 1390-1340 B.C.)

LM Cemetery of Armenoi, Tomb 89

H: 6.2 cm.; D: rim 8.5-9.4 cm., base 3.4 cm.

Restored. Brown-red fabric, grey-yellow
slip. Cylindrical body. Slightly everted
rim. Raised, slightly hollow base.

E.P.

269

270

271

272

273

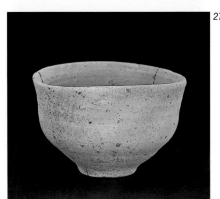
274

OPIUM

One of the most important and powerful drugs in existence, for which we have evidence, is opium. The method of incising an unripe poppy head to produce opium latex, was known on Crete at least by 1250 B.C., if not much earlier, and evidence from the Greek mainland comes with the finding at Tiryns and Kastanas of locally grown opium poppy seeds in levels dating to around 1300 B.C. It may well have been exported in stirrup jars such as these displayed. Raw opium, as well as being a powerful narcotic, is a well-known analgesic and sedative with properties of allaying pain and inducing sleep, having a maximum content of 20% anhydrous morphine. It is possible, for example, that an extract of opium applied directly to a wound if absorbed, might have the same effect as morphine; a piece of wool soaked in a solution of opium and a little saffron, could be effective if used as a suppository to alleviate internal pain. It may also have been used as a primitive anaesthetic, or as a sedative for soothing teething babies by rubbing it upon their gums.

DR. ROBERT ARNOTT
Dept. of Ancient History and Archaeology
University of Birmingham, U.K.

Goddess of the Poppies (H.M. 9305).

275 SIGNET RING

N.M. 942

LH II (c. 1450 B.C.)
Mycenae, Acropolis Treasure
D: bezel 2.5-3.4 cm., hoop 2 cm.;
Weight: 28.6 gr.

Gold. Oval bezel set on a hoop, triangular in section. Depicted on the bezel is a ritual scene, characterized by a number of items of Minoan and Mycenaean religious iconography. A female deity sits beneath a tree and receives offering of poppies and lilies from two female adorants. The female figures behind the tree and in front of the deity are probably her attendants. Behind the women, stylized lion heads frame the whole scene. Towards the top of the scene, are a double axe and, descending from the sky, the tiny figure of a divinity covered by a figure-of-eight shield. In the sky, in an area of the scene depicted by curved wavy lines are the sun and moon.

R.G.A.

275

276 PIN

N.M. 8635

LH I A/B (c. 1550 B.C.)
Grave O, Grave Circle B, Mycenae
L: 16 cm.

Pin with bronze stems and locally made crystal head featuring a slit poppy capsule and its stem. A similar pin comes from Grave III of Grave Circle A.

R.G.A.

277 PIN

N.M. 8636

LH I A/B (c. 1550 B.C.)
Grave O, Grave Circle B, Mycenae
L: 16 cm.

Pin with bronze stems and locally made crystal head featuring a slit poppy capsule and its stem.

R.G.A.

278 PIN

N.M. 8637

LH I A/B (c. 1550 B.C.)
Grave O, Grave Circle B, Mycenae
L: (pres.) 5.5 cm.

Pin with bronze stems and locally made crystal head featuring a slit poppy capsule and its stem.

R.G.A.

276

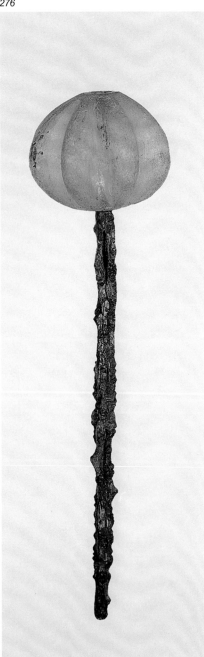

277

278

279 CYLINDRICAL PYXIS WITH LID

H.M. 9501

LM III A1 (c. 1390-1370 B.C.)
Alatsomouri, Pachyammos
H: (with lid) 10.5 cm.; D: base 16.5 cm.

Dense painted decoration in panels. Yellow slip painted with bright red semi-circles, "horns of consecration", and floral motifs. Small monochrome birds on the horns. Cross-hatched antithetic crescent motifs with supplementary little triangles and an almond-shaped cross-hatched motif. On the lid a similar scene of a bird with its wings

folded, accompanied by floral motifs and rock pattern. The scene is bordered by a row of Z-shapes and dots. There is also a band of Z-shapes on the vertical wall of the lid. Fine-grained pure fabric, technique, firing and excellent colour. Intact, slightly worn and chipped.

A.K-E.K.

On the body of the pyxis, poppy heads are depicted alongside small birds. On the lid a bird is tearing apart a poppy capsule.

R.G.A.

280 STIRRUP JAR

R.M. 1567

LM III B (c. 1340-1190 B.C.)
LM Cemetery of Armenoi, Tomb ΣT
H: 10 cm.; D: rim 13.5 cm.

Intact. Pure brown fabric, yellow-grey shiny slip, brown-red paint. Squat conical body (FS 180). Closed cylindrical neck and spout ending at a rim of triangular section. Handles of circular section. Ring base. Zone of shoulder decorated with four Minoan flowers, the petals consisting of four concentric semi-circles dwindling in size towards the bottom.

Either side of each flower is a group of concentric semi-circles. Body down to base encircled by groups of bands.

E.P.

281 STIRRUP JAR

R.M. 21047

LM III B (c. 1340-1190 B.C.)
LM Cemetery of Armenoi, Tomb 211
H: 13 cm.; D: body 13 cm., base 2.3 cm.

Intact. Light brown fabric, yellowish shiny slip, brown-red paint. Globular

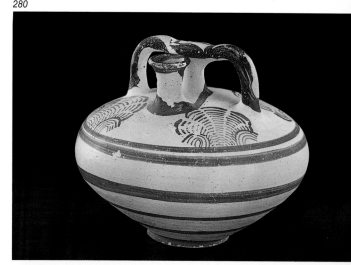

280

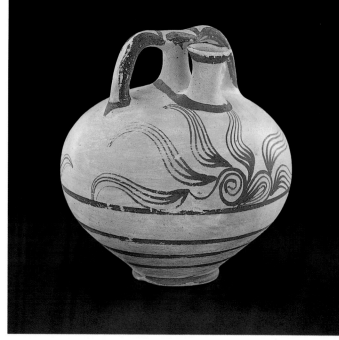

281

body. Closed tubular neck and spout ending in a rim of triangular section. Handles of oval section. Torus base. Upper part of body decorated with two antithetic stylised octopuses (FM 21), with spiral heads and six groups of tentacles. Lower part of body down to base encircled with bands.

E.P.

THE HEALERS

The Minoan and Mycenaean palaces, as with other Late Bronze Age societies of the Eastern Mediterranean and the Near East, will have maintained their own physicians or healers, practising medicine and some minor surgery as well as other forms of community healers - midwives, "wise women" and bone-setters. Their experience would have been based upon observable physical causes, much of it trauma, and they probably knew much about wounds caused by weapons, tools or accidents, and treated them accordingly. However, the causes of strokes or epilepsy, for example, would have been quite mysterious and healers may have regarded these patients as being possessed by a spirit or demon. Whether a palace healer was able to go much beyond sacrifices, spells and incantations, and give a natural explanation to a disease is unclear, but regardless, they would have practised with the **materia medica** at their disposal, tending wounds and setting bones. Considering that the economic and social resources of the palaces were obviously far greater than any other, it is only natural to assume that some healers would have been fully dependent upon the palace in return for rations or land.

Whilst there is no pictorial evidence from the prehistoric Aegean of medical practice, from some of the Linear B texts it is possible to infer that there was a recognized category of individuals specialising in healing. On tablet Eq 146 from Pylos, dated to 1200 B.C., Ventris and Chadwick have identified from the phonetic resemblance to ιατρός, the word *i-ja-te* as a healer or physician and recorded as holding a lease of land, but regrettably there is no occupational context for him. A palace healer, with his position in society, but tied to the *wanax* or the *lawagetas*, may well have owned or leased land. Assuming we are correct in identifying *i-ja-te* as a healer, it is not clear if he had any special position over and above that of, for example, a craftsman, although it must be admitted that his landholding is large, and this may indicate status. Other tablets in the same series from Pylos, concerning land tenure, mention the land holdings of priests, and other palace servants - the king's fuller, the king's potter and the king's armourer also held land. In the *Odyssey* they were classed together with other itinerant labourers.

The existence of a healer, serving a mainland ruling family is also reflected in some of the pathological evidence. The skeleton of a woman, aged approximately 36, found in Tomb Γ of Grave Circle B at Mycenae and dated to approximately 1550 B.C., and a member of one of the ruling families, confirmed by the quality of the grave goods found with her, had a perfectly healed midshaft fracture to her right humerus, a traumatic injury which could not have healed naturally in this way. When compared with many of the lower status occupants of nearby contemporary and earlier cemeteries in the Argolid, such as at Asine and Lerna, where those which had suffered fractures had healed with faulty union and with consequent permanent dysfunction, and clearly without any medical attention, we obviously have here the remains of someone of high status who may have had access to better medical treatment.

Whether there existed religious healers, we cannot tell; but if they did, to them the cause of disease and the operation of remedies would have been so linked with a belief in magic, and diseases would have been considered to be manifestations of the displeasure of deities or spirits, and their prime purpose would be to appease the deity or exorcise the spirit from the body of the sick person. In order to do so they likely employed a number of religious mediums, including spells and incantations, perhaps similar to the Minoan magical healing incantation found in the London Medical

Papyrus found in Egypt and dated to the later part of the XVIII dynasty, to the reign of Pharaoh Amenhotep III, in approximately 1400 B.C., which contains two incantations for the exorcising of a disease, probably chronic conjunctivitis or trachoma, written in the Keftiu or Cretan language. It is mostly unintelligible, but in part reads:

"...Exorcism of the Asian sickness in the Keftiu language... This spell is uttered over ferment, gas, fluid and urine."

We also have evidence for a Mycenaean healing deity. A Hittite divination text (KUB V6), found at the Hittite capital of Hattusas, dates to the reign of King Mursilis II (c. 1350-1320 B.C.) and concerns his illness. It records that, likely in the form of a cult statuette, the god of Ahhiyawa, believed to be part of the Mycenaean world, was brought to help cure him of what is thought to have been aphasia. This suggests that the Mycenaeans worshipped a god of healing whose fame and potency spread as far as central Anatolia.

Amongst the great number of bronze tools found in excavations at Minoan and Mycenaean sites, some would have been available for use in surgery by these healers, such as these examples from the Late Minoan III A-B chamber tombs at Armenoi. The Minoan and Mycenaean healer would also have used tools and other objects to make his medicines and other preparations, such as the mortar and pestle exhibited.

DR. ROBERT ARNOTT
Dept. of Ancient History and Archaeology
University of Birmingham, U.K.

282 LINEAR B TABLET

N.M. 146 (PY Eq 146)
LH III B (c. 1200 B.C.)
Pylos

Clay. Rectangular or page-shaped tablet, used lengthways. The flat surface has a text written in a syllabic script, ideograms and Linear B numbers. This tablet belongs to group Eq, which are lists of land holdings of various officials and individuals. Among these, on Eq 146, which refers to the physical classes of landowners *te-re-ta*, Ventris and Chadwick were the first to propose from the phonetic resemblance to ἰατρός, the word *i-ja-te* as a healer or physician named [..]meno (or -μενος) and recorded as holding a lease of land and issued with one measure of grain. There is no occupational context for him, but a palace healer, like other classes of craftsmen and officials attached to the palace, would have held land.

R.G.A.

283 KNIFE

R.M. 391

LM III A2 (c. 1370-1340 B.C.)
LM Cemetery of Armenoi,
Tomb 46
L: 12 cm.; W: 0.7-2.1 cm.

Bronze. Short bronze knife with a single cutting edge, well preserved. It is a general purpose/type knife found in the Aegean and the Eastern Mediterranean and characterizes Aegean metalwork. Examples have been found from early in the Late Bronze Age until the end of the period. This type probably originated on the Greek mainland and spread to Crete around the middle of the 14th century B.C., during the period of the Mycenaean domination of the Aegean. Its surgical use would have been varied, no less as a form of scalpel or probe.

R.G.A.

284 KNIFE

R.M. 383

LM III A2 (c. 1370-1340 B.C.)
LM Cemetery of Armenoi,
Tomb 46
L: 15.7 cm.; W: 0.5-1.5 cm.

Bronze. Similar to the above, only slightly longer, but will have had very similar uses.

R.G.A.

282

283

28

285 TWEEZERS

R.M. 558

LM III A-B (c. 1390-1190 B.C.)
LM Cemetery of Armenoi,
Tomb 100
L: 8 cm.; W: 0.6-1.97 cm.;
Thickness: 0.12 cm.

Bronze. Bronze tweezers, consisting of a strip of bronze, bent in the middle to form an open loop and with an open ring at the top, with the ends of the legs curving inwards, to give it spring. An incised line along the edge. Usually a small cosmetic or epilation implement, whose shape has remained unchanged from the time of the first examples found on Crete in the Early Bronze Age, around 2300 B.C. However, they are also fundamental in many forms of surgery from the removal of protruding thorns and splinters embedded in the surface of the skin, to more sophisticated use.

R.G.A.

286 TWEEZERS

R.M. 388

LM III A2 (c. 1370-1340 B.C.)
LM Cemetery of Armenoi,
Tomb 46
L: 5.5 cm., W: 0.4-1.1 cm.

Bronze. Smaller and more delicate examples of R.M. 558 above, but with similar uses.

R.G.A.

287 CLEAVER (CURVED BLADED KNIFE)

R.M. 347

LM III B1 (c. 1340-1250 B.C.)
LM Cemetery of Armenoi,
Tomb 55
L: 22 cm.; W: 4-6 cm.;
Thickness: 0.05-0.5 cm.

Bronze. Thick and long triangular cleaver with triangular blade, curved back and thick curved heel, to which a wooden haft would have been attached. The top of the blade has three parallel incised lines running the whole of its length and has a rivet and two holes for attaching it to its haft. Opinions differ as to the likely use of these curved bladed instruments, from chopping meat, the most likely interpretation from the thickness of the blade, to a razor, which might be the use of the smaller types. Common in the Aegean from the beginning of the Late Bronze Age, after which it disappears. Similar objects would have been adopted by surgeons for their repertoire of instruments. Complete, edge slightly damaged.

R.G.A.

285

286

287

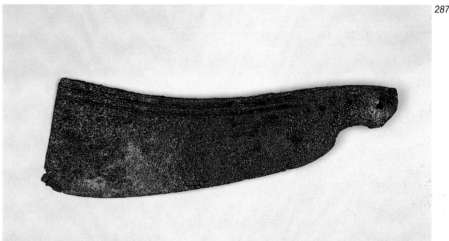

288

288 RAZOR (SMALL CURVED BLADED KNIFE)

R.M. 392

LM III B1 (c. 1340-1250 B.C.)
LM Cemetery of Armenoi,
Tomb 55
L: 14.9 cm.; W: 3-5.3 cm.;
Thickness: 0.05-0.3 cm.

Bronze. Found in the same tomb as the cleaver or curved bladed knife R.M. 347 above, but without the blade decoration, this smaller example may well have been used as a razor and been a handy tool for any surgeon.

R.G.A.

289 GRINDING STONE AND POUNDER

R.M. 2875-2876

MM II (c. 1900-1700 B.C.)
Apodoulou, Room IV
(1) L: (pres.) 17.74 cm.; W: (max) 17.7 cm.;
Thickness: 3.7 cm.
(2) L: 9.37 cm.; W: 4.48 cm.;
Thickness: 3.07 cm.

Stone. Flat oval shaped grinding stone broken at one end, with a rectangular round ended pounder.

R.G.A.

289

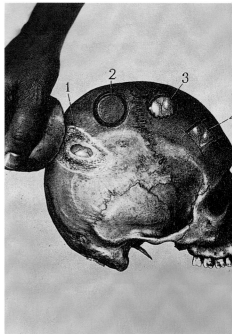

SURGERY FROM SKELETAL EVIDENCE

SURGERY AND SURGICAL TREATMENT

From human skeletal remains found in Minoan and Mycenaean graves, it is sometimes possible to see quite clearly the results of surgery. However, as there are no soft tissue remains, we are unfortunately restricted to the evidence of orthopaedic and cranial surgery. There is evidence from Crete of forms of surgical treatment. In the case of the first of these two individuals from Armenoi, it is possible to detect a small circular depression on the back of the cranium. Recent work shows that similar depressions can be attributed to a swelling of the blood vessels, possibly traumatic aneurysms. An aneurysm may cause severe headaches and, owing to chronic pressure, cause local atrophy and an imprint on the skull such as these. The incisions on this cranium are due to some sort of surgery, in a crude attempt at treating the condition with a knife, the symptoms of which must have been persistent headaches. However, with such forms of surgery, even in Minoan Crete, there must have been a good chance of recovery. There is evidence of venipuncture to the scalp by a flint knife in Babylonian ritual medical texts.

In the second millennium B.C., the breaking of a bone was a serious matter. Bone fractures healing in a position of poor alignment are a common feature amongst the non-elite graves of the period. The large bones, such as the femur, are surrounded by powerful muscles which will contract strongly around the site of a fracture, and are the most common causes of this misalignment. A good healing of a major breakage is perhaps even less likely in the case of compound fractures. When added to the long period of immobilisation, dependence upon others, and the later crippling due to a shortened leg, it may be possible to have some insight into the suffering due to traumatic fractures. Those with fractures affected by osteomyelitis, which gives rise to fever and to delayed healing, may have been forced into an unwise early mobilisation, which often results in deformity of the bones and a major loss of function. As to the treatment of fractures, many of which were brought about by combat, occupational injury, or as the result of being gored by a bull or wild pig, the evidence suggests that those of the forearm were the most common, and the skills of surgeons went beyond a knowledge of simple bone setting.

CRANIAL TREPANATION

Amongst these examples of surgery is cranial trepanation; a procedure performed for the removal of cranial bone. Whilst there are a number of ways the operation might have been carried out, the evidence shows that the Aegean surgeon utilized the scraping technique, using a sharp stone or bronze tool. Avoiding cranial sutures and major blood vessels, he would remove the required area of bone by gradually scraping away the layers of the skull, resulting in a roughly circular opening with bevelled edges. The scraping method probably allowed for a more precise

and controlled penetration of the inner table of bone, and lessened the likelihood of brain injury. A number died as the result of the operation, probably either because of the seriousness of their injuries or from post-operative infection, but there are a number of examples where the operation was successful. The operation was probably performed in the hope of curing intracranial disease or extradural haematoma, persistent migraine or paralysis. But it is more likely that it was a surgical clearing-out for the removal of splinters of bone from a head injury, brought about by combat, hunting, farming or accidents. We cannot rule out, however, the magical or symbolic practice of the operation on the living for the curing of "mental illness" such as epilepsy or schizophrenia, or for the catharsis of "evil spirits".

DR. ROBERT ARNOTT
Dept. of Ancient History and Archaeology
University of Birmingham, U.K.

290 CRANIUM OF YOUNG MALE

R.M. 86 B Exc. No 67B

LM III A (c. 1390-1340 B.C.)
LM Cemetery of Armenoi, Tomb 67

Male, aged approximately 35 years, on which has been observed a small circular depression on the surface of the posterior left parietal. It has an approximate diameter of 1.62 cm., indicating the likely existence of a traumatic aneurysm.

R.G.A.

291 CRANIUM OF YOUNG MALE

R.M. 32 B Exc. No 32B

LM III A (c. 1390-1340 B.C.)
LM Cemetery of Armenoi, Tomb 32

Young male, aged approximately 25 years, where from this fragment it is possible to detect the marks of incisions made by a cutting instrument on the frontal bone of the cranium, the deepest 12.75 cm. long. Another, parallel to it and closer to the midline is 1.1 cm. long. There is a third incision 1.66 cm. long in a corresponding position on the left side of the frontal bone all indicating the possibility of traumatic aneurysms.

R.G.A.

293 CRANIUM OF A MALE INDICATING TREPANATION

M.M. 10.185 (GAMMA 51)

LH I A (c. 1550 B.C.)
Grave Gamma (east body), Grave Circle B, Mycenae

The cranium of an approximately 20-30 year old warrior from Mycenae, indicating that trepanation was performed to on the left side of frontal anterior to left coronal suture. Two roughly semi-circular roundels of bone, 2.7 by 3 cm., that had been cut out survive, and show that the skull had been cut with great skill through the outer table only. The

290 a

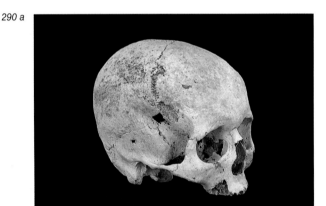

292 HUMERUS OF A FEMALE

M.M. 10.085 (GAMMA 58)

LH I A (c. 1550 B.C.)
Grave Gamma (south body), Grave Circle B, Mycenae

A member of one of the ruling families, confirmed by the quality of the grave goods found with her, this approximately 30-40 year old female had a perfectly healed midshaft three-part fracture to her right humerus, an injury which could not have healed naturally in this way. When compared with many of the lower status occupants of contemporary and earlier cemeteries in the locality, where those which had suffered fractures had healed with faulty union and consequent permanent dysfunction and clearly without any medical attention, we obviously have here the remains of someone of rank who may well have had access to better medical treatment. However, later in the Bronze Age the work of bone-setters would have become more commonplace.

R.G.A.

290 b

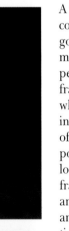

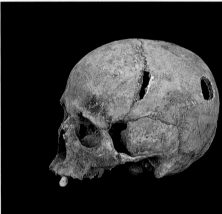

290 c

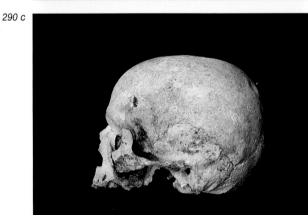

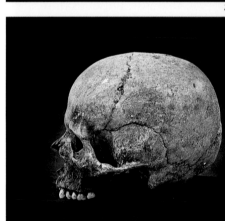

internal diameter of the hole is greater than the external. As it was cut it had sprung away from the head and split into two, curling slightly in the process, probably because it may have been still attached to the scalp. The patient survived at least until the operation had been completed, but as there is no trace of healing or remodelled edges, the patient did not survive for long. From the appearance of the trepanation, it was performed very skilfully with a very keen-edged chisel or gouge. It is possible only to speculate as to why the operation was necessary, but there are two fractures which lead away from the

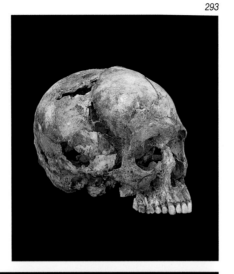

293

294 TRIPOD COOKING POT

. . . .

CH.M. 4460

LM I B (c. 1480-1425 B.C.)
Chania, 1977. Kastelli hill - Greek Swedish Excavations. LM I House I. GSE No 847
H: 42 cm.; D: rim 22 cm.,
body 28 cm., base 22 cm.

Almost complete; restored. Reddish brown, gritty clay. Wheel ridges inside. Tall cylindrical body. Rim slightly incurving with small pulled-out spout. Two small roll handles horizontally set just below rim. Flat base; tall legs, ovoid in section. Plain. Traces of burning outside; heavily burnt inside.

M.A.-V.

292

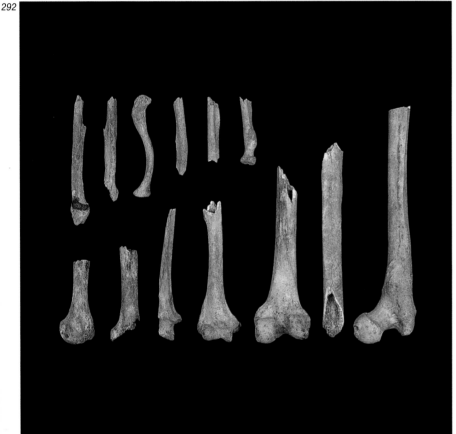

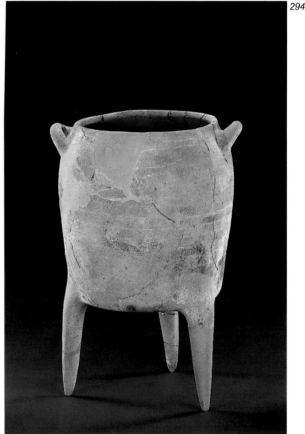

294

trepanation towards the front of the cranium, therefore it is likely that the trepanation had the aim of curing concussion and possibly extradural haemorrhage, following a cranial depressed fracture wound to the head, probably made by a blunt-edged axe, but on closer examination, seems to have been made by a sharper instrument, perhaps a sword. This robust Mycenaean warrior may also have had some form of cranial surgery some years earlier, as he has a healed depression on the right side of his skull.

R.G.A.

Flavours of Their Time

Organic residue analysis has given us tantalising glimpses into ancient activities. Analysis of pottery vessels has revealed some healthy eating habits as evidenced by traces of olive oil and fresh meat with plenty of cereals and fibre. Combinations of these, with the addition of wine, herbs and other ingredients, would have resulted in some interesting recipes.

In order to prise this information out of the pottery we had to resort to scientific equipment but people in the past would only have to sniff the air.

ARCHAEOLOGICAL BIBLIOGRAPHY

ABBREVIATIONS

AA   Archäologischer Anzeiger

AAA   Athens Annals of Archaeology /
Αρχαιολογικά Ανάλεκτα εξ Αθηνών

ΑΔ   Archaeological Bulletin / Αρχαιολογικόν Δελτίον

AJA   American Journal of Archaeology

BSA   Annual of the British School at Athens

BCH   Bulletin de Correspondence Hellénique

CMS   Corpus der minoischen und mykenischen Siegel

SIMA   Studies in Mediterranean Archaeology

ALEXIOU, S. (1954) "Υστερομινωικός Τάφος Παχυάμμου" *Κρητικά Χρονικά*, 8: 399-412.

AMOURETTI, M.-C., BRUN, J.-P. (eds) (1993) *La production du vin et de l'huile en Mèditerranée*, Paris (*BCH* Supplement 25).

ANDRONIKOS, M. (ed) (1975) *The Greek Museums*, Athens/London.

BETANCOURT, P. P. (1985) *The History of Minoan Pottery*, Princeton.

BROWN, J. C. (1996) *RINGS: five passions in world art*, Atlanta High Museum of Art (Exhibition Catalogue).

CATLING, H. W. (1964) *Cypriot Bronzework in the Mycenaean World*, Oxford. (1970) "A Mycenaean pictorial fragment from Palaepaphos" AA: 24-31.

CHADWICK, J. (1972) *Documents in Mycenaean Greek*, 2nd ed., Cambridge

CHADWICK, J., GODART, L., KILLEN, J. T., OLIVIER, J.-P., SACCONI, A., SAKELLARAKIS, I. A. (1986) *Corpus of Mycenaean Inscriptions from Knossos*, vol. I (1-1063), Cambridge.

CLINE, E. (1991) *Sailing the Wing Dark Sea: international trade and the Late Bronze Age Aegean*, Oxford (*British Archaeological Reports* S591)

DAWKINS, R. M. (1904-5) "Excavations at Palaikastro IV" *BSA*, 11: 258-292.

DEMAKOPOULOU. K. (ed) (1986) *The Mycenaean World*, Athens (Exhibition Catalogue).

DOUMAS, C. (1983) *Thera; Pompeii of the Ancient Aegean*, London.

FRENCH, E. B. (1965) "Late Helladic III A2 pottery from Mycenae" *BSA*, 60: 159-202.

FRENCH, E. B., WARDLE, K. A. (eds) (In Progress), *Well Built Mycenae*, Oxford.

FURUMARK, A. (1941a) *Mycenaean Pottery: analysis and classification*, Stockholm. (1941b) *The Chronology of Mycenaean Pottery*, Stockholm.

GEORGIOU, H. S. (1986) *Keos VI. Ayia Irini: specialised domestic and industrial pottery*, Mainz.

GODART, L., TZEDAKIS, Y. (1992) *Témoignages archéologiques et épigraphiques en Crete Occidentale du Néolithe au Minoan Récent IIIB*, Rome (Incunabula Graeca 93).

GRACE, V. (1956) "The Canaanite Jar" in S. S. Weinberg (ed), *The Aegean and the Near East. Studies presented to Hetty Goldman on the occasion of her seventy-fifth birthday*, New York, p.p. 80-109.

HALLAGER, E., HALLAGER, B. P. (eds) (1997) *Late Minoan III Pottery, chronology and terminology* (Acts of a meeting held at the Danish Institute at Athens, August 12-14, 1994), Aarhus.

HALLAGER, B. P., McGEORGE, P. J. P. (1992) *Late Minoan III Burials at Chania: the tombs, finds and deceased in Odos Palama*, Göteborg, Paul Åströms Förlag (Studies in Mediterranean Archaeology 92).

HAWS, H. BODY (1908) *Gournia, Vassiliki and other Prehistoric Sites on the Isthmus of Hierapetra, Crete. Excavations, 1901, 1903, 1904,.* Philadelphia.

HIGGINS, R. A. (1981) *Minoan and Mycenaean Art*, 2nd ed., London.

HOOD, S. (1978) *The Arts in Prehistoric Greece*, Harmondsworth.

KANTA, A. (1980) *The Late Minoan III Period in Crete: A Survey of Sites, Pottery and Their Distribution*, Göteborg (*SIMA* 58).

KANTA, A., ROCCHETTI, L. (1989) "Le ceramica del primo edificio" in Y. Tzedakis and L. Godart (eds), *Scavi a Nerokourou, Kydonias*, Vol. I, Rome, p.p. 101-161. (1999) "Monastiraki and Phaistos, Elements of Protopalatial History", forthcoming.

KRZYSZKOWSKA, O. H. (1988) "Ivory in the Aegean Bronze Age" BSA, 83: 209-234. (1990) *Ivory and Related Materials: an illustrated guide*, London.

LEONARD, A. J. (1995) "Canaanite jars and the Late Bronze Age Aegeo-Levantine wine trade" in P. E. McGovern, S. J. Fleming and S. H. Katz (eds), *The Origins and Ancient History of Wine*, New York (Food and Nutrition in History and Anthropology, Vol.11), p.p. 233-254.

LEVI, D. (1976) *Festòs e la civiltà minoica*, Rome.

LOLLING, H. (1880) *Das Kuppelgrab bei Menidi*, Athens.

MARINATOS, S. (1970) *Excavations at Thera III*, Athens.

MARTLEW, C. HOLLEY (2000) *The Tripod Cooking Pot in Bronze Age Crete*, SIMA, forthcoming.

MARTHARI, M. (1987) "The local pottery wares with painted decoration from the volcanic destruction level at Akrotiri, Thera. A preliminary report" AA: 359-379.

MOMIGLIANO, N. (1991) "MM I A pottery from Evans' excavations at Knossos: a reassessment" BSA, 86: 149-271.

MORGAN, L. (1990) "Island iconography: Thera, Kea, Milos" in D. A. Hardy (ed with others), *Thera and the Aegean World*, vol. I, London, p.p. 252-266.

MORRICONE, M. L. (1979-80) "Vasi della collezione Akavi" *AS Atene*, 57-58: ?

MOUNTJOY, P. A. (1986) *Mycenaean Decorated Pottery*, Göteborg (*SIMA* 73).

NEGBI O., NEGBI, M. (1993) "Stirrup jars versus Canaanite jars: their contents and reciprocal trade" in C. Zerner, P. Zerner and John Winder (eds), *Wace and Blegen. Pottery as evidence of trade in the Aegean Bronze Age*, Amsterdam, p.p. 319-329.

KINDELI-NUNIOU, B. (1995) ΑΔ, 44: Β'2 Χρονικά, 449-451 (Splantzia-Papadopoulos Plot, Chania)

ONASOGLOU, A. (1979) "Ένας νέος μυκηναϊκός θαλαμοειδής τάφος στο Κουκάκι" ΑΔ 34: Α', 15-42.

PALMER, R. (1994) *Wine in the Mycenaean Palace Economy*, Liege (Aegeum 10).

PALMER, L. R. (1963) *On the Interpretation of Mycenaean Greek Texts*, Oxford.

POPHAM, M. R. (1965) "Some Late Minoan III pottery from Crete" *BSA*, 60: 316-342. (1967) "Late Minoan pottery: a summary" *BSA*, 62: 337-351. (1969) "Late Minoan Goblet and Kylix" *BSA*, 64: 299-304.

POURSAT, J.-C. (1977) *Les Ivoires mycéniens*, Paris.

PROTONOTARIOU-DEILAKI, E. (1973) ΑΔ, 28: Β'1 Χρονικά, 90-94.

RUTKOWSKI, B. (1986) *The Cult Places of the Aegean*, New Haven. (1988) "Minoan peak sanctuaries: the topography and architecture" *Aegaeum*, 2: 71-99. (1991) *Petsofas: a Cretan peak sanctuary*, Warsaw.

SANDARS, N. K. (1963) "Later Aegean bronze swords" *AJA*, 67: 117-153.

STAMPOULIDES, N. C., KARETSOU, A., KANTA, A. (eds) (1998) *Eastern Mediterranean: Cyprus, Dodecanese, Crete, 16th-6th centuries B.C.*, Heraklion (Exhibition Catalogue).

TAYLOUR, W. D. (1955) "Mycenae 1939-1954: Part IV. The Perseia Area" *BSA*, 50: 199-237. (1969) "Mycenae, 1968" Antiquity, 43: 91-97. (1970a) "New light on Mycenaean religion" Antiquity, 44: 270-280. (1970b) "Citadel House, Mycenae, 1968 and 1969" *AAA*, 3: 72-80. (1981) *Well Built Mycenae, Fasc. I: The Excavations*, Warminster. (1983) *The Mycenaeans*, 2nd ed., London.

TZEDAKIS, Y. (1969) "L'atelier de ceramique postpalatial à Kydonia" *BCH*, 93: 396-413. (1969) "Ανασκαφή ΥΜ III Α/Β Νεκροταφείου εις περιοχήν Καλαμίου Χανίων" *AAA*, 2: 365-369. (1971) "Minoan globular flasks" BSA, 66: 363-368. (1971) *AΔ*, 26: Β'2 Χρονικά, 635-637.

TZEDAKIS, Y., HALLAGER, E. (1978) "The Greek-Swedish Excavations at Kastelli, Chania 1976 and 1977" *AAA*, 11: 31-46.

TZEDAKIS, Y., KANTA, A. (1966) Καστέλλι Χανίων, Rome (*Incunabula Graeca* 66).

VLAZAKI, M., HALLAGER, E. (1995) "Evidence for seal use in prepalatial Western Crete" *CMS Beiheft*, 5: 251-270.

VENTRIS, M., CHADWICK, J. (1973) *Documents in Mycenaean Greek*, 2nd ed., Cambridge.

VERMEULE, E., KARAGEORGHIS, V. (1982) *Mycenaean Pictorial Vase Painting*, Cambridge, Mass.

VICKERY, K. F. (1936) *Food in Early Greece*, Chicago (*Illinois Studies in the Social Sciences*, 20.3).

ANDREADAKI-VLAZAKI, M. (1987) "Ομάδα νεοανακτορικών αγγείων από τον Σταυρωμένο Ρεθύμνης" in *ΕΙΛΑΠΙΝΗ*: Τόμος τιμητικός για τον Καθηγητή Νικόλαο Πλάτωνα, Heraklion, Βικελαία Βιβλιοθήκη, 1987, p.p. 55-68. (1991) ΑΔ, 46 Β'2 Χρονικά, 426-429 (Chamalevri). (1991-93) "Αρχαιολογικές Ειδήσεις 1989-91" Κρητική Εστία: τ. 5 241-244 (Chamalevri). (1992) ΑΔ, 47 Β'2 Χρονικά, 566-571 (Splantzia-Kaniamou Plot), 583-590 (Chamalevri). (1994-96) "Αρχαιολογικές Ειδήσεις 1992-94" Κρητική Εστία: τ. 4

251-264 (Chamalevri). (1995) "Το αρχαιολογικό ενδιαφέρον στην περιοχή Σταυρωμένου/Χαμαλεύριου Ρεθύμνου" *Κρητολογικά Γράμματα*, II: 367-379. (1997) "Craftsmanship at MM Khamalevri in Rethymnon" in P. Betancourt and R. Laffineur, (eds), *TEXNH: Craftsmen, Craftswomen and Craftsmanship in the Aegean Bronze Age*, (Proceedings of the 6th International Aegean Conference, Philadelphia, 1996), Liege (Aegeum 16), p.p. 37-43.

ANDREADAKI-VLAZAKI, M., PAPADOPOULOU, E. (1997) "LM III A:1 pottery from Khamalevri, Rethymnon" in E. Hallager and B. P. Hallager (eds), *Late Minoan III Pottery, Chronology and Terminology* (Acts of a meeting held at the Danish Institute at Athens, August 12-14, 1994), Aarhus, p.p. 111-155.

WALBERG, G. (1983) *Provincial Middle Minoan Pottery*, Mainz.

WARDLE, K. A. (1969) "A group of Late Helladic III B pottery from within the citadel at Mycenae" *BSA*, 64: 71-93.

WATROUS, L. V. (1992) *Kommos III: The Late Bronze Age pottery*, Princeton.

WARREN, P. M. (1969) *Minoan Stone Vases*, Cambridge. (1972) *Myrtos: An Early Bronze Age Settlement in Crete*, London. (1975) *The Aegean Civilisations: from Ancient Crete to Mycenae*, London.

WARREN, P., VANKEY, V. (1989) *Aegean Bronze Age Chronology*, Bristol.

WRIGHT, J. C. (1985) "Nemea" *AΔ*, 40: Χρονικά, 96.

ZOHARY, D., HOPF, M. (1993) *Domestication of Plants in the Old World*, 2nd ed., Oxford.

Compiled by Dr. Robert Arnott, University of Birmingham (U.K.)

SCIENTIFIC BIBLIOGRAPHY

ADDEO, F., BARLOTTI, L., BOFFA, G., DILUCCIA, A., MALORNI, A., PICCIOLI, G. (1979) "Costituenti acidi di una oleoresina di conifere rinvenuta in anfore vinarie durante gli scavi di Oplonti" *Annali della Facolta di Scienze Agrarie, Universita degli Studi, Napoli,* 13: 144-148.

AMBROSE, S.H. (1993) "Isotopic analysis of paleodiets: methodological and interpretive considerations" in M. K. Sandford (ed), *Investigations of Ancient Human Tissue: Chemical Analyses in Anthropology.* Langhorne, Pennsylvania, p.p. 59-130.

ANGEL, J. L. (1954) "Some problems in interpretation of Greek skeletal material: disease, posture, and microevolution" *American Journal of Physical Anthropology,* 12: 284-297. (1971) *The People of Lerna - Analysis of a Prehistoric Aegean Population,* vol. II, *Lerna: a preclassical site in the Argolid: the people,* Princeton (American School of Classical Studies at Athens). (1973) "Humans from Grave Circles at Mycenae" in G. E. Mylonas, Ο Ταφικός κύκλος Β′ των Μυκηνών, Athens, p.p. 379-397. (1974) "Patterns of fractures from Neolithic to modern times" *Anthrop. Kozlemenyek,* 18: 9-18. (1975) "Paleoecology, paleodemography and health" in Steven Polgar (ed), *Population, Ecology and Social Evolution,* The Hague, p.p. 167-190. (1978) "Porotic hyperostosis in the eastern Mediterranean" *Medical College of Virginia Quarterly.,* 14(1): 10-16. (1982) "Ancient skeletons from Asine" in S. Dietz, *Asine II; results of the excavations east of the Acropolis 1970-1974,* Fasc. 1 - *General stratigraphical analysis and architectural remains,* vol. XXXIV, (Acta Instituti Atheniensis Regni Sueciae), Stockholm, p.p. 105-138. (1984) "Health as a crucial factor in the change from hunting to developed agriculture in the eastern Mediterranean" in M. N. Cohen and G. L. Armelagos (eds.), *Paleopathology and the Origins of Agriculture,* Orlando, p.p. 51-73.

ARNOTT, R. (1996) "Healing and medicine in the Aegean Bronze Age" *Journal of the Royal Society of Medicine,* 89: 265-270. (1997) "Surgical practice in the prehistoric Aegean" *Medizinhistorisches Journal,* 32: 249-278. (1999) *Disease, Healing and Medicine in the Aegean Bronze Age,* Leiden (*Studies in Ancient Medicine*), in press. (1999) "Disease and the prehistory of the Aegean" in Karen Stears (ed), *Health in Antiquity,* London, in press.

AUFDERHEIDE, A. C., RODRIGUEZ-MARTIN, C. (1998) *The Cambridge Encyclopedia of Human Paleopathology,* Cambridge.

BADLER, V. R., McGOVERN, P. E., MICHEL, R. H. (1990) "Drink and be merry! Infrared spectroscopy and ancient Near Eastern wine" in W. R. Biers and P. E. McGovern (eds), *Organic Contents of Ancient Vessels: materials analysis and archaeological investigation,* Philadelphia, MASCA, University of Pennsylvania Museum (MASCA Research Papers in Science and Archaeology no. 7), p.p. 25-36.

BARBER, E. J. W. (1991) *Prehistoric Textiles: the development of cloth in the Neolithic and Bronze Ages with special reference to the Aegean,* Princeton.

BARBUJANI, G., BERTORELLE G., CHIKHI, L. (1998) "Evidence for paleolithic and neolithic gene flow in Europe" *American Journal of Human Genetics,* 62: 488-491.

BASCH, A. (1972) "Analyses of Oil from two Roman glass bottles" *Israel Exploration Journal,* 22: 27-32.

BASS, W. M. (1987) *Human Osteology,* 3rd ed., Columbus.

BENDALL, K. E., MACAULAY, V. A., BAKER, J. R., SYKES, B. (1996) "Heterosplasmic point mutations in the human mtDNA control region" *American Journal of Human Genetics,* 59: 1276-1287.

BERGMAN, A., YANAI, Y., WEISS, Y., BELL, D., DAVID, M. P. (1983) "Acceleration of wound healing by topical application of honey" *American Journal of Surgery,* 145: 374-376.

BERTHELOT, M. (1877a) "Analyse d' un vin antique" *Annales de la Chimie et de la Physique,* 12: 413-418. (1877b) "Analyse d' un vin antique conserve dans un vase de verre scelle par fusion" *Revue Archeologique,* n.s. 33: 392-396. (1877c) "Nouvelle note sur une liquide renferme dans un vase de verre tres ancien" *Revue Archeologique,* n.s. 34: 394.

BAUMANN, H. (1993) *Greek Wild flowers and Plant Lore in Ancient Greece,* London.

BIERS, W. R., McGOVERN, P. E. (1990) *Organic Contents of Ancient Vessels: Materials analysis and archaeological investigation,* Philadelphia, MASCA, University of Pennsylvania Museum (MASCA Research Papers in Science and Archaeology no. 7).

BISEL, S., ANGEL, J. L. (1985) "Health and nutrition in Mycenaean Greece: a study in human skeletal remains" in Nancy Wilkie and William D. E. Coulson (eds), *Contributions to Aegean Archaeology: Studies in Honor of W. A. McDonald,* Minnesota, Center for Ancient Studies, University of Minnesota, p.p. 197-209.

BROOKS, S., SUCHEY, J. M. (1990) "Skeletal age determination on the Os pubis: a comparison of the Ascadi-Nemeskeri and Suchey-Brooks Methods" *Human Evolution,* 5: 227-238.

BROTHWELL, D., BROTHWELL, P. (1998) *Food in Antiquity: a survey of the diet of early peoples,* 2nd (expanded) ed., Baltimore.

BROTHWELL, D., SANDISON, A. T. (1967) *Diseases in Antiquity. A survey of the diseases, injuries and surgery of early populations,* Springfield.

BROWN, T. A. (1998) *Genetics: A Molecular Approach,* 3rd ed., London.

BROWN, T. A., BROWN, K. A. (1992) "Ancient DNA and the archaeologist" *Antiquity,* 66: 10-23. (1994) "Ancient DNA: using molecular biology to explore the past" *BioEssays,* 16: 719-726.

BUIKSTRA, J. E., UBELAKER, D. (1994) *Standards for Data Collection from Human Skeletal Remains,* Fayettville.

CALNAN, K.A. (1992) *The Health Status of Bronze Age Greek Women,* unpublished PhD thesis, University of Cincinnati.

CANN, R. L., M. STONEKING, WILSON, A. C. (1987) "Mitochondrial DNA and human evolution" *Nature,* 325: 31-36.

CARR, H. G. (1960) "Some dental characteristics of the Middle Minoans" *Man,* 60: 119-122.

CASTLE, S. A., HARTLEY, K. F., MACKENNA, S. A., WHITE, R., HUGHES, M. J. (1978) "Amphorae from Brockley Hill, 1975" *Britannia,* 9: 383-392.

CAVALLI-SFORZA, L. L., MENOZZI, P., PIAZZA, A. (1994) *The History and Geography of Human Genes,* Princeton.

CAVALLI-SFORZA, L. L., EDWARDS, A. W. F. (1967) "Phylogenetic analysis - models and estimation procedure" *American Journal of Human Genetics,* 19: 233-257.

CAVALLI-SFORZA, L. L., MINCH, E. (1997) "Paleolithic and neolithic lineages in the European mitochondrial gene pool" *American Journal of Human Genetics,* 61: 247-251.

CELORIA, F. S. C. (1970). "Food archaeology in Britain 1900-1970" *Science and Archaeology,* 4: 8-14.

CHARTERS, S., EVERSHED, R. P., BLINKHORN, P. W., DENHAM, V. (1995) "Evidence for the mixing of fats and waxes in archaeological ceramics" *Archaeometry*, 37: 113-127.

CHARTERS, S., EVERSHED, R. P., GOAD, L. J., LEYDEN, A., BLINKHORN, P. W., DENHAM, V. (1993) "Quantification and distribution of lipid in archaeological ceramics: Implications for sampling potsherds for organic residue analysis and the classification of vessel use" *Archaeometry*, 35: 211-223.

CHARTERS, S., EVERSHED, R. P., QUYE, A., BLINKHORN, P. W., AND REECES, V. (1997) "Simulation experiments for determining the use of ancient pottery vessels: the behaviour of epicuticular leaf wax during boiling of a leafy vegetable." *Journal of Archaeological Science*, 24: 1-7.

CLARK, W. A. (1937) "History of fracture treatment up to the sixteenth century" *Journal of Bone and Joint Surgery*, 19: 47-63.

CONDAMIN, J., FORMENTI, F. (1976) "Recherche de trace d' huile d' olive et de vin dans les amphores antiques" *Figlina*, 1: 143-158.

CONDAMIN, J., FORMENTI, F., METAIS, M. O., MICHEL, M., BLOND, P. (1976) "The application of gas chromatography to the tracing of oil in ancient amphorae" *Archaeometry*, 18: 195-201.

CONDAMIN, J., FORMENTI, F. (1978) "Detection du contenu d' amphores antiques (huiles, vin). Etude methodologique" *Revue d' Archeometrie*, 2: 43-58.

DALBY, A. (1996) *Siren Feasts: A History of Food and Gastronomy in Greece*, London.

DAVIES, W. V., WALKER, R. (eds) (1993) *Biological Anthropology and the Study of Ancient Egypt*, London.

DEAL, M. (1990) "Exploratory analyses of food residues from prehistoric pottery and other artefacts from Eastern Canada" *Society for Archaeological Science Bulletin*, 13: 6-12.

DEGUSTA, D., WHITE, T.D. (1996) "On the use of skeletal collections for DNA analysis" *Ancient Biomolecules*, 1: 89-92.

DENIRO, M. (1987) "Stable isotopy and archaeology" *American Scientist*, 75: 182-191.

DENIGES, G. (1910) "Sur la presence de residus tartariques du vin dans un vase antique" *Comptes rendus hebdomaires des seances d' Academie des Sciences, Paris*, 150: 1330.

DICKSON, J. (1978) "Bronze Age mead" *Antiquity*, 52:108-113.

EVANS, J. (1977) *Food remains. Excavations in the Roman kiln field at Brampton 1973-1974*, Norwich, East Anglian Archaeology Report No. 5. (1990) "Come back, King Alfred, all is forgiven!" in W. R. Biers and P. E. McGovern (eds), *Organic Contents of Ancient Vessels: materials analysis and archaeological investigation*, Philadelphia, MASCA, University of Pennsylvania Museum (MASCA Research Papers in Science and Archaeology no. 7), p.p. 7-9.

EVANS, J., BIEK, L. (1976) "Overcooked food residues on potsherds" in *Archaeometry and Archaeological Prospection: Proceedings of the 16th International Symposium on Archaeometry*, Edinburgh, p.p. 90-95.

EVANS, J., HILL, H. E. (1982) "Dietetic information by chemical analysis of Danish Neolithic potsherds: a progress report" in *Proceedings of the 22nd International Symposium on Archaeometry*, Bradford, p.p. 224-228.

EVERSHED, R. (1993) "Archaeology and analysis: GC/MS studies of pottery fragments shed new light on the past" *Spectroscopy in Europe*, 5: 21-26.

EVERSHED, R. P., HERON, C., CHARTERS, S., GOAD, L. J. (1992) "The survival of food residues: new methods of analysis, interpretation and application" *Proceedings of the British Academy*, 77: 187-208.

EVERSHED, R. P., HERON, C., GOAD, L. J. (1990) "Analysis of organic residues of archaeological origin by high-temperature gas chromatography and gas chromatography - mass spectrometry" *The Analyst*, 115: 1339-1342.

EVERSHED, R. P., HERON, C., GOAD, L. J. (1991) "Epicuticular wax components preserved in potsherds as chemical indicators of leafy vegetables in ancient diets" *Antiquity*, 65: 540-544.

EVERSHED, R. P., ARNOT, K. I., COLLISTER, EGLINTON, J. G., CHARTERS, S. (1994) "Application of isotope ratio monitoring gas chromatography - mass spectrometry to the analysis of organic residues of archaeological origin" *The Analyst*, 119: 909-914.

EVERSHED, R. P., STOTT, A. W., RAVEN, A., DUDD, S. N., CHARTERS, S., LEYDEN, A. (1995) "Formation of long-chain ketones in ancient pottery vessels by pyrolysis of acyl lipids" *Tetrahedron Letters*, 36: 8875-8878.

FANKHAUSER, B. L. (1991) "Chemical analysis of food residues on pottery: from the field to the laboratory" in B. L. Fankhauser and J. R. Bird (eds), Archaeometry: Australasian Studies 1991, Canberra. (1993) "Residue analysis on Maori earth ovens" in B. L. Fankhauser, J. R. Bird (eds), *Archaeometry: Current Australasian Research*, Canberra, p.p. 13-20.

FEL, E., HOFER, T. (1988) "Pots and tastes at Atany in Hungary" in A. Fenton and J. Myrdal (eds), *Food and Drink and Travelling Accessories: Essays in Honor of Gosta Berg*, London, p.p. 28-37.

FIE, S. M., FOUNTAIN, J., HUNT, E. D., ZUBROW, E., JACOBI, R., BARTALOTTA, K., BRENNAN, J., ALLEN, K., BUSH, P. (1990) "Encrustations in Iroquois ceramic vessels and food resource areas" in W. R. Biers and P. E. McGovern (eds), *Organic Contents of Ancient Vessels: materials analysis and archaeological investigation*, Philadelphia, MASCA, University of Pennsylvania Museum (MASCA *Research Papers in Science and Archaeology no. 7*), p.p.11-23.

FORMENTI, F., HESNARD, A., TCHERNIA, A. (1978) "Note sur le contenu d'une amphore "Lamboglia 2" de l' epave de la Madrague de la Giens" *Archeonautica*, 2: 95-100.

FORSTER, P., HARDING, R., TORRONI, A., BANDELY, H.-J. (1996) "Origin and evolution of Native American mtDNA variation: a reappraisal" *American Journal of Human Genetics*, 59: 935-945.

GELLER, J. (1992) "Bread and beer in fourth-millennium Egypt" Food and Foodways, 5(3): 1-13.

GRMEK, M. D. (1989) *Diseases in the Ancient Greek World*, Baltimore. (Translation by Mireille Muellner and Leonard Muellner of *Les Maladies a l'aube de la civilisation occidentale*, Paris, 1983).

GRUSS, J. (1932) "Zwei altgermanische Trinkhorner mit Bier und Metresten" *Forschungen und Fortschritte*, 8: 289. (1934). "Uber den altesten Weinrest aus der romischen Kaiserzeit auf deutschem Boden" *Forschungen und Fortschritte*, 10: 18-19.

GURFINKEL, D. M., FRANKLIN, U. M. (1988) "The analysis of organic archaeological residue: An evaluation of thin layer chromatography" in R. Farquhar, R. G. V. Hancock, L. Paulish (eds), *Proceedings of the 26th International Archaeometry Symposium*, Toronto, p.p. 85-88.

HAEVERNICK, T. A. (1967) "Romischer Wein?" *Acta Archaeologica Academiae Scientarum Hungaricae*, 19: 15-23.

HASTORF, C., DE NIRO, M. (1985) "Reconstruction of prehistoric plant production and cooking practices by a new isotopic method" *Nature* 315: 489-491.

HEIN, W.-H. (1961) "Die Bedeutung der Entzifferung des Linear B fur die Arzneimittel-geschichte" *Pharm. Ztg.*, 106: 1145-1148.

HERON, C., EVERSHED, R. P. (1993) "The analysis of organic residues and the study of pottery use" *Archaeological Method and Theory*, 5: 247-284.

HERON, C., POLLARD, A. M. (1988) "The analysis of natural resinous materials from Roman amphoras" in E. A. Slater and J. O. Tate (eds), *Science and Archaeology. The Application of Scientific Techniques to Archaeology*, Oxford, British Archaeological Reports (196), p.p. 429-447.

HILL, H. E., EVANS, J. (1987) "The identification of plants used in prehistory from organic residues" in W. R. Ambrose and J. M. J. Mummery (eds), Archaeometry: *further Australian studies*, Canberra, p.p. 90-96. (1989) "Crops of the Pacific: New evidence from the chemical analysis of organic residues in pottery" in D. R. Harris and G. C. Hillman (eds), *Foraging and Farming*, London, p.p. 418-425.

HILL, H. E., EVANS, J., CARD, M. (1985) "Organic residues on 3000 year old potsherds from Nantunky, Fiji" *New Zealand Journal of Archaeology*, 7: 125-128.

HILLMAN, G., WALES, S., McLAREN, F., EVANS, J., BUTLER, A. (1993) "Identifying problematic remains of ancient plant foods: a comparison of chemical, histological, and morphological criteria" *World Archaeology*, 25: 94-121.

HIRSCHFELD, L., HIRSCHFELD, H. (1919) "Serological differences between the blood of different races" *Lancet:* 675-678.

HOSTETTER, E., BECK, C. W., AND STEWART, D. (1993) "A Bronze situla from Tomb 128, Valle Trebba: Chemical evidence of resinated wine at Spina" *Studi Etruschi* (Serie III), 59: 211-225.

HOUSLEY, R. A., GAMBLE, C. S., STREET, M., PETTITT, P. (1997) "Radiocarbon evidence for the late glacial human recolonisation of Northern Europe" *Proceedings of the Prehistoric Society*, 63: 25-54.

HOWELL, N., KUBACKA, I., MACKEY, D. A. (1996) "How rapidly does the human mitochondrial genome evolve?" *American Journal of Human Genetics*, 59: 501-509.

JAZIN, E., SOODYALL, H., JALONEN, P., LINDHOLM, E., STONEKING, M., GYLLENSTEN, U. (1998) "Mitochondrial mutation rate revisited: hot spots and polymorphism" *Nature Genetics*, 18: 109-110.

JANKO, R. (1981) "Un 1314: Herbal remedies at Pylos" *Minos*, 17: 30-34.

JAKY, M., PEREDI, J., PALOS, L. (1964) "Untersuchungen eines aus romischen Zeiten stammenden Fettproduktes" *Fette, Seifen, Anstrichmittel*, 66: 1012-1017.

KATZ, S. H. (1987) "Fava bean consumption: a case for the co-evolution of genes and culture" in M. Harris and E. B. Ross (eds), *Food and evolution: towards a theory of human food habits, Philadelphia*, p.p. 133-159.

KENIG, F., DAMSTE, J. S. S., DE LEEUW, J. W. (1994) "Molecular palaeontological evidence for food-web relationships" *Naturwissenschaften*, 81(3): 128-130.

KNÖRZER, K. H. (1983) "Funde prohistorischer Olpflanzen aus dem nordlichen Rheinland" in H. Muller-Beck, R. Rottlander (eds), *Naturwissenschaftliche Untersuchungen zur Ermittlung prohistorischer Nahrungsmittel. Ein Symposionsbericht*, Tubingen, p.p. 105-111.

KROGMAN, W. M., ISCAN, M. Y. (1986) *The Human Skeleton in Forensic Medicine*, 2nd ed., Springfield.

LARSEN, C. S. (1997) *Bioarchaeology: interpreting behaviour from the human skeleton, Cambridge*, (Cambridge Studies in Biological Anthropology 27).

LEWIN, R. (1997) "Ancestral echoes" *New Scientist*, 2089: 32-37.

MACAULAY, V. A., RICHARDS, M. B., FORSTER, P., BENDALL, K. E., WATSON, E., SYKES, B., BANDELT, H.-J. (1997) "mtDNA mutation rate - no need to panic" *American Journal of Human Genetics*, 61: 983-986.

McGEORGE, P. J. P. (1987) "Biosocial evolution in Bronze Age Crete" in *ΕΛΑΠΙΝΗ: Τόμος τιμητικός για τον Καθηγητή Νικόλαο Πλάτωνα*, Heraklion, Βικελαία Βιβλιοθήκη, 1987, p.p. 406-416. (1988) "Health and diet in Minoan times" in R. E. Jones and H. W. Catling (eds), *New Aspects of Archaeological Science in Greece*, Occasional Paper No. 3 of the Fitch Laboratory of the British School at Athens, Athens, p.p. 47-54.

McGOVERN, P. E. (1992) "The chemical confirmation of beer from protohistoric lowland Greater Mesopotamia" *Nature*, 360: 24 (1997) "Wine of Egypt's Golden Age: an archaeochemical perspective" *Journal of Egyptian Archaeology*, 83: 69-108. (1998) "Wine for Eternity" *Archaeology*, 51(4): 28-34.

McGOVERN, P. E., FLEMING, S. J., KATZ, S. H. (1995) *The Origins and Ancient History of Wine*, New York (Food and Nutrition in History and Anthropology, Vol.11).

McGOVERN, P. E., GLUSKER, D. L., EXNER, L. J., VOIGT, M. M. (1996) "Neolithic resinated wine" *Nature*, 381: 480-481.

McGOVERN, P. E., HARTUNG, U., BADLER, V. R., GLUSKER, D. L., EXNER, L. J. (1997) "The beginnings of winemaking and viticulture in the Ancient Near East and Egypt" *Expedition*, 39: 2-21.

MEINDL, R. S., LOVEJOY, C. O., MENSFORTH, R. P., CARLOS, L. D. (1985) "Accuracy and direction of error in the sexing of the skeleton" *American Journal of Physical Anthropology*, 68: 79-85.

MICHEL, R. H., McGOVERN, P. E., BADLER, V. R. (1992) "Chemical evidence for ancient beer" *Nature*, 360: 24. (1993) "The first wine and beer. Chemical detection of ancient fermented beverages" *Analytical Chemistry*, 65: 408A-413A.

MUSGRAVE, J. H., NEAVE, R. A. H., PRAG, A. J. N. W. (1995) "Seven faces from Grave Circle B at Mycenae" Annual of the British School at Athens, 90: 107-136.

NEEDHAM, S., EVANS, J. (1987) "Honey and Dripping; Neolithic food residues from Runnymede Bridge" *Oxford Journal of Archaeology*, 6: 21-28.

OHSHIMA, T., MIYAMOTO, K., SAKAI, R. (1993) "Simultaneous separation and sensitive measurement of free fatty acids in ancient pottery by high performance liquid chromatography" *Journal of Liquid Chromatography*, 16: 3217-3227.

ORTNER, D. J., PUTSCHAR, W. G. J. (1985) *Identification of pathological conditions in human skeletal remains*, Washington DC, (Smithsonian Contributions to Anthropology 28).

OUDEMANS, T. F. M., BOON, J. J. (1991) "Molecular archaeology: analysis of charred (food) remains from prehistoric pottery by pyrolysis - gas chromatography / mass spectrometry" *Journal of Analytical and Applied Pyrolysis*, 20: 197-227. (1993) "Experimental polysaccharide chars and their "fingerprints" in charred archaeological food residues." *Journal of Analytical and Applied Pyrolysis*, 25: 63-75.

OUDEMANS, T. M. F., BOON, J. J., EVERSHED, R. P. (1991) "Tracing vessel use: Quantitative comparison between absorbed lipids and lipids in surface residues on prehistoric pottery" *Proceedings of the Third National Archaeological Science Conference*, York.

PALMER, R. (1994) *Wine in the Mycenaean Palace Economy*, Liege (*Aegaeum* 10). (1995) "Wine and viticulture in Linear A and B texts" in P. E. McGovern, S. J. Fleming and S. H. Katz (eds), *The Origins and Ancient History of Wine*, New York (Food and Nutrition in History and Anthropology, Vol. 11), p.p. 269-285.

PARET, O. (1934) "Wie steinzeitliche Speisereste untersucht werden" *Kosmos*, 31: 185.

PASSI, S., ROTHSCHILD-BOROS, M., FASELLA, P., NAZARRO-PORRO, M., WHITEHOUSE, D. (1981) "An application of high performance liquid chromatography of lipids in archaeological samples" *Journal of Lipid Research*, 22: 778-784.

PASTOROVA, I. (1997) *Chemically linking past and present: comparative studies of chars and resins*, Amsterdam.

PASTOROVA, I., OUDEMANS, T. M. F., BOON, J. J. (1993) "Experimental polysaccharide chars and their 'fingerprints' in charred archaeological residues" *Journal of Analytical and Applied Pyrolysis*, 25: 63-75.

PATRICK, M., DE KONING, A. J., SMITH, A. B. (1985) "Gas-liquid chromatographic analysis of fatty acids in food residues from ceramics found in the southwestern Cape, South Africa" *Archaeometry*, 27: 231-236.

PEATFIELD, A. A. D. (1990) "Minoan peak sanctuaries: history and society" *Opuscula Atheniensia*, 18: 117-131. (1992) "Rural ritual in Bronze Age Crete: the peak sanctuary at Atsipadhes" *Cambridge Archaeological Journal*, 2: 59-87.

POLLARD, A.M. (1993) "Tales told by dry bones" *Chemistry and Industry*: 359-362.

PRAG, J., NEAVE, R. (1997) *Making Faces: Using Forensic and Archaeological Evidence,* London.

REGERT, M., ROLANDO, C. (1996) "Archeologie des residus organiques. De la chimie analytique a archeologie: un etat de la question" *Techne* 3: 118-128.

RENFREW, J. M. (1995) "Palaeoethnobotanical finds of vitis in Greece" in P. E. McGovern, S. J. Fleming and S. H. Katz (eds), *The Origins and Ancient History of Wine*, New York (Food and Nutrition in History and Anthropology, Vol.11), p.p. 255-267.

RICHARDS, M.B., SMALLEY, K., SYKES, B., HEDGES. R. (1993) "Archaeology and genetics: analysis of DNA from skeletal remains" *World Archaeology*, 25(1): 18-28.

RICHARDS, M. R., CÔRTE-REAL, H., FORSTER, P., MACAULAY, V., WILKINSON-HERBOTS, H., DEMAINE, A., PAPIHA, S., HEDGES, R., BANDELT, H.-J., SYKES, B. (1996) "Paleolithic and neolithic lineages in the European mitochondrial gene pool" *American Journal of Human Genetics*, 59: 185-203.

RICHARDS, M. P., MOLLESON, T. I., VOGEL, J. C., HEDGES, R. E. M. (1998) "Stable isotope analysis reveals variations in human diet at the Poundbury Camp Cemetery site" *Journal of Archaeological Science,* 25:1247-1252.

ROBERTS, C. A., MANCHESTER, K. (1995) *The Archaeology of Disease*, 2nd ed., Stroud.

ROTTLÄNDER, R. C. A. (1979) "Der Speisezettel der Steinzeit-Bauern war erstaunlich reichhaltig" *Umschau*, 79: 752-753. (1983) "Chemische Analyse pröhistorischer Gefassinhalte" in *Enzyklopadie Naturwissenschaft und Technik, Jahresband*, Landsberg, p.p. 72-80. (1986) "Chemical investigation of potsherds of the Heuneberg, Upper Danube" in J. S. Olin and M. J. Blackman (eds), *Proceedings of the 24th International Archaeometry Symposium*, Washington DC, p.p. 403-406. (1990a) "Die Resultate der modernen Fettanalytik und ihre Anwendung auf die pröhistorische Forschung" *Archaeo-Physika*, 12: 1-354. (1990b) "Lipid analysis in the identification of vessel contents" in W. R. Biers and P. E. McGovern (eds), *Organic contents of ancient vessels: Materials analysis and archaeological investigation*, Philadelphia, MASCA, University of Pennsylvania Museum (MASCA Research Papers in Science and Archaeology no. 7), p.p. 37-40. (1991) "Gefassinhaltsuntersuchungen an Keramik von der Heuneburg." in H. van den Boom, *Heuneburgstudien. Grossgefasse und Topfe der Heuneburg*, Mainz, p.p. 77-86. (1992) "Untersuchung der Gefassinhalte aus dem Grabhugel von Thunstetten-Tannwaldli." in H. Hennig, *Zwei hallstattzeitliche Grabhugel aus dem Berner Mittelland*, Bern, p.p. 53-54.

ROTTLÄNDER, R. C. A., BLUME, M. (1980) "Chemische Untersuchungen an Michelsberger Scherben" *Archaeo-Physika*, 7: 71-86.

ROTTLÄNDER, R. C. A., SCHLICHTHERLE, H. (1979) "Food identification of samples from archaeological sites" *Archaeo-Physika*, 10: 260-267. (1980) "GefaBinhalte. Eine kurzkommentierte Bibliographie" *Archaeo-Physika*, 7: 61-70. (1983) "Analyse fruhgeschichtlicher GefaBinhalte" *Naturwissenschaften* 70: 33-38.

SALLARES, R. (1991) *The ecology of the ancient Greek world,* London.

SCHOENINGER, M., DENIRO, M., TAUBER, H. (1983) "Stable nitrogen isotope ratios of bone collagen reflect marine and terrestrial components of prehistoric human diet" Science, 220:1381-1383.

SEHER, A., SCHILLER, H., KROHN, M., AND WERNER, G. (1980) "Untersuchungen von 'Olproben' aus archaologischen Funden" *Fette, Seifen, Anstrichmittel*, 82: 395-399.

SHACKLEY, M. (1982) "Gas chromatographic identification of a resinous deposit from a 6th century storage jar and its possible identification" *Journal of Archaeological Science*, 9: 305-306.

SHERIFF, B. L., TISDALE, M. A., SAYER, B. G., SCHWARCZ, H. P., KNYF, M. (1995) "Nuclear magnetic resonance spectroscopic and isotopic analysis of carbonised residues from subarctic Canadian prehistoric pottery" *Archaeometry*, 37: 95-111.

SYKES, B. C. (1999) "The molecular genetics of European ancestry" *Philosophical Transactions of the Royal Society: Biological Sciences*, 354: 131-139.

TODD, T. WINGATE (1920-21) "Age changes in the pubic bone" (Parts I-IV), *American Journal of Physical Anthropology*, 3: 285-334; 4: 1-70, 334-424.

TORRONI, A., HUOPONEN, K., FRANCALACCI, P., PETROZZI, M., MORELLI, L., SCOZZARI, R., et.al. (1996) "Classification of European mtDNAs from an analysis of three European populations" *Genetics*, 144: 1835-1850.

TROTTER, M., GLESER, G. C. (1958) "A re-evaluation of estimation of stature based on measurements of stature taken duing life and long bones after death" *American Journal of Physican Anthropology*, 16: 79-123.

TURKER, L., DEMIRCI, S., AND MELIKOGLU, T. (1992) "The role of cholesterol in identification of archaeological food residues" *Turkish Journal of Chemistry*, 16(4): 246-251.

VAN DER MERWE, N. J. (1982) "Carbon isotopes, photosynthesis, and archaeology" *American Scientist*, 70:209-215.

VELEGRAKIS, G., SKOULAKIS, C., BIZAKIS, J., SEGAS, J., HELIDONIS, E. (1983) "Otorhinolaryngological diseases in the Minoan era" Journal of Laryngology and Otology, 107: 879-882.

WRIGHT, J. C. (1995) "Empty cups and empty jugs" in P. E. McGovern, S. J. Fleming and S. H. Katz (eds), *The Origins and Ancient History of Wine,* New York (Food and Nutrition in History and Anthropology, Vol. 11), p.p. 287-309.

Compiled by Dr. Robert Arnott, University of Birmingham (U.K.).

PHOTOGRAPHS

Stefanos Alexandrou, Graham Norrie, Stefanos Stournaras, Manolis Floures

PHOTOGRAPH ARCHIVES

Metropolitan Museum of Art, New York, U.S.A.,

Kapon Editions, Image Bank, University of Birmingham (U.K.),

University of Manchester (U.K.), Archaeological Receipts Fund

DESIGN: Rachel Misdrachi-Kapon

ARTISTIC ADVISER: Moses Kapon

TRANSLATION TO ENGLISH: David Hardy

TEXT EDITED BY: Vassilis Charalambacos

COMPUTER PROCESSING OF ILLUSTRATIONS: Panos Stamatas

COMPUTER PROCESSING OF TEXT: Eleni Valma

COLOUR SEPARATIONS: GRAFFITI LTD

MONTAGE - PRINTING: A. PETROULAKIS S.A.

BINDING: I. Iosifidis - V. Eftaxiadis